ENDING INSULT TO INJURY

ENDING INSULT
TO INJURY

———

No-Fault Insurance
for Products and Services

JEFFREY O'CONNELL

———

foreword by Daniel Patrick Moynihan

UNIVERSITY OF ILLINOIS PRESS

———

Urbana Chicago London

Quotations from the articles by Jonathan Laing in chapter 1
are reprinted with the permission of the *Wall Street Journal,*
© Dow Jones & Company, Inc. (1972-73).

Excerpts from pp. 5-6, 218-21, 281-82, and 245-47 of *Intern*
by Doctor X copyright © 1965 by Harper & Row, Publishers,
Inc. By permission of the publishers.

Library of Congress Cataloging in Publication Data

O'Connell, Jeffrey.
    Ending insult to injury.

    Includes bibliographical references.
    1. Insurance, Liability — United States. 2. Insur-
ance, No-fault automobile — United States. 3. Personal
injuries — United States. I. Title.
KF1215.O26   346′.73′086   74-16243
ISBN 0-252-00451-5

TO
VIRGINIA

Contents

Foreword *by Daniel Patrick Moynihan* ix

Preface xxi

Acknowledgments xxv

1. All's Fair in Love and Litigation 1

2. Adding Insult to Injury 9

3. The Law's Malpractice against Medicine 29

4. Other Torts by Tort Law 48

5. Where Tort Law Has Been Drifting 56

6. A Blind Alley or Two (Part I) 70

7. A Blind Alley or Two (Part II) 89

8. A Promising Approach or Two (Part I) 97

9. A Promising Approach or Two (Part II) 112

10. A Question or Two (Part I) 139

11. A Question or Two (Part II) 152

Coda 167

Summary 171

Appendix I. More Sly Tricks 177

Appendix II. An Expert's Testimony 183

Appendix III. The Complexities of Compulsory No-Fault
Medical Services Insurance 189

Appendix IV. "Does Economics Help?" 195

Appendix V. Is It Constitutional? *with James E. Souk* 204

Index 247

Foreword

Back success? What? How's that?

That *was* a way of going about things, a way of putting them, once quite common to American affairs. It is the essence of the pragmatic, the practical. Try everything. When one thing works, try it again. Try it on something else. Try it twice as big, twice as small. There is a mathematics that will support the proposition. Linear programming argues for it. Yet it has been, in America, overwhelmingly a *popular* principle. "Nothing succeeds like success" is one variant. "You can't argue with success," another. There are others, for until quite recently the idea permeated American life. It was a first principle of the inspired tinkerers and ingenious mechanics who transformed the great forest, the vast plain, and the pleasant coast beyond into what, for better or worse, they are today. At a risk of overreaching one's knowledge, the formulation does not seem to appear with anything like equal force in other industrializing cultures, although surely the bumptious British of the nineteenth century must have produced its equivalent.

Why does it now seem to be receding from American affairs? Why, more ominously, does it depart with an air of being banished? The second question should be dealt with first. It is scarcely a novel idea that American elites have been busily dissatisfied with what the masses have been able to produce for them. Lionel Trilling has traced this disdain as far back, at very least, as Thoreau. Norman Podhoretz has summed it up: the high culture will not accept what the polity can provide. In this setting it should be no surprise that persons of taste in America — they are not fools, you know —

should have come to identify success as the prime source of energy for the system that dismays them so. Three generations ago William James himself called success "the bitch goddess." Three generations later it has become a settled conviction in much of the high culture that success has failed, and so there is little disposition to back it.

But what about the other culture, that of the tinkerers and the mechanics? There a different set of inhibitions seems to have appeared, especially in that area of tinkering and rearranging and redesigning which we call social reform. There has been a very great deal of this reform in recent years, under "conservative" governments as well as "liberal." And, of course, there are a great many governments in the American system. All have been busy passing ever more laws, sometimes carefully, sometimes in a frenzy designed to keep up with a seemingly ever-expanding agenda of social needs. Unavoidably, this lawmaking has been in part a disappointing experience. "Things" are not that much better. Rather, they are not perceived to be. Survey data are quite clear on this point. Indeed, in many respects, "things" are seen to have gotten worse. A range of explanations has been put forward to account for this. Those of a more classical conservative bent harken back to Dr. Johnson's dictum:

> How few of all the ills that human hearts endure,
> That part which laws or kings can cause or cure.

Among those more optimistic about the human condition, some will argue that, appearances to the contrary, American society has *not* been engaged in a truly strenuous and committed effort for social change. Others, possibly more analytic, will note that with respect to a wide range of social intervention it is now arguably the case that we have reached a point of diminishing return, even negative return. More and more, in so many areas, American social policy evokes the image of an ever more powerful hypothecated giant pounding ever more resources into the angle of an ever-tightening asymptotic curve. Surely the Greeks attached a name and a tale to such labors! For they are not uncommon.

What is uncommon is the man or woman who comes along and, seeing the hopelessness of the task as it is being approached, proposes a new and radically simple approach — which succeeds! Such a man is Jeffrey O'Connell, who in 1965, with his associate Robert E. Keeton, proposed "no-fault" automobile insurance, the one incontestably successful reform of the 1960s. This is not to say other reforms were unsuccessful. But no-fault automobile insurance laws not only succeeded in the first states to enact them, but also succeeded visibly, palpably, and almost immediately. In Massachusetts not only did bodily injury premiums promptly go down, *but so did claims for damages!* Overnight it became evident that O'Connell and Keeton had substantially solved a major social problem — that *this* was the way to allocate the costs of personal injuries and property damages that arise through the automobile transportation system. Within the decade the argument had been reduced to the question of whether no-fault insurance should be enacted by federal or by state legislation, the Congress arguing the one, the White House the other.

There is a nice symmetry to O'Connell's role in all this. He has been content to be seen as himself little more than the inspired tinkerer, the ingenious mechanic, of the sort who helped create the problems he has dealt with. In the manner of those who gave us the horseless carriage in the first place, he has approached problems with no very great pronouncements — indeed, with no pronouncements at all. For all that appearances could tell, he and his partner were simply fooling around back there in the stable with something called "no-fault." Then, one day (would you believe it?) the damn thing worked. It may be the time has come, however, to reveal a little more of this man and his achievement. Those mechanics were not intent on introducing profound social change. O'Connell has been. Which is to say that he perceived, in the first instance with respect to the automobile, the extraordinary disequilibrating impact which certain forms of technology had on society. He and Keeton were on the staff of the Harvard Law School at the time of their early collaboration. Jurisprudence was their subject, not accident claims. But they perceived in the ever-mounting volume of accident litigation a threat to the legal system itself. A threat to overwhelm it with complex and unavailing actions; a threat so to diminish the efficacy of the courts as to undermine confidence in the ability — ultimately perhaps, the intent — to do justice. Matters of the most profound concern. It was no accident that O'Connell was first to publish a comprehensive study setting forth the responsibility of automobile manufacturers to design vehicles which would minimize automobile crashes and injuries.* That work behind him, he turned, in association with Professor Keeton, to the matter of the litigation of such crashes and injuries. Just as it could be shown that to a very considerable extent crashes and injuries could be prevented or mitigated by different design, and that obstinate adherence to older designs had reached the point of actionable negligence, so it could be shown that the litigation of crashes and injuries could be greatly reduced by redesigning the legal system. It could also be shown that the refusal, as it were, of the bar to initiate and implement such changes had profoundly disturbing implications. A further parallel may be suggested. The essence of the epidemiological approach to automobile injuries is to minimize crashes through vehicle and road design but to assume that even so there will be a certain number of such crashes and accordingly to incorporate design elements — safety belts, padded dashboards — which minimize the injuries that follow. No-fault automobile insurance followed much the same pattern: to reduce claims and to reduce the "cost" of claims. Which is to say that no-fault attempts to eliminate needless claims in the way automobile design attempts to eliminate needless accidents — the steering wheel need not come off in the driver's hands — and *then* attempts to minimize the consequences of crashes — a settlement for a broken back need not take four years to reach and end up with the injured person getting, say, forty percent of the money spent in the process, the remainder going to lawyers and other expenses.

As with the individual, so with the society. O'Connell's concerns have been jurisprudential from the first. The individual, yes; the society also. The claims on society need to be kept at a manageable level if those claims which are made are to receive an appropriate and equitable response. When O'Connell first involved himself with the problem of automobile accident claims, he encountered a system of justice that had been so immobilized by inundation as to be scarcely a system of justice at all. It would be no great exaggeration

---

* "Taming the Automobile," 58 *Nw. U. L. Rev.* 299–399 (1963), which was followed by a more popular work, *Safety Last: An Indictment of the Auto Industry* (Random House, 1966), written with Arthur Myers.

to describe these nominally legal procedures (still followed in most jurisdictions) as based less on principles of equity than on the ancient *ius naturalis* which Wordsworth evoked in "Rob Roy's Grave":

> The good old rule
> ... the simple plan,
> That they should take, who have the power,
> And they should keep who can.

O'Connell's concern was that right be done, and that it be *seen* to be right. This meant introducing certain principles of efficiency: devising a system in which there would be fewer claims and, in effect, lesser claims, but in which those claims would tend to involve the more serious and genuine instances of loss and would, in consequence, be dealt with promptly and generously. The accident victim would not become victim of the claims system as well. In a word, O'Connell was concerned to do justice to the individual and to maintain the legitimacy of the legal system to which the individual looks for justice. Both things.

This dual objective permeates the argument of *Ending Insult to Injury,* perhaps his most important work to date. The study begins with the recitation of particulars in the careful, inductionist manner of the past. The plight under traditional tort law of those who suffer accidents from faulty products is shown to be worse, much worse, than that of even automobile accident victims. It costs too much to sue; it takes too long; in the end the injured person gets too little. The Final Report of the National Commission on Product Safety is introduced in evidence: the most serious limitation on recovery of damages for product injuries to consumers is the cost of trial. Witnesses testified that it hardly pays to press a defective product claim for less than five to ten thousand dollars. But note: the number of claims is rising. In the ten years prior to 1973 it had increased tenfold. It would appear that the courts are heading for a new inundation comparable to, perhaps greater than, the giant wave of automobile injury claims.

At first this new wave might seem familiar enough: technology again, with its often unexpected and rarely pleasing second-, third-, and fourth-order effects. One may speculate that rotary lawnmowers are causing about as many personal injuries today as did the Tin Lizzie in 1910. One may also speculate that they are also causing *even more* court claims. What is this about? We are not necessarily a more litigious people than we once were. The incidence of lawyers in the population has only slightly worsened. There was one for every 665 persons in 1900; one for every 626 in 1970. But one can discern a rise in the level of organized distrust. This may be seen most dramatically in the transformation of the consumer movement, which began in the progressive era as a kind of genteel counterpart to the labor movement. Its concern was with the presumed excessive power of producers in a free enterprise market system, a power to set the prices of products without reference to the needs or desires of the atomized consumers, much as wages were set for workers. This power led, so the theory went, to substandard wages, inflated prices, and excess profits, all undesirable things. The consumer, moreover, was vaguely socialistic and emphatically middle class. (When I was a youth at the City College of New York there was a co-op restaurant nearby. I longed to eat there as an expression of solidarity, but I never did, fearing my table manners would not be good enough.) There was, in any event, a sectarian quality to it all: meetings and magazines, and, I do not doubt, even the occasional political candidate.

Consumerism sought fair prices and good quality in what was consumed, but it also sought a cooperative style of life. It never quite took hold. Then in the 1960s it gave way to a vastly more popular and militant movement associated primarily with issues of product safety. The medium for this transformation was the issue of automobile safety, the Watergate of American business. If a second, and final, personal intrusion may be permitted, I would like somewhere to record, and this foreword provides an appropriate opportunity, that in the late 1950s and early 1960s, by which time the scandal was fully discernible and the outcome inevitable, I sought to interest leaders of the consumer movement in taking up the cause of automobile safety. I argued that to do so would not only answer a pressing public need but also dramatize their movement and very possibly attract wide public support for more abstract, less immediate and threatening issues such as truth in lending or truth in packaging. (At about this time something like one out of every four automobiles manufactured ended up with blood on it. There was no way to doubt that the public would respond to a responsible demonstration that this proportion could be reduced. Put differently, there was no way the public could not be aware of the problem.) I had *some* success of a generalized sort. It would be agreed that automobile safety, too, was an issue. But no one got fire in his or her belly. It was not the style of those involved with the old consumerism. It was, however, the style of others, and in no time the new consumerism appeared, manifestly more visible, more enterprising, more accusatory — and perhaps even more middle class than its predecessor.

This new consumerism has proved its effectiveness in a whole range of issues and is beginning now to form itself into organizations of a durable character. I believe it fair to say, however, that there has been a change in manner that comes almost to a change in substance. The new consumerism evinces considerably more distrust of institutions, including those of government, and yet calls for ever more government regulation. As this foreword is written, a considerable debate is taking place in Washington concerning the proposed Consumer Protection Agency. This new agency is designed to represent consumer interests in proceedings before federal agencies, such as the Consumer Product Safety Commission (1972), which are themselves *designed to represent consumers*. A Democratic member of Congress not known for hyperbole wrote to a Washington paper that "millions of American families ... are properly angered that their government has been far more responsive to big business interests than consumer needs." He supports the establishment of a Consumer Protection Agency as a means of "finally getting the federal bureaucracy to move more vigorously in the public interest."

The special assistant to the President and director of the Office of Consumer Affairs agrees. In a prepared statement she wrote that the proposed agency would be a "powerful antidote to the poison of alienation and helplessness affecting many of our citizens [who] believe that their pleas for help or understanding are unheeded ... that only the big and powerful have access to decision makers."

Now this is fairly strong language. One can just barely imagine it coming from a White House official in the course of the effort under President Wilson which led to the establishment of the Federal Trade Commission (1915), the primary consumer protection agency, or the Federal Power Commission (1920) of the government. More easily, one can imagine an official of the Roosevelt White House evoking such images — "poison," "antidote" — in making the case for the Securities and Exchange Commission (1934). But for an official of the Nixon administration it seems a bit much — "alienation," "helplessness." And yet this is the point. The most moderate persons have come to employ a most immoderate language with respect to the perils and anxieties of consuming the unequaled abundance of the American economy. Precisely that condition of plenty which in the past was thought would at last bring a sense of security and a measure of social peace to man's troubled passage has, for some, at least, brought almost the opposite. In the past, meat rotted and men went hungry; today meat is preserved and men worry about the effects of the preservatives. Distrust grows — or is alleged to grow — practically in proportion to the measures taken to allay it. Hence, the latest news from Washington is that an enlightened Republican senator, in the course of the debate over the Consumer Protection Agency, has asked who is going to represent the consumer before the agency designed to represent the consumer before the agencies designed to represent the consumer. Literally. I quote:

OMBUDSMAN FOR CONSUMERS: Senator Taft has filed an amendment to the Consumer Protection Bill, now before the Senate, which would create an "Ombudsman Agency" to oversee activities of a new Agency for Consumer Advocacy proposed by the Bill. Taft fears the ACA would become "an irresponsible and unrestrained super-agency, speaking only for a few, more vocal interest groups" while ignoring the real interests of the consuming public.

One recalls a pressing issue from the McCarthy days, formulated, as I recall, by Zero Mostel: "Who's going to investigate the man who investigates the man who investigates me?"

Of all these goings-on a number of observations may be made. Increased consumer advocacy may be seen, in one perspective, as merely a function of increased consumption. It arises not from any growth in the acquisitiveness of American manufacturers and merchants, nor yet in any decline in standards of social responsibility. I perceive neither; only a willful ignorance of history would sustain such contentions. Something of a quite different order has occurred. A natural process has led to an ever greater profusion of products, catering to ever more specialized tastes and needs. (Recall the remark of the founding Ford that customers might purchase the Model T in any color they liked as long as it was black.) This profusion is true of children's toys; it is true of medicines. It arises in part from profit-motivated enterprise, perhaps even more from disinterested science. It is merely the most recent impact of technology, differing only in degree from earlier periods. However, it does mean that to a corresponding degree consumers find themselves making choices from a bewilderingly abundant market where personal experience is a decreasingly dependable guide. Hence, in that spirit of specialization which produced the abundance, the rising demand for surrogate consumers who will acquire the expertise to make intelligent purchases. Hence, for example, the Consumer Product Safety Commission with its Bureau of Epidemiology, its Risk Index, its National Electronic Injury Surveillance System (NEISS, for those who keep abreast of such matters). As with medicines, so with medicine. The *possibilities* of medical care expand almost geometrically. And so, seemingly, do the possibilities of malpractice. It appears that medical malpractice suits are being filed at the rate of eighteen thousand a year. And yet there is nothing to be alarmed at here. Mankind, or at least Americans, decided there were better things than a simple life with a life expectancy of 22.5 years. And so our affairs have become rather more complex.

There is yet another "normal" need being served, or at least a political scientist may be forgiven the suspicion that there is. An economic space is being created for a certain number of college and law school graduates in a job market not notably short of such persons. If the FTC is filled up, one may apply to the CPA. If no luck there, try the "ombudsman" agency. If that is filled, there is always a chance of a place on the staff of the Senate committee that is keeping an eye on all three. An ambassador to India may perhaps be excused for seeing this as more of a normal social dynamic than is generally perceived elsewhere. Again, a normal, untroubling development.

There is an element, however, in the new consumerism which is not reassuring at all. It is here that O'Connell's work assumes an almost unique importance, for while modest seeming, it addresses the largest of questions. To wit: there is a rise in the perception of threat in modern society, a decline in confidence, a decline in trust. This surely must be the judgment of any person of sensibility. It is no accident that a Republican special assistant in a conservative White House speaks of "alienation" — Marx's term for the psychological damage done by an undisputably productive capitalism. The special assistant — or the recent college graduate who most likely wrote the statement — got it a bit wrong (it is the *worker* who is supposed to be alienated, not the consumer). But how is someone who was well educated in the 1960s supposed to know things like that? At the same time, this is the point. Americans seemed to be acquiring a "trained incapacity" — Thorstein Veblen's term — for solving some of the central "problems" created by success. Consumer problems are an example. It is one thing to see such problems as arising from the productiveness of the economic system; it is a very different thing to see them as arising from its venality. I would not wish to suggest a simple dichotomy. The productiveness is in part the reward for a certain insensitivity, for which there is a penalty also. Herman Kahn notes that Veblen coined his term to refer to the inability of sociologists and engineers "to deal with certain simple issues which they could have dealt with if they had not had their training." Just so the automotive engineers of the 1950s when the issues of traffic safety were clarified by epidemiologists. The issue was simple. Any untrained fourteen-year-old could follow it. The engineers at General Motors could not. This, at very least, is my view. I was there. I was one of those who tried to make them understand. I assert that they *could* not. The alternative view that they *would* not is very different, and I do not subscribe to it. I suspect, however, that most of those who have thought about the matter do. And I suspect that this *also* is an instance of trained incapacity.

I fear that American education is increasingly turning out persons of socially active dispositions who do not understand or accept how the American economic system works and that this is going to have the most baleful consequences for that system. It is going to become overregulated and oversued, undercapitalized and underproductive. I shall be happy to be proved wrong, but for the moment the process of Schumpeterian decline seems well advanced. Curiously, the American economic system just now is beginning to find European admirers on the intellectual left. Or perhaps this is not curious: perhaps it is the most certain sign of decline! Be that as it may, European intellectuals can be found who will allow that the extraordinary quality of the American system was how unpolitical it was, in retrospect a blessing in a too politicized world. Even Andre Malraux, a Marxist legend before, even, his time, has said as much in a recent interview:

> Now, something very curious is happening with the United States. It is the first country in history that will have become the most powerful in the world without having sought it. Because it is perfectly true that there has never been a will to political conquest in the United States. There were episodes but that doesn't count. Americans did not enter the great wars with joy in their hearts; they gained little from them politically. They did not seek to gain more.
>
> The Treaty of Versailles and the Treaty of Trianon are worth what they are worth, but it is not true that the United States sought the greatest advantage. Thus they have been master of the world by having wanted to sell what they produced at the best price. That is a completely new fact, it has never happened before. And the consequence is that they have never really had historical designs.

Simply wanting "to sell what they have produced at the best price." A "completely new fact." There is a case to be made that Malraux is right, from which there follows — for some tastes, at all events — a case for keeping such a system in place as long as possible.

It is not for me to state that such is the purpose of Jeffrey O'Connell. It may not be at all. In any event, he is a more than sufficiently able advocate: he can make his own case, whatever it be. But I would contend that this is an aspect of his work that is easily overlooked. He is a conservative jurist in the sense that Justice Frankfurter was conservative. He values highly those things the legal system can do, and he is concerned that it not seek to overdo. An overextended system, dealing with ever more peripheral issues, eventually becomes incapable of dealing with those vital and central issues for which it was created. The image of empires collapsing on their marches comes to mind. O'Connell does not want us litigating ourselves into a stalemated and paranoid society. We could do so. We could take all the fun out of it, all the pride out of it, and that would be such a waste, such a loss.

In this book O'Connell cites a congressional study on medical malpractice, subtitled "The Patient versus the Physician." This is a relation O'Connell does *not* want. It won't help doctors and it won't help patients. Similar confrontational, adversary relations seem to be developing everywhere. They can't succeed. When everyone sues, no one gets satisfied. Our experience with the automobile brought us after the fact to that realization. O'Connell, for whom, with Professor Keeton, our appreciation must go for this realization, now seeks to enlist our support in what is, in effect, an effort at preventive jurisprudence, corresponding in every essential to preventive medicine. He asks us to consider how things are going. They are not going well. The legal system becomes ever more encumbered; the consequences of this burden become ever more pathologic as systemic failure is interpreted as systemic design. Justice, it is judged, is not done, because justice is not intended. Free systems come more and more to be seen as threatening; regulation, ever more normal and necessary. Thereafter, regulation of the regulators. And thence regulation of the regulators of the regulators. This is the way systems die. O'Connell stands for life. Don't pay overmuch attention to his claim merely to be concerned with aspects of tort liability. He is writing about those particulars whereby a free society remains free. He writes in an honored tradition of jurisprudence. And he writes with a record of proven success which deserves to be backed.

DANIEL P. MOYNIHAN

New Delhi
August, 1974

Preface

Good heavens, another book on no-fault insurance from O'Connell! It *is* a little embarrassing (this is the seventh I've written on the topic in eight years), but at least in this effort I am taking a new tack — trying to apply the no-fault concept (whereby accident victims are paid for their losses regardless of who was at fault in the accident) to other than auto accidents — to *any* kind of accident, really.

And I don't really apologize for all that ink spilled over what can be thought a mundane topic. Of course the problem of compensating accident victims for their out-of-pocket loss can seem rather mean and uninspired compared to more noble and ennobling social experiments. But Daniel Patrick Moynihan, in his book *Coping*, has pointed out that there may be merit to thinking small: "After a period of chiliastic vision we have entered a time that requires a more sober assessment of our chances, and a more modest approach to events. . . . [T]he here-and-now and the close-at-hand are the dominant facts of public life, and the proper study of those who would take part in it."[1] Later, Moynihan states, "I have seen something of Government, have served in capacities from speech writer to Cabinet member, on levels from Manhattan's First Assembly District Middle to the United Nations. I would be hard put to recount a half dozen instances in which 'experts' have come forth with confident advice as to the course social or economic policy should take."[2] But as Moynihan is the first to state, no-fault auto insurance is just such an exception.[3] The professors who proposed this reform (among whom I am proud to count myself) are having their confident prom-

Notes on p. xxiii.

ises of a successful system of casualty insurance, to replace a bankrupt one, redeemed by the success of no-fault insurance laws throughout the country in state after state. As Moynihan puts it, "There is nothing grand about any of this, yet there are worse things than commonplace competence addressed to near-term issues, concentrating on what is likely to happen in two and three and five and ten years' time. As one learns more of the world, one comes to value any 'measure of success.' "[4]

Of course, as Moynihan intimates, academics — and others, especially among the young — tend to scorn a "technocratic" focus that limits itself to reforms such as that of casualty insurance. Daniel Bell, in his book *The Coming of Post-Industrial Society,* comments on the pervasive disenchantment with technocrats and their limited horizons and solutions: "A technocratic society is not ennobling. Material goods provide only transient satisfaction or an invidious superiority over those with less. Yet one of the deepest human impulses is to *sanctify* their institutions and beliefs in order to find a meaningful purpose in their lives and to deny the meaninglessness of death. A post-industrial society cannot provide a transcendent ethic. . . . The lack of a rooted moral belief system is the cultural contradiction of the society, the deepest challenge to its survival."[5]

But Naomi Bliven — surely one of the most perceptive critics in contemporary America — has undertaken to answer Bell:

It strikes me that Dr. Bell and almost all the thinkers he cites are too scornful of matter, of material things, of physical comfort. Not to be too hot in summer or too cold in winter, to be clean instead of dirty, to find work less than exhausting, to have pain killers from aspirin and Novacain to general anesthesia — these material comforts are valuable to me. They are new in history and still comparatively rare in the world. It is a legitimate ethical goal to spread and share physical comfort, even if we are not certain of or agreed upon spiritual questions. I suspect that sharing and spreading comfort *is* our ethic — for the present anyhow — and if it is not "transcendent" or "ennobling," it is far from shameful.[6]

Amen, say I. And proud I am to labor in that vineyard, structuring insurance to better share and spread comfort for the injured.

Notes on p. xxiii.

Put that way, it is hard to think of a task ever considered more ennobling.

NOTES

1. D. P. Moynihan, *Coping* 4 (1973).
2. *Ibid.*, 24.
3. *Ibid.*, ch. 4.
4. *Ibid.*, 4.
5. As quoted in Bliven, book review, in *The New Yorker*, Sept. 17, 1973, pp. 151, 153.
6. *Ibid.*, 154.

Acknowledgments

I have been aided in this study by grants from the John Simon Guggenheim Memorial Foundation; Consumers Union; the Foundation for Insurance Research Study and Training (FIRST) of the League Insurance Group, Detroit, Michigan; and the Center for Advanced Study, University of Illinois. I also benefited enormously from the hospitality of the Centre for Socio-Legal Studies, Wolfson College, Oxford University, where I was a Visiting Fellow during Hilary and Trinity terms, 1973.

The writings of many scholars have been of aid to me in this project, perhaps especially those of the late Professor Albert A. Ehrenzweig of the University of California Law School at Berkeley, but also including, although not limited to, Professor Guido Calabresi of the Yale Law School; Professor Marc Franklin of the Stanford University Law School; Anthony Jolowicz, a Fellow of Trinity College, Cambridge University; Professor Harry Kalven of the University of Chicago Law School; and Professor Robert E. Keeton of the Harvard Law School.

I have benefited, too, from conversations with, among others, Professor Robert Keeton; Donald Harris, a Fellow of Balliol College, Oxford; Anthony Honoré, a Fellow of All Souls College, Oxford; Professor Jan Hellner of the Faculty of Law, University of Stockholm; Professor Kenneth Lopatka of the University of Illinois College of Law; the late Allan McCoid of the University of Minnesota Law School; Professor Richard Musgrave of the Department of Economics, Harvard University; Professor Geoffrey Palmer of the Faculty of Law, Victoria University, Wellington, N.Z.; John

Pollard, M.D., of the Carle Clinic, Urbana, Illinois; Professor Ralph Reisner of the University of Illinois College of Law; Professor Julian Simon of the Department of Economics, University of Illinois; Professor André Tunc of the Faculty of Law, University of Paris; and Dean C. Arthur Williams of the School of Business Administration, University of Minnesota.

Professor Alfred Conard of the University of Michigan Law School and Acting Dean Victor E. Schwartz of the University of Cincinnati Law School read the book in manuscript and offered helpful suggestions. I am also grateful to the editors of the University of Virginia Law Review for their editorial help with those portions of this book which first appeared therein and to Professor John Due of the Economics Department, University of Illinois, who read the law review article in manuscript and made thoughtful suggestions.

James Souk of the class of 1974, University of Illinois College of Law, Robert Blain of the class of 1973, Barbara Farrell of the class of 1975, and James Morris of the class of 1976, my research assistants, rendered professionally adept aid in many ways. I am particularly grateful to James Souk, who is coauthor of Appendix V. I am also grateful — this time as so many times — to my secretary Mrs. Ursula Tate for her expert secretarial skills. Noel Parsons of the University of Illinois Press has aided greatly in the whole editorial process.

Finally, I am indebted — as always — to my wife, Virginia Ann (Kearns) O'Connell, for her invaluable editorial advice, especially for her aid in encouraging me to write "with courtesy to the general reader."

Despite all the grand help I have received from so many, full responsibility for any errors or shortcomings in my work is obviously mine.

1

All's Fair in Love and Litigation

In 1966, one Italo Procaccini was operating a power tool when a chip of steel from the tool struck him in his eye. Procaccini was left completely blind by the accident, for his other eye had already been blinded. One year later, Philip Corboy, president of the Chicago Bar Association and one of the leading personal injury lawyers in the nation, filed suit in Cook County Circuit Court on Procaccini's behalf against Sears, Roebuck and Company, where the tool had been purchased, and McPherson Huff Tool Company, the tool's maker, based on an alleged defect in the tool. In May, 1972, some five years later — a typical delay in the trial of personal injury suits in Chicago and only a little longer than the average delay in other major metropolitan areas in America — the case reached trial.

In a deft and evocative article about Corboy in the *Wall Street Journal*, Jonathan Laing described the exhaustive preparation for and conduct of the trial by Corboy and his associates. Corboy immersed himself in the abstruse technicalities of metallurgy, examining more than twenty tomes on the subject. (This is hard work for the typical lawyer. Most young people who go to law school do so because they are skilled verbally and, conversely, have little aptitude for things mechanical.) According to Laing, Corboy had the tool itself subjected to exhaustive tests, "even flying it to California where it was examined under a special electron microscope large enough to permit viewing the entire tool. Some 20 lengthy depositions, or sworn statements, were taken from various experts, witnesses and other persons connected with the case. He had more than 100 exhibits prepared, including a number of poster-sized blowups of the chip and the tool."[1] All in all, preparations for trial on the plaintiff's side alone cost more than $20,000, with the defense, of course, spending substantial sums of its own.

In order to prove the tool defective — an absolute prerequisite for winning his case — Corboy called to the stand a Chicago industrial metallurgist and a professor of metallurgy from Long Beach State College in California. The metallurgist testified that a failure in uniformity in the chemical composition of the tool, as well as other defects in its composition, caused the chipping. An expert witness called by the defense — a professor from the Illinois Institute of Technology in Chicago — contended, however, in equally exhaustive detail, that there was nothing wrong with the tool.

Not all the lengthy trial was concerned with such technicalities, however. Corboy, as one of the highest-paid trial lawyers in the country, knows the importance of theatrics, drama, and human interest before a jury. Talking about the Procaccini trial, Corboy said, "The biggest sin a lawyer can commit is to bore the jury. . . . It isn't enough to get jurors who will find the defendant liable; they must also be willing to give the plaintiff big money." As a result, selecting jurors is a particularly exacting process for Corboy, and it has some fascinating rules of its own. Retired people are rejected by Corboy because they usually live on fixed incomes, and thus "they are too tight with a buck." Corboy warms to blacks and Jews, on the other hand, because "they have tasted discrimination and therefore tend to identify with the underdog plaintiff." Blue-collar workers, too, are prized since "they empathize more with victims because their own bodies are their livelihood."

In playing to jurors' sympathies, Corboy makes elaborate use of color photographs of the victim's injuries and other means of starkly displaying his client's wounds. In the Procaccini case Corboy followed that principle and another of his precepts — holding off presenting his client until late in the trial. Procaccini was Corboy's last witness. Indeed, it was Procaccini's first appearance in the trial, though the case had already consumed two weeks. As Laing describes it, "the doors of the courtroom swung open and in came Mr. Procaccini, wearing sunglasses, led by his 20-year-old son and a seeing-eye dog. The decision to include the dog had only been reached late the previous evening by Mr. Corboy and an associate.

Note on p. 8.

They decided the poignancy of having the dog lying at his master's feet was worth the occasional barks and recesses that the dog required."

For two hours Corboy led his client — a slender, balding man who frequently wiped his tear-filled eyes — through an anguished recital of the miseries of his condition: the continual pain from his injured eye, the sleepless nights, the long, boring days. At one point Procaccini was led by Corboy to the jury box to take off his dark glasses, revealing his "scarred, milky eyes."

In his closing argument, Corboy, as he later stated, "pulled out all the stops." For more than an hour he described in emotional and harrowing terms the hell of the life of the blind. He climaxed his presentation with an impassioned appeal for justice for Procaccini, who had, he said, "been doomed to a life of perpetual midnight."

Even so — withal the appeal of Procaccini's condition and Corboy's almost legendary skills as an advocate — it was, as Wellington said of Waterloo, "the nearest run thing you ever saw in your life." As often happens in such cases, while the jury was out, both parties, fearful of the jury's verdict, agreed to settle — in this case for $752,000, from which, after deducting Corboy's fee and other litigation expenses, Procaccini received $540,000. In point of fact, just before the members of the jury were told that the settlement had rendered their deliberations moot they had already decided on a lesser verdict (which the settlement made a nullity) of about $675,000. But they had been deliberating for about five hours and had spent a substantial portion of their time debating whether Mr. Procaccini should get anything; several jurors had been initially of the opinion he did not deserve payment because, in their view, the accident was due to his own fault.

Conducting such trials, and guessing right about their outcome, is an awesomely tricky business. As one of the very best plaintiff's lawyers in the country, Corboy reaps handsome rewards. According to writer Jonathan Laing's report on him: "He declines to disclose his annual income, but persons close to him estimate it at more than $500,000 a year — roughly $495,000 more than he earned in his first job, a political patronage post in Chicago's corporation counsel's office. Whatever the exact figure, the 47-year-old son of a policeman is clearly affluent — as evidenced by everything from the gleaming

[new] . . . Cadillac he drives to the Picasso lithographs and Steuben glass figurines that grace his office. He, his wife, Doris, and five children live in a commodious $125,000 home in Chicago's North Shore suburbs. He has extensive real estate holdings."

Corboy's well-rewarded skill in obtaining large verdicts and settlements is even more impressive when one understands the skill of opposing counsel in resisting such verdicts, often by the use of tactics also designed to appeal to the sentiments of jurors. Probably the most impressive insurance company lawyer in Corboy's "turf" is Max Wildman, a fifty-three-year-old Chicago lawyer who defends many of the largest insurance companies or corporations in the United States against personal injury claims. Wildman is the senior partner of a firm of thirty-two lawyers, almost all of whom spend all their time defending personal injury cases. The firm occupies an entire floor of the new IBM building in Chicago. But despite his annual six-figure income, according to reporter Laing in another *Wall Street Journal* piece, Wildman "cuts a less-than-impressive figure as he walks into court. . . . He's dressed in a baggy tweed jacket with elbow patches and badly frayed sleeves. One of his scuffed shoes is separating at a seam. He carries a battered briefcase. . . . Shabby courtroom attire is one of the many ploys he has used successfully during his 25-year career to gain the sympathy of juries. . . ."[2] Asks Wildman with a smile, "Why should the other side have a monopoly on sympathy?" According to Nat Ozman, a prominent Chicago plaintiff's lawyer who has often opposed Wildman in court, "What makes him so dangerous is his ability to use emotionalism and other plaintiff-lawyer tactics against the plaintiff. Juries seem to lap up that Hoosier country boy act of his."

Like Corboy, Wildman is a prodigious and meticulous worker. A big case will see Wildman and his associates spending months in painstaking preparation. They will conduct innumerable interviews with witnesses and technical experts such as engineers, burrow in numerous technical manuals as well as law books, and then take as many as sixty sworn statements. Courses in everything from bacteriology to metallurgy are a customary part of Wildman's courtroom preparation.

For Wildman, as for Corboy, jury selection is all-important. "You have to find people able to resist the natural impulse to give the

Note on p. 8.

plaintiff the moon, and that's not easy," says Wildman. Logically enough, since Corboy shuns retired pleople who live on fixed incomes, Wildman prefers them, along with older blue-collar and middle-management workers: "They are accustomed to shifting for themselves and are usually conservative with awards." Wildman resists younger jurors because of what he calls their "tendency to have a social-worker, do-gooder mentality." On the other hand, he often seeks to exploit racial and class differences in jury selection in order to encourage dissension among jurors. "A disunified jury rarely grants large awards," he says.

In order to win a case — or at least to hold down the size of a verdict — Wildman will often resort to a variety of artifices: "You can put on the strongest case in the world, but if you don't use your ingenuity and pull tricks you'll get murdered by the jury anyway. Everything I do in front of a jury, whether done in court, during recesses or in the corridors outside court, is calculated to create a certain impression with them. The facial expression, the physical gesture, the mannerism are often more important than what a lawyer actually says. It's absolutely fatal for a defense lawyer to convey arrogance, prosperity or insouciance about the plaintiff's injuries." And so, as Laing describes it, "Mr. Wildman dresses poorly. He never smokes his cigars, which he has custom-made, in front of the jury. During a trial he makes a point of always eating in the courthouse cafeteria with the jurors rather than at his usual haunt, Chicago's posh University Club."

Although his clients are invariably large insurance companies or corporations, Wildman makes a point of having the nominal defendant (say, an employee of the insured corporation) sit with him at the defense table throughout the trial. The presence of such a "goat," as Wildman calls him, personalizes the defense: "I want to create the impression with the jury that the goat's head is on the block, so that when they retire to the jury room to decide the case, their sympathy for the plaintiff will be offset by their concern over the fate of the goat." Recently Coath & Goss, Inc., a Chicago building contractor, retained Wildman to defend a $1.2 million suit by the widow and three children of a young elevator mechanic's helper who was killed at one of Coath & Goss's construction sites. In that trial the plaintiff's lawyer called a variety of experts, among them a safety engineer from the Illinois Institute of Technology and several witnesses from the Elevator Constructors Union. The case involved the fall of a one-ton elevator platform, held aloft by so-called safety shoes, which crushed the mechanic, who was working four floors under it. The issue was whether the elevator platform was unsafe in light of the alleged failure of the company to follow an industry practice of cabling the elevator to the building in addition to using the safety shoes. As his "goat" Wildman used the general superintendent from Coath & Goss at the site of the accident. Throughout the trial the superintendent, dressed in work clothes, sat at the defense table. Eventually he was called as the defense's only witness. Then Wildman's emotional closing argument tried to imply that the superintendent — and not Coath & Goss, Inc. — was being charged with responsibility for the death.

Wildman is not above resorting to what he himself calls "tricks." "In one case," writes Laing, "in which Mr. Wildman's client was charged with negligence by a middle-aged businessman whose wife died in ... [an accident], he had his attractive blonde secretary come into the courtroom at the end of the trial and sit next to the [plaintiff] widower. Following Mr. Wildman's instructions she asked the man an innocent question, smiled, patted his hand, and quickly left." Smiling at his recollection of the incident, Wildman said to Laing: "Just one look at the cold expressions on the lady jurors' faces was enough to tell me that we were home free. When the jury came back with a not-guilty [that is, a verdict that the defendant was not guilty of responsibility for the accident], the plaintiff's lawyer never knew what hit him. You see, the entire interchange took place while he was facing the jury in the midst of his closing argument."

Similarly, at the trial over the elevator accident, Wildman arranged for a claims supervisor of Liberty Mutual Insurance Company, which had retained him, to sit in on the entire trial and chat amiably with the widow in front of the jury whenever her lawyer was absent in order to give the impression that she had a boyfriend. Defending such practices, Wildman told Laing, "After all, in this day of consumerism and distrust of the establishment, a lawyer defending corporations doesn't have a hell of a lot going for him, so he has to make his breaks."

Although it is hard to justify trickery, one can perhaps better understand the pressures that lead to such practices by understanding the unique nature of personal injury cases, as a class, in engendering one-sided emotional appeal.[3] Personal injury cases often pit a lonely, needy, pathetic injured person against a large, wealthy, impersonal corporate institution (either an insurance company or a large self-insuring corporation). No other class of cases, not even criminal cases, so uniquely, as a general proposition, involves this one-sided aspect. In criminal cases, it is true, the defendants are lonely, often pathetic people facing a large impersonal institution — the state, but the state also has emotional appeal on its side. The individual defendant is charged with a criminal, often a heinous, act. Not only emotional outrage against him but also sympathy for his alleged victim can be exploited. In criminal cases, then, it is often the prosecution — the representative of the large, impersonal, institutionalized party — which can appeal more to emotion than can the opposing side. And the mutual possibility of exploiting sympathy often leads to mutual restraint on each side for fear of retaliatory exploitation.

The same *mutual* possibility of emotional appeal exists for other classes of cases in which human factors are intense, such as divorce or child custody cases. But in personal injury cases there is no such possibility of even-sided emotional appeal. The most the victim is usually guilty of is carelessness — scarcely very heinous. So the plaintiff can indulge in appeals to emotion with relatively little fear of being checked, because, as Wildman indicates, for the defendant to keep objecting to the plaintiff's emotional evidence of, say, the nature and gravity of his injury is to risk appearing heartless or "insouciant." As a result, personal injury cases become uniquely emotional affairs, with the restrained and frustrated defendant often turning to trickery. In sum, all litigation is subject to some irrational, emotional appeal, but personal injury cases seem unique in the strength of that appeal.

This, then, is the ambience of personal injury litigation — fraught with a frightening mixture of arcane technology, raw emotionalism, and sly tricks.* Quite a basis for deciding whether and how the desperately injured should be cared for.

* For a further example taken from a trial transcript, see *infra,* Appendix I. Note on p. 8.

NOTES

1. Laing, "For the Plaintiff . . . ," *Wall St. J.*, Aug. 2, 1972, pp. 1, 12, col. 1. The discussion of Philip Corboy in this chapter is, in large measure, based on this evocative article.

2. Laing, "For the Defense," *Wall St. J.*, July 5, 1973, pp. 1, 10, cols. 1, 2. The discussion of Max Wildman in this chapter is largely based on this companion piece to Laing, "For the Plaintiff . . . ," *supra* note 1.

3. *Cf.* R. Keeton, *Trial Tactics and Methods* 7 (2d ed. 1973).

2

Adding Insult to Injury

In many ways, the cases of Philip Corboy's client, Italo Procaccini, and of others opposed by Max Wildman are typical — typical of the expense, delay, hazards, and frustrations of litigating over personal injury in our society. But in one crucial respect Procaccini's case, at least, was not typical. Procaccini escaped — albeit narrowly — the typical fate of an injured claimant: getting nothing. This, of course, is the end so skillfully sought by lawyers like Max Wildman. How successful the tort liability system is in resisting and defeating claimants like Italo Procaccini is indicated by the *Final Report* of the National Commission on Product Safety, which states, "[M]ost injuries to consumers [from manufactured products] go uncompensated."[1]

In 1972 New York State joined a growing number of states in enacting a so-called no-fault automobile insurance law. Under the New York law, which took effect February 1, 1974, after an automobile accident each victim is automatically paid up to $50,000 for his actual wage loss or medical expenses without regard to faulty conduct on anyone's part.[2] Thereby, the need to qualify for payment by the kind of exhaustive faultfinding exemplified in the Procaccini case will be eliminated in almost every case. Under another feature of the statute, lawsuits for personal injuries based on fault will be prohibited unless a victim's medical bills total at least $500 or unless he is killed or suffers certain serious injuries, such as a complicated fracture, loss of bodily function or limb, or disfigurement.[3]

But the New York no-fault auto insurance law, while assuring much more compensation to auto accident victims, does not in any

Notes on p. 24.

way alleviate the situation of a person injured like Mr. Procaccini in other than an auto accident, nor does it solve the difficulties of auto accident losses above $50,000. The same situation prevails in all the other jurisdictions that have passed genuine no-fault auto insurance laws.[4] Indeed, with the exception of Michigan[5] and Minnesota,[6] the no-fault benefits payable are much lower elsewhere than in New York (in Massachusetts, for example, they are only $2,000).[7]

In essence, the following presents the differences between liability and no-fault auto insurance. Under the old so-called tort liability system, after an accident in a collision between Jones and Smith, Jones could claim against Smith based on the fact that Jones was free from fault and Smith was at fault. Because Jones is an "innocent" party claiming against a "wrongdoer," Jones is allowed to claim not only for his out-of-pocket losses but for the monetary value of his pain and suffering as well. But because it is so difficult in so many cases to establish not only who was at fault but also the pecuniary value of pain (what *is* an aching arm worth?), payment under the so-called fault system is often nonexistent and almost always long delayed, and the insurance pie is always greatly lessened by the need to use up so much of the money to pay expensive experts for haggling over who and what is to be paid.[8]

The solution for auto accident insurance is now seen to be a system whereby after an accident between Jones and Smith each will be paid, regardless of anyone's fault, by his own insurance company, periodically month by month as his losses accrue, for his own out-of-pocket loss (relatively easy to total up from, say, the medical bills, in contrast to fighting to determine what pain is worth in dollars and cents). As a corollary, each will be required to waive his tort claim based on fault against the other. With the savings from the reduction of legal fees (no-fault insurance has been called "no-lawyer" insurance) and from the elimination of nonpecuniary loss payments, more people will be eligible for payment from the insurance pool into which fewer — or surely no more — dollars need be paid.[9] This is, in essence, the "miracle" being wrought by no-fault auto insurance.

Unfortunately, no state — with the possible exception of Michigan, and perhaps Minnesota and New York as well — has enacted a truly respectable no-fault auto insurance law. The National Con-

Notes on pp. 24–25.

ference of Commissioners on Uniform State Laws[10] and the staff of the Senate Commerce Committee[11] have both drafted bills providing comparatively generous no-fault benefits, including provisions for some catastrophic losses, and abolishing most claims based on fault, but state legislatures have not seen fit to follow suit. As long as no-fault laws replace only trivial claims based on fault and provide benefits as meager as the $2,000 provided under the Massachusetts law, smaller claims based on fault will continue to waste auto insurance dollars while overpaying many slightly injured victims, and bigger claims based on fault will continue to thwart seriously injured traffic victims, leaving them without prompt or adequate — and in many cases significant — payment.

One reason for such inadequate no-fault laws (in addition to simple conservatism, often in the face of powerful lawyer and insurance company lobbying) has been the fear of what relatively unlimited no-fault benefits might cost: "Although the proponents [of the most ambitious no-fault plans] . . . have predicted substantial cost savings even under their unlimited coverage, the costs of covering catastrophic loss could be staggering. For example, Professor Conard and his colleagues estimated in their . . . study [of auto insurance in Michigan] that the three per cent of traffic victims who suffer out-of-pocket loss of $10,000 or more account for 57 per cent of all out-of-pocket loss suffered by all traffic victims. Similarly, the gross underestimations of the cost of Medicare and Medicaid have tended to make skeptics of us all concerning optimistic actuarial estimates of the cost of relatively unlimited insurance coverages."[12]

Because one of the strongest appeals of no-fault insurance has been lower cost, no-fault laws will probably continue to leave many larger losses uncovered. The interests of traffic accident victims would best be served if the savings from no-fault insurance were used to cover the cost of providing higher no-fault benefits, but in light of the resentment over exorbitant auto insurance costs, that alternative appears politically unpalatable. One cannot deny the tragedy involved in this stalemate, for neither is there much likelihood that any catastrophically injured traffic victim is going to recover his tremendous losses in a tort suit. According to the monumental Department of Transportation study of auto accident payments, the typical traffic victim who is permanently and totally disabled sus-

Notes on p. 25.

tains an average out-of-pocket loss of $78,000 but receives compensation of only $12,500 from auto liability insurance.[13] About half of those who are seriously injured in traffic accidents get nothing at all from tort liability claims.[14] Leaving such victims to the tender mercies of a tort liability suit is too often little or no help.

The problem of securing adequate compensation is even more pronounced for those who suffer losses, large or small, in accidents not involving automobiles. At least for auto accidents many people have long been getting paid something. Figures vary, but approximately 85 percent of all traffic victims — those with slight injuries as well as serious ones — get something when a lawyer is hired to claim against the other driver's insurance company.[15] True, the maldistribution of payment is horrendous: those suffering under $100 get on the average seven times their loss if a lawyer is retained,[16] while of those suffering $10,000 or more in out-of-pocket loss, 96 percent get less than their loss.[17] But at least for auto accidents a large total number of people are being paid a large total sum of money. The situation in other areas of tort liability is much darker. For areas such as product liability and medical malpractice, to name the two most significant areas of tort liability other than auto accidents, we have no data of the depth and quality developed for traffic accidents, but everything we know tells us how relatively niggardly and rare are payouts under these other forms of tort liability. In contrast to most auto accident claims, which most lawyers feel competent to handle, "[i]n the best of circumstances, a products case is still a bruising, frequently heartbreaking, always onerous undertaking for client and lawyer."[18]

Why should this be? In the first place, the issues in a product liability case are far more technical and demanding than are those in a typical auto case. Establishing whether a driver was going too fast, was in the wrong lane, or was failing to keep a proper lookout, while perhaps tedious, is well within the ken of almost any adult, not to mention lawyer. But in order to impose liability on a manufacturer for injury caused by his product, that product must be proven in some way defective,[19] and proving a product defective involves engineering evidence and testimony of the most technical and arcane kind, as the description of the Procaccini case illustrated.

According to a legal manual on the trial of products liability cases,

Notes on p. 26.

"Before trial, counsel [on each side, must spend] . . . hours, if not days or weeks, with his expert learning about the technology and the minutiae of the product [in question]."[20] And all the while lawyers and engineers are huddling and conferring and appearing in court, an extremely expensive meter is ticking. In a recent typical accident case, for example, engineer Leslie Williams charged $250 a day for four days' testimony in court, totalling $1,000, plus $30 an hour for extensive pretrial research and consulting.*[21]

Of course, the decision to invest all this time and money and energy is not lightly undertaken. Manufacturers, as we shall see, defend product liability cases with a vengeance and a passion — and often win. The plaintiff's lawyer, on the other hand, is paid on a contingent fee. Thus, if the case is lost the lawyer is out of pocket a rather huge investment in time and money. As a practical matter, a lawyer often will himself pay for the experts' fees and for the elaborate exhibits in the event of an adverse verdict. If the case is won, these costs are taken out of the settlement or verdict, with the lawyer getting one-third or more of either the total verdict or the remainder as his fee, depending on the lawyer's mode of procedure.

Nor are the problems of legal doctrine and factual proof by any means limited to proving a defect. The manufacturer will most often defend with an almost endless variety of technical and legal hurdles that can often only be resolved after exhaustive trials and then appeals, with the latter resulting in lengthy, arcane, technical written opinions many thousands of words in length. For example, it will be contended:

¶ That the product was not unreasonably dangerous.

In a New Jersey case, Edwin Jakubowski, an employee of the Ford Motor Company, was sanding a car body with a pneumatic rotary-type grinding machine that used a sanding disc manufactured by Minnesota Mining and Manufacturing Corporation. The disc snapped in half and struck Jakubowski in the abdomen. In the resulting litigation against 3M, the defendant contended, among other things, that although the disc may have been dangerous, it was not

---

* Some of the flavor of the exhaustive and highly technical nature of the preparation, examination, and cross-examination of such expert witnesses is conveyed by a small portion, set forth in Appendix II, of the testimony of one expert in an actual case.

Notes on p. 26.

unreasonably dangerous in that it must be expected that discs will wear out and break. The defendant won at the trial level. Jakubowski appealed and succeeded in getting an intermediate appellate court to order a new trial in an opinion of some forty-eight hundred words (with the legal and factual issues concerning the disc's defectiveness sufficiently complex also to cause one judge on the three-man panel to write a rather extensive dissenting opinion). Minnesota Mining and Manufacturing then appealed to the Supreme Court of New Jersey, which overruled the intermediate appellate court and reaffirmed the trial court in a 4–3 decision, with the majority opinion running to some three thousand words and the minority opinion to about one thousand words. (Keep in mind that the most Jakubowski could have obtained from the state supreme court at this point was an order for a new trial so he could start all over again.)[22]

¶ That it was not the product that in fact injured the plaintiff.

On September 12, 1964, Doris Elliott had a shampoo and permanent at Marguerite's Beauty Parlor in Franklin, New Hampshire. When she arrived home, "all my hair was on my shoulders. Then I looked in the mirror and it kept coming out. For almost a week or so it kept coming out." She sued the beauty parlor, which defended on the ground that there was no showing that her condition was caused by the beauty parlor or any shampoo or other material the beauty parlor had applied to her hair. Ms. Elliott won at the trial, the beauty parlor appealed to the Supreme Court of New Hampshire, and on July 30, 1969 (almost five years after the accident), a verdict for the beauty parlor was ordered in a two-thousand-word opinion.[23]

¶ That the injury did not occur so much because the product was defective but as a result of some other cause, such as the victim's own idiosyncratic condition.

In June, 1958, Dorothy Cochran of Eugene, Oregon, who suffered from a painful form of arthritis of the spine, was referred to Dr. James Broke, who prescribed a drug called chloroquine manufactured by the Sterling Drug Company. A side effect of the drug, taken over three years, led to Ms. Cochran's virtual blindness. She sued both Dr. Broke and Sterling. The defense was based substantially on the proposition that if "her tragic loss of vision was caused

Notes on p. 26.

by chloroquine, she was one of the rare persons so affected." The defendants won at the trial level, Ms. Cochran appealed to the Supreme Court of Oregon, and the judgment against her was affirmed in an eighteen-hundred-word opinion.[24]

¶ That the defect was not in the product when it left the hands of the party being sued but arose later.

On April 21, 1961, William Sundet of Nebraska was injured by an explosion of the rifle he was firing. He sued Olin Mathieson Chemical Company, which he claimed was the manufacturer of the cartridge in the chamber at the time of the explosion. Olin Mathieson defended on the ground that the package of shells had been opened before sale to Sundet and perhaps reloaded with other than Olin Mathieson's cartridges. In addition, Olin Mathieson contended, there was no reasonable basis for concluding, even assuming the cartridges were Olin Mathieson's, "that any defect at the time of the retail sale [to Sundet] represented a preexistent condition of [Olin Mathieson's] . . . making." At the trial there was judgment for Olin Mathieson, Sundet appealed, and in early 1966 (well over five years after the accident) the Supreme Court of Nebraska, in a relatively short five-hundred-word opinion, affirmed the judgment for Olin Mathieson. (Here, too, the procedure of the case was such that the best Sundet could have obtained at this point would have been a new trial.)[25]

¶ That the injured party, through his own contributory fault, helped cause the accident, thus barring any liability.

On March 5, 1967, Edgar Magnuson was using a snowmobile while fox hunting with some companions near Granite Falls, Minnesota. Traveling at twenty to twenty-five miles an hour, the snowmobile went into a ditch, stopping abruptly. Magnuson smashed his right knee against an exposed spark plug, which had lost its protective insulator some time before the accident. Magnuson sued Rupp Manufacturing, Inc., the maker of the snowmobile. Rupp defended on the basis, among other grounds, that Magnuson should have been aware of the danger. The jury found for the defendant, the trial judge granted Magnuson's motion for a new trial, and Rupp Manufacturing appealed to the Supreme Court of Minnesota, which reinstated the jury verdict against the injured victim in an opinion of some six thousand words. (Once again, the most the

Notes on p. 26.

injured party could have obtained after all this was another trial to start all over again.)[26]

¶ That the manufacturer gave sufficient warning of the danger — express or implied — to the injured party.

Lorna Crane of San Diego undertook to paint premises she and her husband owned while preparing to start a restaurant. She was persuaded by a salesman at Sears, Roebuck and Company to buy a surface preparer. During the process of applying the preparer to a wall in a toilet room, "there was," in the words of the court's opinion, "a 'woosh,' fire leaped into the room [and] plaintiff caught on fire. . . ." She sued both Sears and the Universal Paint Corporation, manufacturer of the preparer. The defense was based, among other things, on the fact that the label contained an express warning that the mixture was flammable and that the plaintiff had failed to heed the warning properly since "there were no windows or ventilation in either the toilet room or the adjoining wash basin compartment in which there was a hot water heater, other than a vent tube in the toilet room." Mrs. Crane gained a verdict at the trial level, the defendants appealed, and the appellate court affirmed the trial court verdict in a twenty-two-hundred-word opinion.[27]

In 1964 Charles Posey was operating a forklift truck manufactured by Clark Equipment Company in his employer's warehouse. He accidentally lifted cartons of furnace units above the height of his seat; they swayed, and the carton on top fell on him. He sued Clark Equipment for failing to provide the forklift with available special overhead protection for "high tiering" or for failing to give warning that such a guard should be installed during high tiering. Clark Equipment defended on the grounds, among others, that the danger was obvious and therefore that in effect the warning was implied. The trial court directed a verdict for the defendant, Posey appealed, and the United States Court of Appeals in 1969 affirmed the verdict against the injured party in a twenty-eight-hundred-word opinion. (And here, once again, the procedure was such that the most Posey would have gained at this point, five years after the accident, was a chance to start all over again with a new trial.)[28]

Keep in mind that these and countless other similar snags can all lead to expensive, prolonged disputes, with that horrendously expensive meter again ticking away for both sides. As far as the defense

Notes on p. 26.

is concerned, according to the report of the National Commission on Product Safety, "[t]he manufacturer employs a battery of attorneys and technical experts with ample resources at their disposal. The consumer must prove [as pointed out above, a variety of complicated propositions]. . . . Meanwhile the defense can muster volumes of evidence against each statement by the consumer. The defense can also stall: it can appeal to the next highest court. While the consumer waits and pays, the defense, if it expects to lose, can offer a modest settlement."[29]

The obstacles facing a victim injured by a manufactured product, in contrast to those faced by a traffic victim (bad as the latter are), are exacerbated by the deep umbrage the typical manufacturer takes at facing or paying a product liability claim. After all, his product is accused of being defective. Quite apart from the adverse publicity involved, it deeply offends the pride of most manufacturers to be thus challenged. It denigrates the prodigious effort they believe they expend on such things as careful design and quality control. As a result, a product liability insurance policy will often give the insured manufacturer a right of veto over any power of the insurance company to settle the claim. In contrast, the typical automobile policy gives the insurance company the right to settle without regard to any protest by the insured motorist. Studies indeed show that insurance companies pay little heed to any insured motorist who in fact does protest payment. Little matter, since such protests are quite rare. After all, does the typical motorist take offense with his liability insurance company for paying out on his behalf? On the contrary, so indifferent are insured motorists to claims against them that, according to one study, for claims settled early in the proceedings fully 64 percent of the insured defendants did not know the outcome of the case. Even when the case went to trial a substantial number did not know the outcome![30] The bitter reluctance of the typical manufacturer, on the other hand, to settle almost *any* case is illustrated by the remark a few years ago of a "lawyer who [defended] . . . bottlers of soft drinks against claims for injuries alleged to have come from foreign matter in their product [who stated] . . . that he never [recommended] . . . a settlement. 'After all,' he said, 'all a man needs to go into business against us is a bug and a nickel.' "[31]

The extent to which the aim of product liability insurance is to

Notes on p. 27.

deny rather than to make payment for injuries is graphically, if unconsciously, illustrated by a recent speech by W. R. Metzgar, an officer at Aetna Life & Casualty, one of the largest product liability insurers in the world. After describing the exhaustive administrative procedures that should be adopted by insurance companies "working as a team" with manufacturers on product liability insurance (including reviewing the manufacturing process as well as test procedures and imparting advice on just what records should be kept and for how long), Metzgar states: "The objective of all this is to finally achieve the utopia of noting where the product claims are coming from and knowing that a successful defense is already built and in operation."[32]

The consequence of this kind of intransigence, according to the report of the National Commission on Product Safety, is that "[t]he most serious limitation on recovery of damages for [product] injuries to consumers is the cost of trial: witnesses testified that it hardly pays to press a defective product claim for less than $5,000 to $10,000." As a result, says the report, "most injuries to consumers [from manufactured products] go uncompensated." Indeed, in light of the difficulty of prosecuting a product liability claim, the report comments, it is "[s]mall wonder that some manufacturers do not even respond to letters claiming compensation for injuries: they know that more than two-thirds will never pursue the claim. A survey of 276 persons in Denver and Boston who had reported their injuries to the Food and Drug Administration Survey teams showed that only 4 percent contacted an attorney to investigate possible legal redress." And of those 4 percent, less than 1 percent (2 out of 276) did so with intent of claiming against the manufacturer. "To advise a battered consumer to sue," says the commission, "may simply add insult to injury."[33]

All this would be tragic enough even without the huge losses due to personal injury inflicted by manufactured products in this country. The National Commission on Product Safety found that 20 million Americans annually are injured "in the home as a result of incidents connected with consumer products," with "a number of makes, models, or types" of products harboring especially "unreasonable hazards to the American consumer: architectural glass, color television sets, fireworks, floor furnaces, glass bottles, high-rise bicycles,

Notes on p. 27.

hot-water vaporizers, household chemicals, infant furniture, ladders, power tools, protective headgear, rotary lawnmowers, toys, unvented gas heaters, and wringer washers."[34]

Of the 20 million injured, 110,000 are permanently disabled and 30,000 are killed.[35] The annual cost to society from such injuries may well exceed $5.5 billion, with a calculation of over $4 billion in "costs to the injured persons, their families, and close friends or relatives, whether or not the monies are reimbursed."[36]

Of the particular products, architectural glass or ordinary window glass injures 150,000 annually, with 100,000 of these injuries alone caused by people walking through glass doors;[37] fireworks injure from 5,000 to 15,000 people each year;[38] injuries resulting from the use of ladders amount to 125,000 to 200,000 every year, with 400 to 600 of these resulting in death;[39] power tools injure some 125,000 people annually;[40] rotary lawnmowers have caused an estimated 140,000 injuries in one year;[41] children's toys and play equipment cause at least 1,400,000 injuries each year;[42] and 100,000 to 200,000 injuries each year are related to wringer washing machines.[43]

Lest these statistics glide too impersonally by, some excerpts from the commission's report quite literally flesh them out:

> Two eighth-grade football players collided on their school's athletic field. Both were wearing the school's prescribed protective helmet, but it did not protect one. He required six operations (five involving brain surgery). Medical bills exceeded $12,000. At age 20, he is partially paralyzed, handicapped by a speech disorder, and unable to care for himself.[44]

> . . . .

> The McCormack family bought a Hankscraft vaporizer advertised as tip-proof, foolproof, and safe. It bore the seals of *Good Housekeeping* and *Parents'* magazines, and the mark of Underwriters' Laboratories. They placed it on a stool in their home, plugged in the house circuit, and waited for the steam to rise. While it was steaming, their 3-year-old daughter caught herself in its electric cord. The vaporizer tipped and spilled scalding water onto the child. Andrea McCormack spent 5 months in the hospital enduring a series of painful operations. She will bear the scars all her life.[45]

> . . . .

Notes on p. 27.

On the first warm Saturday in spring, hospital emergency room crews expect a parade of patients holding a bloody towel around a lacerated or amputated hand or foot. On opening day of the grass-grooming season, the rotary power mower begins its work of trimming lawns, fingers, and toes. About 70% of the injuries from power mowers are lacerations, amputations, and fractures that result from the cutting and crushing action of the fast whirling blade.

In addition, there are high-velocity ejections of wire, glass, stones, and debris that can puncture vital body parts.

Thomas Cohiles regularly cut two or three lawns in his hometown of Marysville, California, to earn pocket money. One day in September 1965, Tom stood nearly 30 feet from a friend operating a power mower. As the machine turned sharply right, a rock hurtled from the discharge opening and struck Cohiles' right eye. Today, that eye is blind.[46]

. . . .

Eugene McDaniel in Georgia was a normal 19-year-old when he turned up the heat in his room. Now he has a mental age of about 8.

The cause . . . was something the [victim] . . . couldn't see, hear, or smell: carbon monoxide (CO). And the source of CO . . . was an innocent-looking unvented gas heater.[47]

. . . .

On August 14, 1968, in Columbus, Ohio, a washing machine strangled a 3-year-old girl. The mother had left the machine running while she went to look for her child outdoors. Upon returning, the mother found her daughter with head and arm caught inside the moving wringer.

These wringers use two motor-driven rollers which squeeze water out of rinsed clothes with a pressure of 500 or more pounds. Their velocity is about 300 inches per minute.[48]

Despite such harrowing but actuarially predictable death and mutilation, the total amount of compensation available to victims from product liability insurance is negligible, even when compared with the exiguous benefits flowing to traffic victims from automobile liability insurance. For auto accidents, a Department of Transportation study found that, with compensable losses totalling $5.1 billion in serious injuries and death cases, auto liability insurance paid out

Notes on p. 27.

only $800 million, or 15 percent of compensable losses.[49] For consumer products the percentage is apparently much less. According to the National Commission on Product Safety, product liability insurance covers "only a few per cent of the medical cost of injuries."[50] In another way, too, the sickeningly bad auto liability insurance system nonetheless makes the product liability insurance system look that much worse by comparison: more than half — 56 cents — of every auto insurance premium dollar is chewed up in administrative and legal costs.[51] This is in contrast to administrative and legal expenses of 3 cents per dollar for social security, 7 cents per dollar for Blue Cross, and 17 cents per dollar for health and accident plans.[52] Although precise figures for product liability insurance are not available, given what we know about the greater need for expensive experts and the greater likelihood of recalcitrant resistance to claims, along with the lack of payment of smaller nuisance claims, the percentage of the premium dollar spent on administrative and legal expenses for product liability insurance is considerably greater even than that for auto insurance.[53]

Fewer than ten years ago there were about 50,000 product liability claims in U.S. courts; today there are about 500,000.[54] Similarly, the gross amount of product liability premiums has skyrocketed: between 1950 and 1970, according to one estimate, premiums grew by 500 percent.[55] But because of the complexity and inefficiency of product liability litigation and insurance, the public has derived little benefit from the vaunted explosion of product liability suits. Except for a few victims "lucky" enough (1) to be seriously injured by a product with a demonstrably provable defect, (2) to hire a Philip Corboy, and (3) to possess a case which — miracle of miracles — can run the gauntlet of countless legal and practical pitfalls, the recipients of money which could help to compensate injured consumers are for the most part a few highly skilled lawyers on both sides, a few highly skilled engineers and technical experts, and a few casualty insurance companies, constantly complaining about how much money they are losing on the whole operation.

There might be one public benefit which could compensate for this disgraceful state of affairs: if all this energy, talent, and money expended by expert witnesses, the bar, and the insurance industry resulted in deterrent feedback to manufacturers and a reduction in

Notes on p. 27.

accidents, then all the expense and frustration of product liability might be justified. Certainly this is a justification for tort liability often urged by the trial bar.[56]

Unfortunately, tort liability does not succeed as a deterrent, either.

The National Commission on Product Safety commissioned law professor William Whitford to do an empirical study "to assess the impact of product liability litigation on the decisions of manufacturers regarding the design of their products and the content of the warnings issued about dangers connected with their products' use." "The circumstantial evidence uncovered in this project," wrote Whitford, "together with what direct evidence there is, suggests that products liability litigation usually has little direct impact on product design or warning decisions." The evidence supporting this conclusion was of three types, said Whitford: "First, in many of the cases studied, the time period between the occurrence of the injury and the final outcome of the litigation exceed 5 years, and in almost every case the time period was at least 2 years. The design of many products is changed periodically for reasons unconnected with safety, and when these products are involved in litigation, the court is usually asked to determine whether a design no longer in use was sufficiently safe."[57] Second, although manufacturers probably interest themselves in product liability litigation more than, say, motorists,[58] nonetheless

a number of ... manufacturers ... indicated that their insurers handled all products liability claims. In some instances, the manufacturers apparently do not even inform themselves of the final resolution of the claims, and for these manufacturers it is obvious that a court decision will have no direct effect on product design or warning decisions. A manufacturer who intended to take account of litigation results would be likely to exert more control over the claim setting process since the other interests that enter into design decisions could be undesirably affected by an adverse outcome.

Finally, a majority of the rotary mower manufacturers who replied responsively [to this survey] indicated that they did not routinely keep track of litigation involving other manufacturers. A manufacturer taking account of products liability litigation in

Notes on p. 28.

its design decisions would logically inform himself of the outcome of litigation involving manufacturers of similar products, particularly in an industry in which there has been so much litigation.[59]

Well, if tort litigation serves little, if any, deterrent purpose on manufacturers directly, how about an indirect effect? Do insurance companies encourage manufacturers to show a more general concern for safety?

No luck there, either. Herbert Denenberg, then a professor of insurance at the Wharton School of the University of Pennsylvania and later the much-publicized insurance commissioner of Pennsylvania, conducted another study for the National Commission on Product Safety on the activities of the casualty insurance industry in encouraging safer products. According to Denenberg, "the insurance industry is in a strategically perfect place to promote loss prevention, to find new and better methods of saving life, limb, and property, to prevent needless and tragic accidents and catastrophies, and to make our productive process work more efficiently and more humanely. Insurance industry opportunity and insurance industry self-interest for loss prevention should blend into a near perfect picture."[60] But in reporting on a survey of product liability insurance companies, agents, brokers, and insureds, Professor Denenberg found the following patterns:

¶ Insurance companies — including "some of the billion dollar companies [and] . . . several considered to be among the top handful of insurers with a 'blue-chip' reputation for loss prevention and engineering" — failed to analyze their claims files, underwriting documents, or other records to "obtain principles and guides for preventing future products liability claims."[61]

¶ Insurance companies did not know — or even bother to try to know — "what the payoff is for loss prevention service." Most companies had not studied, for example, "the impact on products liability [losses] of different types or intensities of inspections and other loss prevention services."[62]

¶ Insurance companies had no idea — or even interest in — what their various loss prevention and inspection services actually cost them.[63]

Notes on p. 28.

¶ Insurance companies had very poorly staffed loss prevention departments, where such departments existed at all.[64]

¶ Insurance companies' agents, brokers, and customers had "grave misgivings about the loss prevention services of the American insurance industry." Indeed, 62 percent of insurance buyers of large American industrial concerns felt that their insurer did not "make an important contribution, by its loss prevention advice, to [their] overall products liability safety effort."[65]

¶ Insurance companies not only failed to utilize pertinent safety information in their own files, but refused to let others in government, academe, or the like have access to their records "in order to extract life-saving information."[66]

NOTES

1. National Commission on Product Safety, *Final Report* 74 (1970) [hereinafter cited as *Final Report*].
2. Comprehensive Insurance Reparations Act, ch. 13, art. 18, §§ 671(1) and (2) and 672(1) (1973), 1 McKinney's Session Law of New York 9. See *N.Y. Times,* Feb. 14, 1973, p. 50, col. 1.
3. Comprehensive Insurance Reparations Act, ch. 13, art. 18, §§ 671(4)(a) and 673(1) (1973), 1 McKinney's Session Law of New York 9.
4. For a discussion of the distinction between a genuine no-fault law and a "spurious" or so-called add-on law, see *N.Y. Times,* Nov. 27, 1972, p. 55, cols. 1–2. Under a genuine no-fault law along with no-fault benefits there is to some extent an abolition of the right to sue based on who was at fault in the accident. An "add-on" no-fault law provides only no-fault benefits with no abolition of the right to sue based on fault. As of this writing, fifteen states have enacted genuine no-fault laws: Colorado, Connecticut, Florida, Georgia, Hawaii, Kansas, Kentucky, Massachusetts, Michigan, Minnesota, Nevada, New Jersey, New York, Pennsylvania, and Utah.
5. The bill passed by the Michigan legislature in October, 1972, which took effect in October, 1973, provides for no-fault benefits up to a maximum of $36,000 in wage loss plus unlimited reimbursement for hospital, medical, and rehabilitation costs. It eliminates the tort action unless there is death, permanent disability, serious disfigurement, or serious impairment of bodily function (28 Mich. Compiled Laws Ann., ch. 31, §§ 3101–79 [Supp. 1973–74]). The economic feasibility of the bill would seem to turn on the courts' definition of the word *serious.*
6. The Minnesota bill provides no-fault benefits of $20,000 in medical expenses and $10,000 in other economic loss, including wage loss of 85 percent of salary to a maximum of $200 a week, $1,250 death benefits, and $15 a day for replacement service (for, say, a substitute housekeeper). The tort threshold is $2,000 in medical expenses or disability exceeding sixty days, death, permanent injury, or disfigurement (ch. 408 [1974], Minn. Laws). For

ADDING INSULT TO INJURY

a report on a Pennsylvania statute, passed as this book is in the press, providing unlimited medical benefits and up to $15,000 in wage loss, with a tort threshold of $750 in medical bills, see *National Underwriter* (Property and Casualty ed.), July 19, 1974, p. 2, cols. 2–4.

7. Ann. Laws of Mass., ch. 90, §§ 34a and 34m (1970).

8. J. O'Connell, *The Injury Industry and the Remedy of No-Fault Insurance* 4–8 (1971).

9. "[T]he Massachusetts law has resulted in substantial savings in bodily injury premiums as well as an unexpected decline in claims for damages. Favorable reports on the state's experience were largely responsible for the enactment of a no-fault law by its neighbor Connecticut" (*N.Y. Times,* Oct. 3, 1972, p. 23, col. 5). For a favorable report on the similar Florida no-fault law, see *N.Y. Times,* Nov. 24, 1972, p. 59, cols. 2–3. The New Jersey no-fault, too, has been the subject of favorable reports (*N.Y. Times,* Dec. 24, 1973, p. 17, cols. 7–8).

10. National Conference of Commissioners on Uniform State Laws, *Uniform Motor Vehicle Accident Reparation Act (UMVARA)* (1972).

11. The Senate bill was redrafted late in 1972 to utilize as "[t]he technical basis for the bill [many of the provisions of]...the Uniform Motor Vehicle Accident Reparations Act [UMVARA], which was promulgated in August 1972 by the National Conference of Commissioners on Uniform State Laws ..." (Senate Committee on Commerce, *The National No-Fault Motor Vehicle Insurance Act,* S. Rep. No. 93-382, 93d Cong., 1st Sess., 1–2 [Comm. Print 1973]). The bill, in slightly modified form (S. 354, 93d Cong., 2d Sess.), passed the Senate on May 1, 1974, by a 53–42 vote, but its fate in the House of Representatives remains uncertain (*N.Y. Times,* May 2, 1974, p. 86, cols. 1–4).

12. O'Connell, *supra* note 8, at 118. On the other hand, cost projections under New York's new law (*N.Y. Times,* Jan. 29, 1974, p. 29, cols. 1–3) and for the law proposed by the commissioners on uniform state laws, both of which have very extensive benefits (see *supra* notes 2, 10), indicate that the cost of even substantial no-fault benefits, if combined with a tort exemption (see *supra* note 4), can be surprisingly low compared to tort liability insurance. "For example, the estimates submitted to the Special Committee on UMVARA [the Uniform Motor Vehicle Accident Reparation Act, *supra* note 10 and accompanying text, which would provide lifetime no-fault benefits for wage loss and medical expenses with no overall limit] from the three major segments of the [insurance] industry who disagree sharply about the desirability of no-fault insurance, ranged only from modest savings to modest increases in comparison with costs of the existing [tort liability] system, on average, for policyholders carrying liability insurance of $25,000 per person and $50,000 per accident" (Keeton, "No-Fault Insurance Developments in Perspective," *North Atlantic Regional Business L. Rev.* 14, 18 [Fall, 1972], also printed in testimony of R. Keeton, *Hearings on H.R. 5448 before the Subcommittee on Business, Commerce and Taxation of the House Committee on the District of Columbia,* 93d. Cong., 1st Sess. 188–93 [1973]; see also Keeton, "Compensation Systems and Utah's No-Fault Statute," 3 *Utah L. Rev.* 383, 398-99 [1973]).

13. U.S. Department of Transportation, *Motor Vehicle Crash Losses and Their Compensation in the United States* 90 (1971).

14. 1 U.S. Department of Transportation, *Economic Consequences of Automobile Accident Injuries: Report of the Westat Research Corp.* 38 (1970) [hereinafter cited as *Economic Consequences*]. "In interpreting this number, it should be kept in mind that recovery is presumably dependent on the injured person not having contributed to the accident in the fault sense" (*ibid.*). See also A. Conard *et al., Automobile Accident Costs and Payments: Studies in the Economics of Injury Reparation* 172, 186 (1964).

15. R. Keeton and J. O'Connell, *Basic Protection for the Traffic Victim: A Blueprint for Reforming Automobile Insurance* 55 (1965).

16. American Insurance Association, "Exhibit X," in *Report of Special Committee to Study and Evaluate the Keeton-O'Connell Basic Protection Plan and Automobile Accident Reparations* (1968). See also U.S. Department of Transportation, *Automobile Personal Injury Claims* 114 (1970).

17. *Economic Consequences, supra* note 14, at 235.

18. *Final Report, supra* note 1, at 73.

19. For a good discussion of the defective product requirement, see R. Keeton, *Venturing to Do Justice* 108–12 (1969). A recent decision by the California Supreme Court at least attempted to ease the task of the over-burdened plaintiff by holding that he need not prove that the product was in a "defective condition unreasonably dangerous to the user or consumer" as required by Restatement (Second) of Torts § 402A (1965), but need prove only that the product was defective (Cronin v. J. B. E. Olson Corp., 104 Cal. Rptr. 433, 501 P.2d 1153 [1972]; see also Glass v. Ford Motor Company, 123 N.J. Super. 599, 304 A.2d 562 [1973]). As a practical matter, however, the plaintiff most often still faces an awesome task as long as he must prove a defect existed in the product.

20. Bushnell, "Defendant's Trial Techniques," in *Products Liability: Law, Practice, Science* 13:47 (ed. S. Schreiber and P. Rheingold, 1967).

21. *Wall St. J.*, April 20, 1971, p. 1, col. 1. "Most of us who are directly connected with the insurance industry can relate to individual cases where verdict or settlement of $500,000 or more is not uncommon. Just as severe, and possibly more important in some respects, we also can individually cite cases where the defense costs equal or exceed that same $500,000 figure" (address by James H. Killian, Executive Vice President, Fireman's Fund American Insurance Companies, to the Product Liability Prevention Conference, Newark College of Engineering, Newark, N.J., Aug. 23, 1973).

22. Jakubowski v. Minnesota Mining and Manufacturing Corp., 42 N.J. 177, 199 A.2d 826 (1964).

23. Elliott v. Lachance, 109 N.H. 481, 256 A.2d 153 (1969).

24. Cochran v. Brooke, 243 Ore. 89, 409 P.2d 904 (1966).

25. Sundet v. Olin Mathieson Chemical Corp., 179 Neb. 587, 139 N.W.2d 368 (1966).

26. Magnuson v. Rupp Manufacturing, Inc., 285 Minn. 32, 171 N.W.2d 201 (1969).

27. Crane v. Sears, Roebuck & Co., 218 Cal.2d 855, 32 Cal. Rep. 754 (1963).

28. Posey v. Clark Equipment Co., 409 F.2d 560 (7th Cir. 1969).

29. *Final Report, supra* note 1, at 73.

30. Conard *et al., supra* note 14, at 296–97. See also U.S. Department of Transportation, *Public Attitudes toward Auto Insurance: A Report of the Survey Research Center, Institute for Social Research, University of Michigan* 55–57 (1970).

31. C. Morris, *Morris on Torts* 3 (1953).

32. Metzgar, "Products Liability: Problems Are Complex," *National Underwriter* (Property and Casualty ed.), Sept. 15, 1972, p. 17, col. 1.

33. *Final Report, supra* note 1, at 74 (footnotes omitted).

34. *Ibid.,* 1.

35. *Ibid.*

36. *Ibid.,* 68.

37. *Ibid.,* 12.

38. *Ibid.,* 14.

39. *Ibid.,* 25.

40. *Ibid.,* 26.

41. *Ibid.,* 28–29. The year of this estimate was 1969.

42. *Ibid.,* 30.

43. *Ibid.,* 33.

44. *Ibid.,* 28.

45. *Ibid.,* 20.

46. *Ibid.,* 28.

47. *Ibid.,* 32.

48. *Ibid.,* 33.

49. *Economic Consequences, supra* note 14, at 146–47, Table 15 FS (1970).

50. *Final Report, supra* note 1, at 70 (footnotes omitted).

51. R. Keeton, *Compensation Systems: The Search for a Viable Alternative to Negligence Law* 33 (1969).

52. Warne, "Let's Hear From the Insurance Consumer," 36 *Ins. Counsel J.* 494, 496 (1969). See also Conard *et al., supra* note 14, at 59.

53. "Adjusting expenses average in the miscellaneous liability field about 21.8% of earned premium for stock and mutual companies. If it were possible to segregate the product liability portion of this field, no doubt the loss expense ratio would be even higher" (Killian, *supra* note 21).

54. *National Underwriter* (Property and Casualty ed.) Sept. 8, 1972, p. 48, col. 4; p. 49, col. 1.

55. *Business Insurance,* Nov. 6, 1972, p. 55, col. 2. According to the *New York Times,* which expresses a commonly held feeling, "an effect of no-fault auto laws will be that instead of bringing [automobile] negligence cases, lawyers may focus on such fields as product liability and medical malpractice" (*N.Y. Times,* Jan. 29, 1974, p. 53, col. 4). Indeed, according to Joseph Kelner, one of the leading personal injury lawyers in the country, "In the future, the volume of litigation that will emanate from product cases will either equal or surpass the litigation arising out of automobile collision cases" (Kelner, "Plaintiff's Trial Techniques in Product Liability Cases," in Schreiber and Rheingold, *supra* note 20, at 13:15, 16). For expectations of a rise in medical malpractice cases, see *infra,* ch. 3, notes 28–29 and accompanying text. On the other hand, the complexity of product and medical

cases (see, for example, *supra* notes 18–21 and accompanying text and *infra,* ch. 3, notes 1–6 and accompanying text) means that the number of lawyers handling auto cases who are capable of handling product and medical cases are very few. And it is the marginal — not the expert — auto negligence lawyer who is adversely affected by no-fault laws, at least where small thresholds on tort exemptions are involved (*supra* note 4 and accompanying text). "A preliminary survey in Massachusetts found that a small percentage of lawyers had, in fact, quit private practice [after the introduction of no-fault auto insurance]. 'The few lawyers who will be affected probably should be weeded out anyway,' says Leonard Ring, president of the American Trial Lawyers Association" (*N.Y. Times,* Jan. 29, 1974, p. 53, col. 4). Of course, to the extent the tort exemption in auto no-fault laws eliminates almost all auto cases, the spillover effect in more cases for other types of injuries may be felt.

56. *Cf.* address by Charles Hvass to the Independent Insurance Agents of Minneapolis, Oct. 11, 1967, in American Trial Lawyers Association, *Justice and the Adversary System* 334, 343 (n.d.).

57. Whitford, "Products Liability," in *Supplemental Studies, 3 Product Safety Law and Administration: Federal, State, Local, and Common Law* 221, 228 (1970).

58. *Supra* notes 30–31 and accompanying text.

59. Whitford, *supra* note 57 at 228–29.

60. Statement of H. Denenberg, 9a *Hearings of the National Commission on Product Safety* 311, 312–17 (1970).

61. *Ibid.,* 314.

62. *Ibid.*

63. *Ibid.,* 315.

64. *Ibid.,* 315–17.

65. *Ibid.,* 317.

66. *Ibid.,* 318.

3

The Law's Malpractice against Medicine

The scenario for medical malpractice cases closely follows that for product liability. Here, too, one finds (1) liability turning on quite complicated fact situations, with concomitant expense and delay, (2) deeply offended defendants whose instinct is to resist settlement strongly, (3) such expenses and bother of litigation that only the largest claims are brought, (4) relatively little of the total loss being paid from liability insurance, (5) rapidly rising claims and premiums, and (6) most of the money going to lawyers and insurance companies rather than to the accident victims.

Because the human body is incalculably more complex and less easily understood than any item a consumer can buy, medical malpractice suits almost necessarily involve factual issues even more esoteric and intricate than those found in product liability litigation. One lawyer who has intensively studied medical malpractice has recently spoken of "the almost Byzantine nature of trying to find fault in malpractice litigation. . . ."[1] David Harney of Los Angeles, one of the nation's foremost medical malpractice trial lawyers, in trying to convey the frustrations of this kind of litigation, told a special congressional study of medical malpractice of a case involving "a failure to diagnose a fracture of the spine following a traumatic injury, which led to paralysis of the patient":[2]

> Under the standard form of contingent fee agreement I, as the plaintiff's attorney, was required to advance all of the necessary court costs [in preparation for trial], and the figure . . . approximated or exceeded $50,000. I was able to secure the testimony of an out-of-town physician as an expert witness, but the defense kept

him on the stand under cross examination for approximately 10 days, to my great expense and to the great inconvenience of the witness.

. . . .

The defense was able, as usual, to parade experts onto the witness stand and the experts testified either that there was no violation of any applicable standard of [medical] practice or that the failure to have diagnosed the fracture in question would have made no difference in the ultimate outcome of the patient. On the main issue involved in the trial, the jury was unable to reach a decision ("hung jury") and a mistrial was declared following the 17-week jury trial.[3]

Prior to retrial a settlement was reached, but, says Harney, only after defense costs that were "three times or more greater than my demand for settlement."[4]

According to the recent report of the Department of Health, Education, and Welfare (HEW) Secretary's Commission on Medical Malpractice, "Medical malpractice cases are among the most difficult to try. They usually take two to three times longer than other personal injury cases because of the complexity of the requisite expert medical testimony. Thus, although few in total number, they contribute significantly to the congestion and overload of the court system."[5] So complex are medical malpractice cases that they are not only extraordinarily long to try *in* court but also to settle *out* of court. Says the HEW secretary's commission, "It takes a long time to close a malpractice claim file on the average, only half are closed within 18 months after they are opened; ten percent remain open 6½ years after they are opened."[6]

The problem of complexity of issues and the need for expert witnesses is greatly exacerbated in medical malpractice cases by the so-called conspiracy of silence among doctors. Despite denials by the American Medical Association and other medical groups, as Dr. Ruth Alexander has put it:

Most doctors and surgeons tend to shy away from testifying under oath as witnesses against a colleague. Almost the entire profession of medicine fairly reeks with secrecy and silence. Many doctors, surgeons, nurses, and hospitals are prone to cover up for each other, in keeping with an "ethical" exclusiveness character-

Notes on p. 44.

istic of few other professions. Anyone who may testify against a colleague in any one of these [medical] fields, because his own integrity or indignation gets the better of his fear of reprisal, is apt to be penalized as a traitor to the profession and may be medically, economically, or socially ostracized. . . .[7]

Many grim examples can be cited of such reluctance to speak out and of the retaliatory professional action which can follow testimony adverse to a fellow professional. For example, doctors were asked by the Boston University Law-Medicine Institute whether they would testify in behalf of a claimant in a malpractice case in which a surgeon had mistakenly removed a wrong kidney. Seventy percent of the doctors stated they would refuse to testify despite the clear merit of the claim.[8]

The bitter and pervasive flavor of this reluctance has been illustrated by the indoctrination of an idealistic young intern, as revealed in his published diary:

Monday, October 31

. . . .

. . . [T]here was one case that came in Saturday night that stirred the place up a bit, even though I didn't really get in on it. It's all very hush-hush except that every doctor in the place is talking about it. This patient was a girl who has been a long-time cocktail waitress down at the Hacienda, who was sent in by Dr. Frank Harlow, one of the really top-rate outside surgeons. This in itself was funny, because Harlow does most of his surgery at St. Christopher's and rarely indeed brings anybody here — I guess on the theory that there's not room enough for him and Nathan Slater [the leading "in-house" surgeon] in the same hospital. Anyway, this gal came in by ambulance, and the nurse called me, all confused; Harlow had called ahead to schedule emergency surgery, but he'd said specifically *not* to call out any intern or resident, he'd come in himself. He wasn't there yet, and the patient was, and the nurse said the woman was obviously having a lot of pain and she didn't know what to do.

So I went up to the floor, but before I saw the girl, who should come buzzing in but Hank Ruggles and Harlow together. Apparently, Harlow had called him to scrub on the case with him as a special favor. And they both were very vague and insisted that I needn't bother to scrub.

Notes on pp. 44–45.

That was about 7:30 P.M. Saturday. About 11:00 I was down at midnight supper wondering if I was really hungry enough to try the hot pot or not when Hank appeared, so mad he was actually swearing under his breath, and he told me what the story was. It seems this woman had a varicose vein ligation done at St. Christopher's Hospital about a week before by some general practitioner — Hank wouldn't say which one. Anyway, a day or so later she had developed this sore, swollen leg and complained of pain in the leg and cramps when she walked; she'd called the GP on the phone, and the GP had told her not to worry, there always was some pain and swelling after a vein ligation and it would go away. Next day it was worse, so the woman went to the GP's office, and the doctor ordered some quinine for her leg cramps, and said, "There, there, my good woman, everything's going to be all right," but was too busy to examine her leg.

A couple of days later the leg was so painful that the woman went back and this time insisted that the GP call another surgeon in for a second opinion. This time the doctor looked at the leg, and then called Harlow in because he discovered that the leg was blue and cold from mid-thigh on down. Harlow had shipped her in to Graystone on the spot, and set up emergency surgery, and he and Hank had opened up the incision again and discovered that the GP had ligated the woman's femoral artery just below the groin, so she had no arterial circulation to her leg for four days. So Hank and Harlow had just finished doing a thromboendarterectomy, cutting out the ligated section of the artery and sewing the ends back together again, and then had the anesthetist give her a splanchnic block, which helps dilate the blood vessels in the leg, in hopes of opening the circulation back up again. There on the operating table, after they joined the artery together again, the leg turned pink down to the knee, and after the splanchnic block it was pink to the ankle, but the foot stayed slate gray. It now looks as if the girl may have to have an amputation just above the ankle and lose a foot, all because some jackass couldn't tell the saphenous vein from the femoral artery.

Well, it sounded incredible to me that any doctor could make a mistake like that in the first place, and even more incredible that he could just ignore the woman's complaints, particularly those complaints, for four days postoperatively. If the mistake had been picked up within twenty-four hours, chances are her foot could have been saved. And now neither Hank nor Harlow know what to tell the woman; she's sitting on a $100,000 malpractice claim and doesn't know it. Hank said the GP would probably lose his surgical privileges at St. Christopher's for a while, or at least have them limited, but he didn't think the woman should be told that she was the victim of incompetent surgery compounded by negligence. I got sore as hell at this, told Hank it seemed to me that the gal should sue for every nickel she could get and that every doctor in town should be with her right down the line.

Hank just shook his head and said, "It could be you next time just as well, and then what?" I said, "Well, I wouldn't do a vein ligation without looking at what I was doing, for one thing, and nobody in his right mind could get that big pulsating artery confused with a vein." Hank said, "My ass they couldn't, I've done it myself. I had a big, fat 2-0 silk tie around a femoral artery once, all set to pull it down and tie it before somebody noticed it and hollered. You just can't nail the man for making the mistake, and as for negligence, there isn't a doctor alive that isn't negligent one way or another every week of the year. So how can you crucify this guy just because he happened to get caught? You go pointing fingers and you may find yourself in a very slippery spot sometime with a whole lot of fingers pointing at you."

Well, I can't agree with him, or at least I don't think I can, but I'm not so sure about it as I might have been before I came to this place. I guess nobody is going to say anything much, just tell the woman that this was an unfortunate complication of her surgery, and see what happens. I mean see whether she actually needs an amputation or not, and see what she does. And I know about it, but I don't think I'm going to walk in and say to her, "Gee, you ought to sue that bird for everything he's got," either....

Friday, January 13

. . . .

... [T]he cocktail waitress who had her femoral artery tied off by mistake is back in, and I've been seeing her from time to time. Dr. Harlow had done a below-the-knee amputation, and then the girl got gangrene in the stump and they had to do an above-the-knee amputation. This hasn't healed well, and now she's in the hospital again to attempt a skin graft on the stump, with the very distinct possibility that an even higher amputation may be necessary.

This girl is really just about at the end of her tether emotionally; Thursday night when she was admitted and found out she might have to have more surgery beyond the skin graft, she was just literally weeping, and she sits around and does the best she can to keep a stiff upper lip. She has already been thrown to over $3,000 worth of hospital costs and surgeons' fees, and as far as I know this is still being represented to her as one of the regrettable but uncontrollable complications of a vein ligation. There's been no blame cast on the guy that did the ligation in the first place, nor has anybody come forward offering to pay the girl's doctor and hospital bills for her, as far as I know, so there she is stuck with it. Can't really blame her for having low morale, but I still wonder just exactly where medical ethics come into a picture like this. Or whether they only come into it when it's convenient for the doctor.[9]

As a counterweight to this tragic tale, another entry in the diary indicates how vulnerable to unfair second guessing the medical profession considers itself, even when it performs as well as possible.

Wednesday, November 30

. . . .

. . . [A]bout 5:00 . . . I went down to see my old friend Ed Arnquist, who was back in on Leo Richards' service. This is a big Swede admitted in July, a forty-four-year-old man who was complaining then of unsteadiness and loss of balance. He's had a very bizarre story since, and now has everybody in a big flap, especially Cal Cornell and the radiologist, who is really standing on his ear. Seems when Ed had been in before, Cornell was called for a neurological consultation. He had examined the man carefully then, but couldn't find any explanation for his balance loss, couldn't find anything wrong with him really except that he couldn't keep his balance when he stood on one foot, and had nystagmus — an odd kind of involuntary jerky movement of the eyes when he looked out of the corner of his eye. They'd sent him home without a diagnosis then; even though Cornell knew he had something going on in his brain he couldn't find.

Later, after I was off the service, Ed Arnquist came in again because the balance loss was getting steadily worse, and this time an electroencephalogram showed changes suggesting that he had

Note on p. 45.

a mass lesion in his brain somewhere. Cornell then did a ventric-
ulogram — a sort of grisly diagnostic procedure involving introduction of some air into the interior chambers of the brain that
are normally filled with cerebrospinal fluid — and these studies
showed the outline of a brain tumor located in a place Cornell
could get at. So Cornell had opened Ed's skull and peeled out
this big tumor that was growing there. The thing was so sharply
defined and peeled out so neatly that Cornell was certain it was
benign, and had one of his rare days of elation when he thought
he'd cured a patient. Everybody was happy for Ed for about three
days until the pathologist got a careful look at the slides of the
tumor and declared that it was a metastatic cancer that looked
very suspiciously like bronchogenic carcinoma under the microscope.

Well, this was in October, and Ed had had many chest X-rays,
all reported normal, so they hauled him back down to X-ray for
some special chest films including stereos and sectional tomograms,
and, sure enough, without any question there was a tiny little
soft-tissue mass in the upper lobe of his left lung. The thing that
jarred everybody was that once this soft fuzzy shadow was located
and he knew where to look for it, the radiologist got out all the
old films of Ed's chest that he'd read as negative and found the
barest suggestion of this same lesion visible on a chest film taken
back in July, and still present on all taken since. The X-ray man
was all shaken up; six months lost on a lung cancer is dreadful, and
it practically *has* to be an X-ray diagnosis early. But he insisted
that to spot this shadow on the film at all you not only had to
know that it was there; you also had to know exactly where to
look for it. Of course, now *everybody* can see it.

Unfortunately, all these little niceties are all the same to old
Ed. He had a carcinoma of the lung which has been sitting there
for well over six months, and has seeded to his brain. Leo Richards
now wants to do an exploratory and take out the lung lesion. He
feels that Ed's only possible chance would be if the brain lesion
were somehow a single metastasis, and that by taking out the lung
tumor he might catch the cancer before it has seeded anywhere
else. Of course, the odds against a single metastasis are just astronomical, but I guess with that disease even a million-to-one chance
is worth taking. Very probably they'll find a chestful of metastatic
nodes along with the primary cancer, and that will be that. But

if they leave the thing in there, Ed's odds for survival are 0.00 . . . to a hundred decimal places; with it in there he is already dead and just hasn't quit breathing yet. Anyway he's to be done on Thursday.

[*Post hoc:* I was obviously shaken up about Ed Arnquist, as were most of the clinic men, especially the X-ray man. And Ed *did* have metastatic nodes in his chest, and died of his lung cancer about four months later. At the time I know I felt that the radiologist had made a hideous and inexcusable error, and thought he was just making excuses for himself when he said the lung lesion couldn't have been identified in July unless you already knew it was there and where to look for it. Curiously enough, those films of Ed Arnquist's chest have since become teaching classics; they have been presented in clinical conferences on chest disease all over the country, and repeatedly the best and most experienced X-ray specialists, without exception, have missed the fatal shadow that was visible on the July films until it was pointed out to them. And this was under conditions where they *knew* something was funny about the chest film because it wouldn't have been shown to them if it were really as normal as it looked. They still couldn't pick it up.

So I suppose this vindicates the radiologist insofar as it vindicates anybody in a case like Ed Arnquist's. More than anything else, though, I think it points out the kind of fight medical men are up against constantly, and are totally aware of constantly, with every patient they see. Every practicing doctor has more than one Ed Arnquist on his record that he blames himself for, rightly or wrongly. In a way, you could say it points out the guile and craftiness of the Enemy. I think now that Ed probably had the best, most expert, careful and interested medical care he could have gotten anywhere, and the Enemy whipped even the best. Medical students joke about the "almost-visible chest lesion" or the "almost-audible heart murmur." They laughingly define a "Grade I" murmur as the murmur you can hear only if the Professor of Medicine insists that it's there. And they laugh because they know that that "almost-visible chest lesion" is no joke at all, that it happens to be very real; it is the cancer of the lung that they are going to miss one day until it's too late, and it is better to laugh than to think too much about it.][10]

The young intern comments in the introduction to his diary on Note on p. 45.

the strange combination of arrogance and humility — and selfishness and selflessness — among the medical profession concerning its mistakes.

> This journal ... does not really convey the depth of Dr. Fred Kidder's wrath the night the medical resident and I nearly killed his patient, old Jerry Dykeman, by giving him a medicine that knocked out the only natural breathing mechanism the old man had left. Very little was said at the time — we were all too busy breathing for old Jerry with a resuscitator until the effect of the drug wore off — but Dr. Kidder was simply furious. We had failed to recognize a treacherous situation and had ignored principles of medicine that we both knew backward. Dr. Kidder never really forgave us that incident for the rest of the year, and he has not let me forget it to this day.
>
> Of course, the profession has not been eager to publicize such incidents, however critical they may be to the education of the doctor-in-training. Such reporting is taboo. As a result, people have never realized that the Jerry Dykemans are the price that they, collectively, have always had to pay for the privilege of having well-trained and competent physicians. Dreadful and frightening as this seems, it is true. People need to understand how a doctor becomes a doctor, what the practice of medicine is all about, what it is that a doctor must put into the game; and, above all, they need some insight into the human limitations upon a doctor's powers.
>
> To understand these things would be to answer a great many ugly questions about the profession of medicine. It would explain why doctors guard their independence so jealously, and regard any move toward political control of their work with such dread. It would explain why doctors feel that their fees are just and equitable, however high or low, and why they resent public criticism so bitterly. It would explain why doctors rally to protect each other from attack whether it is justified or not, why they regard malpractice actions with such indignation, and why they hate the incompetents in their ranks so viciously yet are so slow to censure them — because every doctor is haunted by the knowledge that *next time it could so easily be me.*[11]

The tone of that *cri de coeur* is the tone of anyone in the front line of human endeavor who faces backbiting and second guessing

Note on p. 45.

from those far from the arrows and wounds. It is the tone of the professional soldier or the policeman responding to after-the-fact criticism of how he reacted in the heat of combat — criticism from those safe and aloof. In the case of the medical profession, its insistence on being its only arbiter is increased by its being a proud — perhaps now the proudest — profession. A profession has two essential characteristics distinguishing it from mere "jobs." First, a profession, as Daniel Bell has put it, "is a learned (i.e., scholarly) activity, and thus involves formal training, but within a broad intellectual context. To be within the profession means to be certified, formally or informally, by one's peers or by some established body within the profession."[12] Second — and flowing from the initial certification by one's peers or their representatives — is the continuing reliance on peer review rather than on outside control. In Bell's words, "One might say that business is called to account by its customers through the market, whereas a professional is called to account by his peers through the professional group."[13]

But, of course, no one, at least in a democratic society, can be allowed to be above any outside review and discipline, no matter how difficult or demanding or proud his role. Witness the need for civilian control of the military and, more prosaically, the recent upsurge of interest in civilian review boards for the police.[14] But the tension inevitably caused by such outside "interference" makes it all the more necessary to structure such control in as rational and helpful a way as possible. Little wonder, then, that the circus atmosphere of adversarial combat involving "arcane technology, raw emotionalism, and sly tricks"[15] pervading the personal injury trial has raised medical resentment toward malpractice litigation to paranoidal heights, culminating in the common view that no decent doctor should take any part in it.

Some idea of the resultant pressure on doctors to remain silent is illustrated by the experience of a New York surgeon whose permission to admit patients was revoked by several hospitals after he testified in court about an obstetrician's crucial error which had caused brain damage to a child during its birth. Cancellation of a doctor's own malpractice insurance can also result if he testifies against another doctor.[16]

The medical ranks are so closed because, as has been suggested,

Notes on p. 45.

the doctor — even more than the manufacturer — resents and resists a lawsuit so deeply and bitterly. The widely held view of the medical profession is that responsibility for most medical malpractice suits can be laid at the feet of greedy, grasping, unethical shysters, stirred by their unconscionable contingent fees, who in turn stir up, or at least join with, ungrateful, unrealistic, and ignorant patients. According to a recent congressional study entitled *Medical Malpractice: The Patient versus the Physician:* "Physicians contend that a large number of claims and suits filed against them have no basis — that no negligence is involved. The physicians believe their patients regard them as 'easy targets' for litigation and sizable judgments and claims."[17] The main objective of attorneys in medical malpractice suits, according to Dr. Emil Seletz, a prominent neurosurgeon, in his address to a convention of the International College of Surgeons, is to "aid in the holdup and run with the loot."[18] Speaking of Melvin Belli, personal injury lawyer personified, one county medical society president spat, "Hanging is much too good for him. He should be made to suffer as we [doctors] have suffered."[19]

Recent years have seen extensive efforts to improve malpractice proceedings and relations between doctors and lawyers. For example, so-called screening panels, composed of physicians (sometimes with advice from an outside party such as a lawyer or clergyman) have been established in some areas. According to the HEW Secretary's Commission on Medical Malpractice, a "claimant may submit his case to the panel either before or after he has formally filed suit, though most plans encourage the use of the panel before filing. There is usually a *quid pro quo;* if the panel finds that a claim has merit, it will provide the claimant with an expert witness; if it finds against him, he must agree to drop the claim." But the most the HEW secretary's commission report could say on such panels was that "while we are not able to endorse all of such plans as truly workable or calculated to alleviate the tensions and problems that exist in this field, we do believe they merit continued experimentation."[20] The simple fact is that screening panels — or arbitration of claims — are inevitably going to be peripheral in their effect because the basic problem of malpractice claims is not the form of the forum for disposing of claims, but rather the

Notes on p. 45.

complexity of the issues presented by those claims. And neither screening panels nor arbitration address themselves to the core of this problem, helpful as they may be on occasion in softening the impact of adversary proceedings.

The futility of cosmetic approaches is perhaps best illustrated by journalist Larry King's report of what happened when

> [r]ecently the medical doctors and lawyers of West Texas decided to bury their various hatchets arising from lawsuits which keep on splitting the two professions into hostile camps. The doctors hosted at Odessa Country Club. There was first a two-hour cocktail party, which in retrospect looks like bad planning, and then a banquet at which the biggest doctor muckety-muck there welcomed the lawyers with a stiff, formal little speech. Warren Burnett, one of the best-known trial lawyers of the Southwest, a master of the high sardonic, who had been in dogged attendance at the cocktail party, had been tapped to respond on behalf of the lawyers. He made a short but memorable speech. Rising, he dropped his voice low and said, "During the course of these festivities, I have taken judicial notice of the arrival of our doctor-hosts and their ladies, in limousines and mink, all or most of them wearing expressions of superior knowledge or secrets known only to themselves and/or God. I feel moved to remind our hosts that while *their* professional antecessors were bleeding George Washington with leeches and teaching that the night air was poisonous, *my* professional antecessors were drawing up the Constitution of these United States — as noble a document as known to the minds of men or angels. I thank you one and all." End of party.[21]

The degree to which doctors resent and resist malpractice suits is perhaps best shown by their attitude towards even arguably valid claims. In one survey of doctors, the question was asked: "If you were sued for medical malpractice by a patient who sincerely believed you to be negligent, and he had obtained an expert to testify against you, and there was some question as to your negligence, would you favor your insurance company vigorously defending the suit or settling the action out of court?" Ninety-six percent of the respondent doctors said they would favor a vigorous defense under those circumstances, 2 percent were unsure, and only 2 percent favored settlement.[22]

Notes on p. 45.

As the result of such factors, only the most profitable claims for medical malpractice are pursued. According to Dr. David Rubsaman, who holds both medical and law degrees and is an expert on medical malpractice,

[a] considerable number of patients who have a medical injury, even though probably negligently caused, and who go to see a first-class malpractice attorney, will not be accepted by him. A patient may have lost a month's work and be out of pocket a thousand dollars for medical expenses because of the doctor's negligence. Assume he is now completely recovered and feels fine. That month of work and a thousand dollars for medical expenses is a heavy burden for a man making five hundred dollars a month. But no first-class attorney in California will take that case because the malpractice insurance carriers will not settle, and it just costs too much money for the plaintiff's attorney to try them. There is an excellent plaintiff's attorney in Northern California who will not accept a case of probable liability that will bring in less than twenty-five thousand dollars. He will not accept a case of absolutely certain, clear-cut liability if it is worth less than ten thousand.[23]

All this means, too, that very little of the total loss suffered as a result of medical treatment is compensated. According to a recent publication on medical malpractice by the Center for the Study of Democratic Institutions:

Although the number of malpractice lawsuits and claims is increasing and the publicity attached to large awards or settlements may give the impression that a fair and just compensation system is flourishing, the consensus at the [center's] conference [on medical malpractice] was that most people who sustain medical injuries, either through negligence or unavoidable accident, do not get into the claims system. They receive no compensation.

Mr. [Eli P.] Bernzweig, [an attorney and executive director of the HEW Secretary's Commission on Medical Malpractice] cited an American Medical Association professional liability survey which indicated that for every patient who files a malpractice suit "there are probably ten times as many who never become aware of the fact that they have legitimate fault claims under our system."[24]

Notes on pp. 45–46.

Unquestionably, however, as the center's paper indicates, medical malpractice claims and premiums are increasing dramatically. Medical malpractice suits are being filed at the rate of 18,000 a year,[25] with a total cost in premiums to health care providers of about $300 million a year.[26] Claims for some have increased by 1,000 percent in a ten-year period.[27] As a corollary, "[i]ndividual [health care] providers are understandably alarmed when one considers that they have had to increase their coverage and that premium rates have also increased tremendously. Premiums for dentists rose 115 percent between 1960 and 1970; those for hospitals, 262.7 percent; those for physicians other than surgeons, 540.8 percent; and those for surgeons, 949.2 percent."[28] At the present time it is not unusual for a doctor to pay from $5,000 to $12,000 *annually* in medical malpractice insurance premiums.[29]

But malpractice victims, like their product-injured counterparts, have benefited but little from increased premiums, claims, and litigation. According to the center's study, "The lion's share of the total cost to the insurance companies of malpractice suits and claims goes to the legal community."[30] One witness before the HEW secretary's malpractice commission — whose testimony, along with others on this point, the commission found "compelling" — testified: "I had a serious back injury, and was out of work for two years. I made a $22,000 settlement, and after that I realized $3,000. The attorneys got the balance of the profits and split it with the doctors [who acted as expert witnesses]."[31]

Of course, as in the case of product liability, the enormous expenditure of time and energy and talent and money in tort liability litigation might be justified in the case of medical malpractice if it served as a deterrent to unsafe medical procedures. But the HEW secretary's commission tended toward the conclusion not only that the tort liability system apparently fails to deter much medical malpractice, but also that on the whole it leads to *unsafe* practices. A physician will often fail to "perform a procedure or conduct a test because of [his] ... fear of a later malpractice suit, even though the patient is likely to benefit from the test or procedure in question."[32] The commission specifically described:

¶ Many doctors who were so fearful of a malpractice suit that they refused to render emergency aid at the scene of an accident.[33]

Notes on p. 46.

¶ Hospitals and doctors who were reluctant for the same reason to participate on lifesaving rescue teams organized to handle emergency situations in the hospital.[34]

¶ Doctors who failed to fully utilize the services of nurses and other allied health care personnel for fear of increased exposure to malpractice suits.[35]

¶ Physicians who were reluctant "to publish in medical journals case reports describing in detail noted adverse effects of diagnostic and therapeutic procedures [out of] . . . fear . . . that the material will be picked up and used as evidence in a lawsuit."[36]

In addition, fear of malpractice suits often adds prodigiously to the cost of medicine, apparently without providing any benefit to the patient. The commission focused on an aspect of what it called "defensive medicine" — defined in this regard by the commission as "the conducting of a test or performance of a diagnostic or therapeutic procedure which is not medically justified but is carried out primarily (if not solely) to prevent or defend against the threat of medical-legal liability."[37] According to the commission, "nearly every physician who testified before the Commission cited the practice of defensive medicine as an example of the harmful effect resulting from the increasing number of malpractice suits. Recent opinion surveys report that between 50 to 70 percent of the physicians polled said they engaged in various forms of so-called defensive medicine."[38] As an indication of the rife nature of needless treatment, "a study of 570 consecutive children admitted to a hospital emergency room for head trauma [showed that] the treatment of only one was altered as a result of the skull X-rays taken."[39] The staggering costs involved in such overgenerous use of X-rays is suggested by an estimate from another source that "one of every 3 X-rays taken in the U.S. was for legal reasons. Since X-rays cost Americans about $3 billion annually . . . the public spends $1 billion a year on medically useless films. That is not to mention the hazard of exposing people to excess radiation."[40]

Granted that, in the words of the HEW commission, "in a particular case one man's defensive medicine may be — and often is — another's good practice,"[41] and that the amount of so-called defensive medicine being practiced is still very much unknown,[42] the contrast between all the money and energy being spent on medical

Notes on pp. 46–47.

malpractice claims and any evidence that it encourages good medicine — not to speak of encouraging bad medicine or discouraging good medicine — is damning indeed.

Certainly, it is common knowledge that the results of malpractice litigation rarely, if ever, serve as the basis for disciplinary action by either professional or governmental bodies. Similarly, accreditation procedures for health care facilities do not consult malpractice litigation records in appraising permissible levels of performance. Medical malpractice is viewed by health care providers at best as a private, unpleasant dogfight. And the more usual response of health care providers — both informally in social contacts and in professional review procedures — toward someone who is sued is one of sympathy rather than criticism or ostracism. A survey conducted by the American Medical Association of state medical society officials found them expressing "the belief that generally a medical professional liability claim or suit does not have a serious or extended effect on the physician's practice or reputation."[43]

In point of fact, as suggested earlier, the closed ranks caused by the beleaguered feeling of health care providers concerning malpractice claims means that malpractice litigation inhibits discovery of malpractice more than uncovering it. Dr. Robert Derbyshire, author of the leading text on medical disciplinary proceedings,[44] recently opined that health care providers are led to protect, rather than to unearth and discipline, unethical doctors because of their fear of lawsuits, which, he says, "borders on paranoia."[45]

NOTES

1. D. McDonald, ed., *Medical Malpractice: A Discussion of Alternative Compensation and Quality Control Systems* 17 (Center for the Study of Democratic Institutions Occasional Paper, 1971).

2. Subcommittee on Executive Reorganization of the Senate Committee on Government Operations, *Medical Malpractice: The Patient versus the Physician,* 91st Cong., 2d Sess. 27 (Comm. Print 1969).

3. *Ibid.*

4. *Ibid.*

5. U.S. Department of Health, Education, and Welfare, *Report of the Secretary's Commission on Medical Malpractice* 18 (1973) [hereinafter cited as HEW Secretary's Commission Report].

6. *Ibid.*, 11.

7. 3 A. Averbach, *Handling Accident Cases* 3:9–10 (1960). The HEW

Secretary's Commission on Medical Malpractice believes that the so-called conspiracy of silence among doctors "if it did exist, is much less prevalent now," but it then goes on to admit that it is really unable to state very firmly the extent of the problem as it exists today and admits that the problem may very well be a considerable one still (HEW Secretary's Commission Report, *supra* note 5, at 36–37).

8. M. Gross, *The Doctors* 520 (1966).

9. Doctor X, *Intern* 218–21, 281–82 (1965).

10. *Ibid.,* 245–47.

11. *Ibid.,* 5–6.

12. D. Bell, *The Coming of Post-Industrial Society* 374 (1973).

13. *Ibid.,* n. 6.

14. For an interesting example of overlapping conflicts here, consider the following: "With the Chicago Bar Assn. calling for a civilian review board for the police department, some of [Chicago's] . . . police organizations are planning a counterattack — by urging an independent board to review the ethics and practices of lawyers under fire. One incensed top police executive put it this way: 'If, as the Bar Ass'n maintains, self-regulation doesn't work for us, why should we believe it works for them? After all, with Watergate and the Equity Funding cases, lawyers are catching as much heat as police'" (Kupcinet, "Kup's Column," *Chicago Sun-Times,* Nov. 26, 1973, p. 66, cols. 1–2).

15. See *supra,* ch. 1, p. 7.

16. Carlson, "Suing the Doctor," *Wall St. J.,* Feb. 28, 1969, p. 1, col. 1.

17. Subcommittee on Executive Reorganization, *supra* note 2, at 5. On the other hand, consider the following: "Many health-care providers are convinced that the vast majority of malpractice claims asserted by patients are entirely without foundation. In order to test the validity of this assertion, the Commission's study of closed claim files asked malpractice insurers to indicate whether or not each claim file was or was not 'legally meritorious in terms of liability.' The results indicated that the insurance carriers judged 46 percent of the claims to be meritorious. This percentage is slightly higher than the percentage of all claims paid (45%); however, cross tabulations are not yet available to establish any possible correlation between claims paid and claims judged to be meritorious. Viewed together, the number of claims judged to be meritorious by malpractice insurers and the number in which payment was made to the claimant would seem to indicate that the vast majority of malpractice claims are not 'entirely baseless,' as often alleged" (HEW Secretary's Commission Report, *supra* note 5, at 10).

18. Silverman, "Medicine's Legal Nightmare" (Part II), *Saturday Evening Post,* April 18, 1959, pp. 31, 118.

19. *Ibid.* (Part I), April 11, 1959, p. 13.

20. HEW Secretary's Commission Report, *supra* note 5, at 91.

21. As quoted in Bazelon, "Clients Against Lawyers," *Harper's Magazine,* Sept., 1967, pp. 104, 114.

22. Sinow, "Professional Liability Insurance" (unpublished manuscript, University of Illinois College of Law, 1972).

23. McDonald, ed., *supra* note 1, at 4. See also Deitz, Baird, and Berul,

"The Medical Malpractice Legal System," in *Appendix*, HEW Secretary's Commission Report, *supra* note 5, at 87, 117–18.

24. McDonald, ed., *supra* note 1, at 4.

25. HEW Secretary's Commission Report, *supra* note 5, at 6.

26. *Ibid.*, 12. This estimate strikes some as very low. New York State alone, according to one informal estimate, produces $125 million annually in court judgments and out-of-court settlements, not to speak of premiums.

27. Averbach, "Rx for Malpractice," 1970 *Ins. L. J.* 69.

28. HEW Secretary's Commission Report, *supra* note 5, at 13. For a discussion of dental malpractice, see P. Revere, *Dentistry and Its Victims* (1970). "[S]ome actuaries dealing with medical malpractice are now saying if malpractice judgments continue to spiral upwards liability insurance payments for such losses will in the foreseeable future outstrip all other forms of liability insurance awards" ("Editorial," *Business Insurance*, Jan. 7, 1974, p. 18, cols. 1–2). For a discussion of the astronomical rise in medical malpractice premiums in New York State in recent years and yet a concomitant abandonment of the field as unprofitable by the insurance company which has written almost all New York State physicians for the last twenty-five years, see *N.Y. Times*, Jan. 8, 1974, p. 1, cols. 6–7. Rick Carlson, a lawyer specializing in the study of medical malpractice, has ventured that the occasions for medical injuries are increasing. He cites, for example, the "steady decline in physicians per 100,000 of population. There will also be a projected shortage of 100,000 nurses by 1975" (Carlson, "A Conceptualization of a No-Fault Compensation System for Medical Injuries," 3 *Law & Society Rev.* 329, 342 [1973]). Also, under so-called prepayment schemes (whereby insureds will pay a flat fee in advance to have all their health care provided), "providers may tend to under-utilize and under-serve" (*ibid.*, 345; see *infra*, ch. 9, notes 59–61). Finally, "the advent of broad-based deep coverage of health care services through a national health insurance plan will unquestionably increase utilization of services for the segments of the population benefiting from expanded coverage. Thus, an ineluctable increase in demand will be exerted on a system marked by critical shortages of personnel" (Carlson, *supra* this note, at 352).

29. Keeton, "Compensation for Medical Accidents," 121 *U. Pa. L. Rev.* 590, 595, n. 16 (1973). See also *N.Y. Times*, *supra* note 28.

30. McDonald, ed., *supra* note 1, at 2.

31. HEW Secretary's Commission Report, *supra* note 5, at 34.

32. *Ibid.*, 14.

33. *Ibid.*, 15.

34. *Ibid.*, 16.

35. *Ibid.*, 17–18.

36. *Ibid.*, 14.

37. *Ibid.*

38. *Ibid.*

39. Bernzweig, "Defensive Medicine," in *Appendix*, HEW Secretary's Commission Report, *supra* note 5, at 38, 40, citing "Child Head X-Rays: Value Doubted after a Study of 570 Cases," 11 *Medical Tribune* no. 54, at 1ff. (Oct. 26, 1970).

40. *Business Insurance*, Sept. 10, 1973, p. 3, col. 2.

41. HEW Secretary's Commission Report, *supra* note 5, at 14.

42. Note "The Medical Malpractice Threat: A Study of Defensive Medicine," 5 *Duke L. J.* 939 (1971); Hershey, "The Defensive Practice of Medicine: Myth or Reality," 1 *Milbank Memorial Fund Q.* 69 (1972).

43. "How State Medical Society Executives Size Up Professional Liability," 164 *J.A.M.A.* 580, 582 (1957).

44. R. Derbyshire, *Medical Licensure and Discipline in the United States* (1959).

45. As quoted in Shearer, "Intelligence Report," *Parade Magazine,* Sept. 16, 1973, p. 8, col. 2.

4

Other Torts by Tort Law

Cases of auto accidents, product liability, and professional mal-practice constitute the most significant cases of tort litigation in our society. (Industrial accidents, the other great category of accidents, were largely removed from the torts system by no-fault workers' compensation statutes passed by the various states, for the most part early in this century.) Other categories remain, however, such as falls in stores, hunting accidents, and other almost countless ways accidents can happen. For these cases, too, the cumbersomeness of the fault system operates with its heavy hand. Nor are the problems by any means limited to the difficulties of establishing the defendant's fault or defect. Myriad other legal barriers remain to an intelligent — not to say humane — way of compensating victims of accidents.

In the first place, for the most part the plaintiff, in order to re-ceive compensation, must prove not only that the defendant was at fault in the accident but also that he himself was free from con-tributory fault in the form of either contributory negligence or assumption of risk. The issue of the claimant's contributory fault involves the same wasteful, agonizing dissection of the appropriate-ness of human conduct in the causation of accidents. More and more states — apparently in an effort to ward off no-fault legislation — have passed so-called comparative negligence legislation under which the plaintiff is not completely barred from payment by his negligence; rather, the respective negligence of the two parties is compared, and damages are calibrated accordingly. For example, if the defendant's fault were determined to be twice that of the plaintiff, the plaintiff would be paid two-thirds of his losses and would bear the remainder himself. Such a rule, by allowing more injured people to be paid, nonetheless often complicates the already cumbersome process of faultfinding by requiring not only the fact but some quantification of fault to be ascertained.[1]

The law of damages in tort cases — that is, when and how such payment has to be made — is also a nightmare of inefficiency and inequity. Under the law, only one lump-sum payment is called for once liability has been determined. This means that nothing is paid "on account" as losses accrue. On the contrary, an insurance company will (understandably, in terms of its bargaining position) use the fact that it will be many months or even years before trial is reached (so clogged are the courts with other personal injury cases) to induce the injured person to accept much less payment than might otherwise be due him in order to get some desperately needed cash. This is in contrast, of course, to other forms of insurance, such as medical and disability insurance, in which payment is made periodically. This requirement of one lump-sum payment means that when payment is made — *if* it is made — it covers not only all the losses already accrued but also a *final* estimate of all the losses ever to occur in the future. Once the damages are fixed by a settlement or verdict, the amount ordinarily cannot be reviewed even if it turns out to be woefully inadequate or wildly excessive. This means oftentimes that the settlement process and trial see the plaintiff's doctor grossly exaggerating the aftereffects of an injury while the insurance doctor is equally grossly disparaging them — with the hapless and ignorant jury left eventually to decide between the warring experts.[2]

The lump-sum method of payment also means that the badly injured victim is often encouraged — consciously or unconsciously, by his lawyer, his doctor, or himself — to remain as pathetically handicapped as possible, as long as possible, in order to appeal to the jury's sympathy and thereby increase his verdict. This, too, is in contrast to other forms of insurance — including workers' compensation — in which the aim of the whole health insurance process is to begin to rehabilitate the patient to productivity and maximum health as soon as possible. Testifying before a congressional committee, Professor Alfred Conard of the University of Michigan Law

Notes on p. 54.

School stated: "The first objective of any [compensation] . . . system should be to rehabilitate injury victims, using 'rehabilitation' in a broad sense to embrace comprehensive care from first aid through occupational retraining (if needed). Rehabilitation not only relieves the individual's own misery, but enables him to carry his weight in society. The tort liability system is a failure in this connection, because its payments come too uncertainly and too late; even when the victim is certain of payment, he has to make an agonizing choice between money and treatment."[3] The tort system's medieval posture of accusation, retribution, and delay flies in the face, of course, of the *enormous* savings — both human and economic — that ambitious rehabilitation efforts with accident victims can mean. Although in a few traffic cases of clear liability so-called advance payments to meet the accruing needs of accident victims are being made,[4] no comparable effort is as widespread in other accident cases.[5]

Still another feature of the damages part of the tort law operates with appalling waste and cruelty: under tort law, the fact that a person has already been paid from, say, sick leave or health insurance does not prevent him from being paid the same amount all over again under a tort liability insurance claim based on fault. Such a rule grew up at a time when these so-called collateral sources ("collateral" to the tort defendant, that is) of health insurance and sick leave were relatively rare. Thus, there was an understandable reluctance to see the "wrongdoer" benefit from the prudence of his victim by allowing him to subtract from what he owed the victim those benefits the victim had purchased for himself. But the rule makes less and less sense with each passing year, for these collateral sources have mushroomed in size and importance. They have reached the point where over two-thirds of what is paid in traffic cases of serious injury and fatality comes from nontort sources, such as sick leave and health insurance. But the rule calling for these (now huge) amounts to be paid all over again under a fault claim often means either a wasteful duplication of payment to an accident victim or, on occasion, wasteful paperwork as money is shuffled back and forth between insurance companies. By way of contrast, the two oldest major lines of casualty insurance (fire and marine) have never allowed duplication of payment to the accident victim, but instead have always sensibly paid the claimant his net economic loss.[6]

The evils of the so-called collateral source rule are also compounded by practices which have arisen in trying to measure the pain and suffering for which an accident victim with a valid tort claim is entitled to be reimbursed. Because pain and suffering are so amorphous and unmeasurable, very often an arbitrary rule of thumb is adopted which pays a multiple of, say, two or three, or even seven or ten, times the medical bills to compensate for pain and suffering. The precise multiple depends on the bargaining position of the parties, but regardless of the multiple, the medical bills are already paid by health or hospitalization insurance; this means that the victim can profit not only one dollar for every dollar of medical costs he incurs (at a time when the medical profession has raised to a new art the creation of costly services) but a multiple of two or three or even seven or ten times the already inflated medical bill! If you sat down to design a system for wasting and dissipating precious medical and insurance resources, you could not do any better than that. And of course knowledgeable personal injury laywers — working often with cooperative doctors — have themselves learned to exploit these rules to the level of a new art. A lawyer quickly recognizes that padding on medical costs is really as good as coining money — at no real risk to anyone. The patient's medical expenses are being paid by his health insurance, and he retains the lawyer on a contingent fee. The lawyer has a stable of cases, so he can afford an occasional one that goes awry, and at any rate he may be inclined to pad only the more likely ones; in addition, the mere act of padding makes it more likely that a settlement will be forthcoming from an insurance company fearful of letting the process drag on. The doctor finds himself being paid to take care of people who are not really very sick — by definition a rather easy task — as he assigns his nurse to supervise an almost endless and automatic regimen of diathermy treatment and the like.

It is important to recognize that all this is done neither dishonestly nor even necessarily cynically. After all, the victim *has* been in an accident. At the least he has been shaken up — perhaps badly and perhaps with broken bones. Prestigious experts — doctors and lawyers — urge him to take special care of himself, with the

Note on p. 54.

result that he is often only too glad to oblige, uncertain and afraid as he is about matters legal and medical. This uncertainty and fear may be especially true of those in lower socioeconomic groups. Freud pointed out, for example: "We shall probably discover that the poor are even less ready to part with their neurosis than the rich, because the hard life that awaits them when they recover has no attraction, and illness . . . gives them more claim to the help of others."[7] His observation is probably true of physical as well as psychic ills. The lawyer, too, can convince himself that the system rewards such elaborate concern and care for his client, and, after all, who is to say at what point medical care for an injured person becomes excessive? (Indeed, it is the impossibility of doing so — except in egregious cases — that makes padding such a safe procedure.) And the doctor as well convinces himself that extra care certainly cannot hurt. Also keep in mind that the orthopedic specialist — largely dealing in broken bones — is dependent on accident victims for his business. If he is "uncooperative" with their legal claims, he may find himself with fewer referrals from lawyers and others. And of course everyone is in a position, if he is ever gnawed by doubts, to reassure himself that " 'everybody' does it." So everybody gains — and everybody loses.

Not all padding is quite so innocent, however. Mrs. Lydia Jiminez, of Perth Amboy, New Jersey, was injured in an auto accident in 1969. The Woodbridge, New Jersey, law firm of Rabb and Zeitler, specialists in personal injury cases, directed her to a doctor for treatment of her back injury. Then, after she complained of feeling "very nervous," her lawyers sent her to a Dr. Herbert Boehm for twice-a-week neuropsychiatric treatment. According to Mrs. Jiminez, in her testimony before the New Jersey State Commission of Investigation, "He locked me up in a small closet with a heat lamp with a pair of dark glasses." After the sixth visit she told the doctor, "I can do this at home," and she never returned. But that did not stop the doctor's "treatment." He submitted a bill for $630 to Rabb and Zeitler supposedly for treating Mrs. Jiminez thirty-nine times. (Mr. William Rabb, one of Mrs. Jiminez's lawyers, told her he would ask for a refund of $250 from the doctor which he would repay to her, but, testified Mrs. Jiminez, "I never got the money.") Dr. Boehm's mysterious treatment was quite clearly no clerical

Note on p. 54.

error; other auto accident victims, Mr. and Mrs. Antonio Elias of Newark, testified that they, too, had visited Dr. Boehm together "eight or nine times," primarily for heat therapy to treat their headaches and "tension." These treatments also consisted largely of ten minutes of heat lamp therapy, according to the couple's testimony. But, the testimony continued, Dr. Boehm submitted a bill for sixteen visits, charging his patients for the administration of "analgesics, tranquilizers and reassurance." According to Mrs. Elias, however, she had not been given any tranquilizers because she had been pregnant at the time.[8]

Several recent newspaper, bar, and grand jury investigations in major cities have revealed widespread rings of ambulance chasing in which professional runners, who are hardened criminals, work with lawyers not only to round up cases, pad claims, and submit totally phony claims, but collusively to "stage" accidents as well![9]

Of course, it is true that padding of small claims is more rampant in cases other than medical malpractice or product liability cases, where the smaller nuisance claim is less often pursued, but padding can certainly occur in these cases; in medical malpractice claims, for example, "more than half of the claimants who receive payment get less than $3,000,"[10] a range surely susceptible to padding.[11] And padding is surely operative in many other kinds of accidents not related to traffic accidents, such as falls on commercial or even private premises and so on.

Finally, the fact of payment for pain and suffering often turns personal injury case trials from rational procedures designed to allocate losses into emotional and even theatrical extravaganzas which are often quite unrelated to the real needs and losses of accident victims. Lawyers expend awesome efforts and skill to play on a jury's sympathy, gullibility, and biases in order to increase or decrease the amount of payment for pain and suffering, as the tactics of Messrs. Corboy and Wildman in chapter 1 illustrate. Although the amount payable for economic loss such as wage loss and medical expenses is often relatively inelastic, it is in evaluating pain and suffering that a jury can "reward" or "punish" with almost no opportunity for rational supervision by a court, given the basically irrational judgment being made. Veteran personal injury attorney Verne Lawyer, speaking at a legal seminar on personal injury cases,

Notes on pp. 54–55.

stated: "I put in my book ... the appearance of the plaintiff as number one in attempting to evaluate a [personal injury] lawsuit because I think that a good ... type, one who'd be likeable and one that the jury is going to want to do something for, can make your case worth double at least ... what it would be otherwise and a bad-appearing plaintiff could make the case worth perhaps less than half of what it might be otherwise."[12] What the plaintiff's appearance has to do with the amount of his suffering is something that Lawyer does not undertake to explain.

This, then, is the present tort insurance system: not a system for paying accident victims from accident insurance (as sensible as that simple idea would seem to be), but a system for *fighting* accident victims about paying them from accident insurance; a system so cumbersome and tricky that the typical accident victim, even after consulting a lawyer (even a highly skilled specialist), cannot know *what* he will be paid, *when* he will be paid, or *if* he will be paid; a system hugely wasteful of insurance dollars that puts so much into the pockets of lawyers and insurance companies and gives so little to the victims themselves; a dilatory system that, when it finally gets around to disposing of cases, is usually cruelly vindictive to most and occasionally relatively generous to others, with the outcome more dependent on luck and emotion than on need and reason.

NOTES

1. J. O'Connell, *The Injury Industry and the Remedy of No-Fault Insurance* 13–14 (1971).

2. *Ibid.*, 16–17.

3. Testimony of A. Conard, *Hearings on H.R.J. Res. 958 before the Subcommittee on Commerce and Finance of the House Committee on Interstate and Foreign Commerce,* 90th Cong., 2d Sess. 85 (1968).

4. O'Connell, *supra* note 1, at 22–27.

5. For an indication of advanced payments being made in medical malpractice cases, see Kendall and Haldi, "The Medical Malpractice Insurance Market," in U.S. Department of Health, Education, and Welfare, *Appendix, Report of the Secretary's Commission on Medical Malpractice* 494, 516 (1973) [hereinafter cited as HEW Secretary's Commission Report].

6. N.Y. Insurance Department, *Automobile Insurance ... For Whose Benefit: A Report to Governor Nelson A. Rockefeller* 31, n. 50 (1970).

7. Sigmund Freud as quoted in M. Harrington, *The Other America* 119 (1962).

8. *N.Y. Times,* May 9, 1973, p. 45, cols. 7–8.

9. O'Connell, *supra* note 1, at 60.

10. HEW Secretary's Commission Report, *supra* note 5, at 10 (1973). But for an indication of a relative lack of smaller, nuisance medical malpractice claims, see Dietz, Baird, and Berul, "The Medical Malpractice Legal System," in *Appendix, ibid.,* 87, 117–18. See also *supra,* ch. 3, note 23 and accompanying text.

11. But see O'Connell, *supra* note 1, at 118, indicating that the likelihood of padded medical bills decreases with the seriousness of the injury.

12. As quoted in R. Keeton and J. O'Connell, *Basic Protection for the Traffic Victim: A Blueprint for Reforming Automobile Insurance* 29–30 (1965), citing Iowa Academy of Trial Lawyers, *Legal-Medical Seminar* 119–21 (State University of Iowa, College of Law, 1963).

5

Where Tort Law Has Been Drifting

Many reforms of tort law — apart from no-fault auto insurance — have been put into effect in recent years, but these reforms have been marginal — though you would never guess it from listening to us lawyers. In the case of product liability, for example, there has been, as the late Dean William Prosser of the University of California Law School at Berkeley termed it, first the "assault" and then the "fall" of the "citadel." Prosser used this apocalyptic language to describe the switch from the requirement that the injured party prove the manufacturer of the offending product guilty of negligence to a new rule of so-called strict liability under which no proof of the manufacturer's negligence is required.[1] In 1966 he wrote:

> The fall of a citadel is a dramatic moment....
>
> In the field of products liability, the date of the fall...can be fixed with some certainty. It was May 9, 1960, when the Supreme Court of New Jersey announced the decision in *Henningsen v. Bloomfield Motors, Inc.*[2] The leaguer had been an epic one of more than fifty years. [A] sister fortress...had fallen, after an equally prolonged defense, in 1916. Much sapping and mining had finally carried a whole south wing of the strict liability citadel, involving food and drink; and further inroads had been made into an adjoining area of products for what might be called intimate bodily use, such as hair dye and cosmetics. Heavy artillery had made no less than eight major breaches in the main wall, all of them still stoutly defended.

Notes on p. 67.

Then came the Henningsen case. . . .

What has followed has been the most rapid and altogether spectacular overturn of an established rule in the entire history of the law of torts.[3]

Well, everything is relative. But Prosser's prose aptly illustrates the extent to which we lawyers and judges have long been preoccupied with trivia in personal injury law while deceiving ourselves that we are moving the world, because, despite the dean's pretentious language, so-called strict liability in cases involving an injury from a manufactured product still entails the process of proving the product defective. The result is that the change in the law has been largely one of terminology, not substance.[4] According to the editors of the *Harvard Law Review,* writing in 1965 (five years after *Henningsen* and one year before Prosser wrote), the switch from a negligence criterion to strict liability had by then made precious little difference in insurance rates: "Indeed, current insurance practices permit a manufacturer to insure his products at roughly the same cost whether he makes them in a negligence state or a strict [liability] state."[5] The gap between substance and verbiage in tort law is surely starkly demonstrated when "the most rapid and altogether most spectacular overturn of established rule in the entire history of torts" was not significant enough to be reflected in tort liability insurance rates.

In the case of the law of medical malpractice the changes have been even more modest. Even the name of the game has remained the same. True, small incremental changes have been made: for example, the so-called locality rule formerly required a plaintiff in a medical malpractice suit to hire an expert medical witness from the defendant doctor's own locality. This requirement made proof all the more difficult because one had to get a neighboring colleague to testify against a defendant doctor, and the close nature of local medical societies thereby increased the burden of trying to avoid the notorious "conspiracy of silence" under which all doctors are so reluctant to testify against one another.[6] But abrogation of the locality rule to allow doctors from elsewhere to testify,[7] while commendable, scarcely eases the burden of proof in a complex factual case to any remarkable extent. Proving medical malpractice remains

Notes on p. 67.

long, expensive, and arduous. Other examples, such as allowing the plaintiff to prove his case by making use of medical textbooks in court, as opposed to calling an expert medical witness in person,[8] are in the same category.

Similarly, changes in other liability rules, such as finally allowing a wife, as well as a husband, to recover for loss of so-called consortium (comfort, companionship, sexual relations, and so on) as a result of injury to her spouse, really bespeak more the law's prior timidity than present liberality.[9]

In short, despite the spate of recent changes the structure of tort law remains "gothic," to use Harry Kalven's word — overly complex and rich in its shadings and structure.[10] It is gothic in two dimensions. First, the factual determinations *within* any given case are overly complex; for example, Was the step in the store "properly" lighted? Was the cable able to withstand "appropriate" stress? Second, its doctrines for rationalizing law as *between* cases and categories of cases are overly complex. To illustrate the latter problem, Kalven has recently traced "the utter incoherence of the formulation of the rule" that imposes liability without regard to fault on ultrahazardous activities such as blasting with dynamite.[11] This "utter incoherence" manifests itself in two ways. The first is in attempts to rationalize the rule itself in the face of such totally irrational distinctions as whether the damage was done by actual physical intrusion of debris (for which no-fault liability is imposed) or by concussion (for which only liability based on fault is imposed). More importantly, though, "the utter incoherence" manifests itself in the courts' attempts to decide why, as a general proposition, liability without fault should ever exist and the concomitant attempts to decide why that proposition should be applied in some cases and not in others. In point of fact, as we shall see, the imposition of liability without fault by courts has been rigidly restricted by (1) imposing it only on abnormally dangerous activities and (2) by further imposing it only on abnormally dangerous activities which are *not* the subject of common usage. As a result, no-fault liability, except under workers' compensation — which was imposed by legislatures, not courts — has rarely been imposed. Consequently, no-fault liability has been isolated and

Notes on pp. 67–68.

largely unimportant in its total impact in the common law of torts.

Kalven goes on to point out that the law's treatment of the irrational distinction between direct physical intrusion by debris and concussion illustrates that there is, in case-by-case decisions of judges under the common law, "the ultimate instability of a minor irrational distinction . . . ; sooner or later the law will work itself pure." Just so; the distinction between direct physical intrusion and concussion is disappearing in the common law. But a corollary of that capacity of the law to grow and rid itself of minor irrational distinctions is, in Kalven's words, an "indifference of the legal system to major inconsistencies. The role of logic in law is to iron out the small contradictions, the big ones we leave alone." Kalven posits as an illustration of this tragicomic plight the law's inability to rationalize when to impose no-fault — or strict — liability. He writes of "the weakness at the moment of any over-all theory of tort liability, the lack especially of any coherent theory of strict liability and of any criteria for allocating 'jurisdiction' as between negligence and strict liability as principles of liability."[12]

Kalven then proceeds to examine the ludicrously tortuous attempts by the New York courts over 122 years to apply a doctrine of no-fault liability in cases involving the use of explosives — a tale so full of intellectual oddities and inconsistencies that "one could derive a course in jurisprudence from it."[13] As indicated, the New York courts eventually succeeded — after that long period — in shucking the silly distinction between debris and concussion, but never in their ordeal did they succeed in formulating a cogent reason why there should be a rule of strict liability in some instances and negligence in others — and this despite the issue being eventually placed in 1969 squarely before Judge Stanley Fuld of the New York Court of Appeals,[14] "surely," in Kalven's words, "one of the most deservedly admired, able and scholarly judges of our time."[15] While Fuld succeeded in finally imposing no-fault liability for concussion as well as for debris, he was wary of the traditional and most obvious basis for applying the stricter rule to all blasting cases — the idea that the activity is unusually dangerous.

Notes on p. 68.

Kalven sympathizes with him. The law *is* in an awful mess on the matter of deciding which activities are sufficiently dangerous to call for no-fault liability and which are not. Why, in this day and age, should the airplane be considered so abnormally dangerous that the damage to a farmer's field caused by an aircraft out of control must be paid for regardless of fault, whereas similar damage by an automobile out of control must be paid for only if the operator of the automobile was negligent? Actually, airplanes are safer than cars today. And even if airplanes are considered abnormally hazardous, are they not unquestionably today items of "common usage" and therefore on that basis ineligible for no-fault liability? Writes Kalven: "One suspects that the extra hazardous activities of the popular mind, like flying airplanes, using explosives, and utilizing nuclear energy [for which activities no-fault liability is imposed] are probably unusually safe because of the expertise with which they are handled; and if there were some way of arraying systematically various activities in terms of their risk, the result would turn current evaluations upside down. One irony of the New York story may well be that blasting is not so dangerous after all."[16] In other words, if degrees of danger and risk were really the basis for imposing liability regardless of fault, categories like driving motor vehicles would be subject to no-fault liability and flying airplanes and dynamiting would *not* be.

More particularly, Kalven goes on to examine the plight of the bystander, that is, not the purchaser of a car, but, say, an injured pedestrian, under strict product liability law. Early expansion of liability for injuries from manufactured products was grounded in the law governing the sale of goods. The theory seems to have been that any special right to be paid for injuries caused by a product was granted only to the purchaser and his immediate family — the "consumer." As Kalven points out, the new strict (no-fault) product liability was "closely linked with the rhetoric of consumer protection," stemming from a kind of sales warranty concerning the safety of the goods in the transfer from the seller to the buyer; it was applied first and foremost to food products.[17] But most food purchases are consumed by the purchaser and his family, and injuries to bystanders by food products are quite rare. So the hunch

Notes on p. 68.

of many lawyers was that no-fault liability would not be extended by the courts in their case-by-case rulings to protect bystanders, as distinguished from purchasers. In other words, given the rationale for justifying the extension of special no-fault protection to purchasers, refusing to protect bystanders would have seemed to present a logical stopping place for the new no-fault product liability.

As a corollary, if the bystander were to be protected under such no-fault liability, a new rationale would seem necessary for applying such broad no-fault liability to all product injuries but not to other kinds of injuries. Prosser has expressed it best:

> Bystanders and other nonusers . . . present a fundamental question of policy. If the philosophy of strict [no-fault] liability is that all injured plaintiffs are to be compensated by holding the suppliers of products to strict [products] liability for all the harm they do in the world, and expecting them to insure against the liability and pass the cost on to society by adding it to the price, then there is no reason whatever to distinguish the pedestrian hit by an automobile with bad brakes from the injured driver of the car. [But i]f the supplier is to be held liable because of his representation [to the purchaser] of safety in marketing the goods, then the pedestrian stands on quite a different footing. He is not the man the supplier has sought to reach, and no implied representation [or warranty] has been made to him that the product is safe for his use; nor has he relied upon any assurance of safety whatever. He has only been there when the accident happened; and in this he differs from no other plaintiff. Thus far, with the emotional drive and the public concern and demand centering on the consumer, it has been the second theory that has prevailed; and those who have no connection with the product except as victims have been denied the strict [products] liability, and left to negligence.[18]

Prosser was writing in 1966. But in fact, after considerable and agonized judicial hesitation (during which period a lot of victims left courtrooms uncompensated and nearly everyone left confused), the bystander barrier finally proved "to be no obstacle after all."[19] Once again, after gothic permutations and endlessly convoluted rationale, as in the case of distinguishing between debris and concussion, distinctions between purchaser and bystander were rejected.

Notes on p. 68.

To paraphrase Kalven, the small contradiction was worked out. But also once again, despite the mounds of judicial print piled over the issue, the big contradiction was left alone. According to Kalven, "The courts have uniformly seen the issue of the bystander as technical, as involving only an incremental change in the ambit of liability."[20]

But if the courts refuse to face up to the real issues confronting them, Kalven does not share their diffidence — at least up to a point. To him the step to protecting the bystander seems to "involve bigger things":

As I see it, it has served to sever the new products liability from its historic connections with warranty and the consumer which made it a doctrine with some profile and some parameters; the key term for the liability is no longer *product*, but *enterprise*. The idea of enterprise liability has been in the wind for years, originally in an effort to explain the doctrines of agency [whereby a principal was liable for the negligence of his agent, regardless of any negligence on the principal's part in hiring him or otherwise]. On this view what is important is [not that the defendant or his product were faulty or defective but] that the defendant is an enterprise, that is, is *systematically* engaged in generating the risks, *and* has access to the mechanism of *the market* [to spread those risks]. [This]...is thought to make him a superior risk-bearer able to pass on the loss into channels of wide distribution. There is undoubted power in these policy notions and this is not the place to debate them seriously. We would merely note that the premises now have considerable reach, and if we are serious about enterprise liability, a good part of contemporary tort law will need to be revised accordingly, and very little of its once spacious domain is likely to be left to the negligence principle.

If there is a complaint about the way the courts have handled the bystander cases, it is simply that they have apparently not noted that in ironing out the inconsistency in treatment between user and bystander they were sharpening the inconsistency between products liability and other areas of tort law. In extending recovery to the bystander the law has, we would suggest, severed the connection between products liability and a product.[21]

But the common law's irrational floundering in deciding whether

Notes on p. 68.

and when to impose liability regardless of fault* does not cause
Kalven to lose faith. He writes: "For those who have a taste for
the common law, the process, although we have seen it at work a
hundred times before, retains its fascination on each new occasion.
What is perhaps most striking at the moment is that the common-
law judges in the tort system, while the [tort] system stands deep
in the shadow of formidable legislative change, continue so ener-
getically, and so gallantly, with their traditional daily business of
[working things out on a case-by-case basis by what might be
termed] 'interstitial legislation.' "[22] But, to speak bluntly, it is the
fascination of us lawyers with our own "energetic and gallant"
ratiocinations — ratiocinations that, as Kalven indicates, ignore the
big issues while taking years and sometimes even generations to
work out the small ones — which has so largely caused the almost
unimaginable grief that the tort liability system inflicts on everyone
(except us lawyers).

So Kalven has raised — but not answered — the crucial question
which the law has so long ducked: How do we decide when to
impose no-fault liability? A corollary question is, Why not impose
it all the time? Why ever require proof of the defendant's fault —
or its equivalent, proof of a defect in his product — before imposing
liability on him? The real key to the requirement of proof of fault
or defect has been that it is a way of limiting liability, long a
matter of morbid concern in the common law of torts. If I am held
liable for all the harm I cause regardless of whether I was at fault,
the question is asked, won't my liability be endless?[23] For example,

* So-called strict liability in product liability cases is actually a sort of half-
way house between traditional fault liability and the no-fault liability exem-
plified in the blasting cases. Although fault on the part of the defendant is not
required under the new strict liability formulation in product cases, a defect
in the product still is. In the case of blasting, on the other hand, as long as
the explosion causes injury, the blaster must pay, regardless of any fault *or*
defect. Although the results of the change in product liability law are not
often important in practice (this chapter, notes 4–5 and accompanying text),
the philosophical implications of moving away from negligence as a basis of
liability are important. And so, although Professor Kalven, like so many others
in this area, identifies strict liability in product cases too closely with strict
liability in extrahazardous cases, avoidance of a requirement of proving
negligence *is* present in both cases.

Notes on p. 68.

is the manufacturer, wholesaler, or retailer of a stove to be liable
for any and all injuries to persons who burn themselves by stoves,
regardless of any fault on the businessman's part or any defect in
the stove? Such open-ended liability would be crushing, wouldn't
it, threatening many businesses with bankruptcy? Indeed, the law
has long feared the extent of liability even when it is limited by
being tied to the defendant's fault. In the famous *Palsgraf* case,
railroad employees were apparently negligent in helping a passenger trying to board a starting train. Unbeknownst to the railroad
employees, the passenger had firecrackers in the paper bag he was
carrying; they fell to the ground, exploding, and the concussion
in turn caused a weighing machine some thirty feet away to topple
and injure the plaintiff. Chief Judge Cardozo of the New York
Court of Appeals, in one of the most famous common law opinions
ever written, refused to hold the railroad liable on the ground that
even though the railroad was at fault, the resulting injury was
too bizarre a result to hold the railroad responsible for it. In order
to consider the defendant's negligence "the proximate cause" of
the plaintiff's injury, that injury must be a foreseeable consequence
of the defendant's negligence, not highly unpredictable. Otherwise,
Cardozo argued — and generations of judges and lawyers have
agreed — the extent of liability would be too unpredictable.[24] Similarly, suppose I negligently injure an attractive young girl in an
auto accident, causing her severe facial scars. She falls into a state
of deep depression and, as a result of her depressed emotional
state, dies a year and a half later. Even though the court might
concede the accident "caused" the death, it would not impose
liability for the death on me, the death being too "remote." As
Prosser has put it, requiring the defendant's act to be the "proximate cause" of the plaintiff's injury "is merely the limitation
which the courts have placed upon the actor's responsibility for
the consequences of his conduct. In a philosophical sense, the
consequences of an act go forward to eternity, and the causes of
an event go back to the discovery of America and beyond. 'The
fatal trespass done by Eve was cause of all our woe.' But any
attempt to impose responsibility upon such a basis would result
in infinite liability for all wrongful acts, and would 'set society
on edge and fill the courts with endless litigation.'[25] As a practical

Notes on p. 68.

matter ... [s]ome boundary must be set to liability for the consequences of any act. . . ."[26]

Similarly, although we lawyers — and judges — have "talked big" about extending liability in products cases through the adoption of so-called strict product liability, the law has been conscious of a need to limit liability. In fact, by retaining the requirement that the product be defective the law has kept about as severe a limitation on liability as was traditionally provided by the common law requirement of proof of negligence on the part of the defendant. Without such a limitation, it is thought, we would be confronted with that perilous situation in which the manufacturer, wholesaler, or retailer of stoves is to be liable for any and all injuries to persons who are burned by stoves, regardless of any fault on the businessman's part or any defect in his product.[27]

But in an increasingly sophisticated and sensitive age the plight of the broken and battered accident victim has had more and more appeal, and to turn him away without compensation has caused the law more and more anguish. Professor Charles Gregory of the University of Virginia Law School, for example, has analyzed what the New York Court of Appeals was up to in its tortured wrestling through the years with injuries stemming from blasting: "My belief is that the New York court had a sort of Freudian fixation on a concept which it consciously and outwardly purported to loathe ... liability without fault for the consequences of extra hazardous conduct. It was obviously fascinated by this sinister concept but did not dare to come out into the open and admit it. . . ."[28]

And so, despite such anguish, a strong undertow in tort liability for personal injuries has been toward payment to more and more accident victims. Fleming James and Fowler Harper, in their great treatise on tort liability, have pointed out that despite continuing reliance on traditional rules on the surface, "[g]reat changes are going on under the surface which have profoundly affected the operation ... of tort liability ... ,"[29] changes which have been in the direction of assuring compensation to increasing numbers of accident victims, often under principles applicable to social insurance.

Notes on pp. 68–69.

Although Harper and James applaud this trend of accident law toward more compensation, others have bitterly resented it. To them, it was not only distorting the law of torts but doing it surreptitiously, without fairly facing the issues.[30] The insurance industry in particular has deeply resented this often devious sub-surface change. What has happened in their view — and in the eyes of more objective observers[31] — is that judges and jurors have tended to stretch and distort legal rules to force defendants to pay injured plaintiffs, confident in the knowledge that the defendants themselves would not have to pay but rather that the money would come from the vast coffers of large, impersonal insurance companies. The insurance industry has resented the fact that — despite the premise of liability insurance that *insurance attaches because there is liability* — too often under modern court rulings *liability attaches because there is insurance*. The response of the plaintiff's personal injury bar to these trends, on the other hand, has been a fascinating balancing act. Its members have loudly applauded — and indeed often initiated — moves toward increased liability and compensation while stoutly opposing compensation so readily available that lawyers would no longer be necessary to help get it. Perhaps that explains — not too unfairly — the anomaly of trial lawyers fighting for no-fault strict product insurance, in which the requirement of proving a defect leaves them with their litigable issues, while condemning no-fault automobile insurance, in which the litigable issues largely vanish.[32]

In the face of such powerful opposition, movement toward much easier and quicker payment from insurance for accident victims has been neither swift nor extensive. Responding to the contention of visionaries like Harper and James that "insurance already has revolutionized the law of torts," Prosser surmised that a "dispassionate observer, if such a one is to be found in this area, might quite as readily conclude that the 'impact' of insurance on the law of torts has been amazingly slight. . . ."[33]

And in fact, when one considers the number of accident victims unpaid and underpaid after enormous delay and expense in the processing of claims,[34] one is forced to agree with Prosser that the ancient inefficiency of the common law of torts has had little trouble resisting the modern efficiency of insurance.

Notes on p. 69.

It is time we lawyers stopped kidding ourselves, and our constituencies, with our endless — and largely futile — ratiocinations which iron out the small contradictions and leave the big ones alone.[35] It is time we turned to ambitious legislation for reform instead of relying so much on the tortured, tortuous, even torturing tort system with its case-by-case common law crawl — a system from which law professors derive so much fascination, law practitioners so much income, and the general public so few benefits.

NOTES

1. Prosser, "The Assault upon the Citadel (Strict Liability to the Consumer)," 69 *Yale L. J.* 1099 (1960); Prosser, "The Fall of the Citadel (Strict Liability to the Consumer)," 50 *Minn. L. Rev.* 791 (1966).

2. 32 N.J. 358, 161 A.2d 69 (1960).

3. Prosser, "The Fall of the Citadel," *supra* note 1, at 791–92.

4. Switching from negligence to strict liability in product liability cases "would chiefly help the 15 percent of plaintiffs... who may otherwise be unable to prove or pinpoint the actual negligence that produced the defect" (Stoljar, "Accident Costs and Legal Responsibility," 36 *Mod. L. Rev.* 233, 241 [1973]).

5. Note, "Product Liability and the Choice of Law," 78 *Harv. L. Rev.* 1452, 1456 (1965). "Arguably there is some difference between requiring proof of a defect... and requiring proof that the manufacturer was negligent, but the difference is slight in theory, and perhaps even slighter in practical impact. Virtually the same evidence is likely to be marshalled on either issue, and it seems unlikely that juries would often respond differently to the slightly contrasting charges that would be given" (R. Keeton, *Venturing to Do Justice* 109 [1969]). "[T]he need to show the jury an unreasonably dangerous or defective condition is essentially the same regardless of whether you proceed on a negligence, warranty, or strict liability theory" (E. Swartz, *Hazardous Products Litigation* 306 [1973]).

6. *Supra,* ch. 3, note 7 and accompanying text.

7. See, e.g., Wiggins v. Piver, 276 N.C. 134, 171 S.E.2d 393 (1970).

8. See, e.g., Mass. Gen. Laws Ann., ch. 233, § 79c (Supp. 1973).

9. E.g., Dini v. Naiditzh, 20 Ill.2d 406, 170 N.E.2d 881 (1960). For a discussion of the spate of common law decisions overruling tort precedents, see Keeton, "Judicial Law Reform — A Prospective on the Performance of Appellate Courts," 44 *Tex. L. Rev.* 1254, 1255–59 (1966).

10. "Most of the issues pertaining to the liability of manufacturers, and other sellers in the marketing chain, for physical harm arising from the dangerousness of products can be regarded as facets of two broad problems — the meaning of defect and the kind of misconduct on the part of users and others that will insulate a particular seller in the marketing chain from liability if the product is found to be defective.... [T]he tremendous amount of uncertainty regarding the two basic problems as to the meaning of defect and the

effect of misconduct of others must be substantially reduced before there can be effective administration of justice with reference to claims in this area. Hardly any claims based on inherent risks in the way products are designed can be settled at present with any confidence of what the outcome of litigation would have been, and trial judges are faced with an impossible task of describing to the jury in any sort of intelligible manner the scope of the seller's responsibility in such cases" (P. Keeton, "Product Liability and the Meaning of Defect," 5 *St. Mary L. J.* 30 [1973]).

11. Kalven, "Tort Law — Tort Watch," 34 *Am. Trial Lawyers Ass'n J.* 1, 32 (1972).

12. *Ibid.,* 31. Concerning the ambiguity of the term *strict liability,* see footnote, p. 63.

13. *Ibid.,* 38.

14. Spano v. Perini Corp., 25 N.Y.2d 11, 250 N.E.2d 31 (1969).

15. Kalven, *supra* note 11, at 39.

16. *Ibid.,* 42–43.

17. *Ibid.,* 46. As at the text at note 12, *supra,* see footnote, p. 63.

18. Prosser, "The Fall of the Citadel," *supra* note 1, at 819–20.

19. Kalven, *supra* note 11, at 49.

20. *Ibid.,* 56.

21. *Ibid.,* 57.

22. *Ibid.,* 59.

23. Malone, book review of A. Ehrenzweig, *Negligence without Fault,* 25 *So. Calif. L. Rev.* 14, 18–20 (1951).

24. Actually, it appears to have been a very thin case of negligence. A man carrying a package jumped to board a moving train but seemed to be unsteady; thereupon a guard who held the door open reached forward to help him, and another guard on the platform pushed him from behind. During this activity, the apparently innocuous package was dislodged, fell on the rails, and exploded. One wonders where was the negligence on the part of the railroad employees in behaving thus. Indeed, one is prompted to ask whether the appellate judges did not assume the negligence in order to reach the delicious — and historical — question of law! Had they simply decided that the railroad employees were not negligent toward the boarding passenger, the fascinating question of proximate cause would simply have disappeared.

25. Mitchell, J., in North v. Johnson, 58 Minn. 242, 59 N.W. 1012 (1894).

26. W. Prosser, *The Law of Torts* 236–37 (4th ed. 1971).

27. Chief Justice O'Connell of Oregon (no relation to the author) has pointed out the illogic of limiting any theory of enterprise liability to cases where the product is defective. In his view, the rationale of risk spreading "has no special relevancy to cases involving injuries resulting from the use of defective goods. The reasoning would seem to apply . . . to any case where an injury results from the risk creating conduct of the seller in any stage of the production and distribution of goods. Thus a manufacturer would be strictly liable even in the absence of fault for an injury to a person struck by one of the manufacturer's trucks being used in transporting his goods to market" (Wights v. Staff Jennings, Inc., 241 Ore. 301, 309, 405 P.2d 624, 628 [1965]). As a result, O'Connell refused in the aforementioned case to apply a broad theory of enterprise liability because, as he said, it "proves too much" (*ibid.*).

28. Gregory, "Trespass to Negligence to Absolute Liability," 37 *Va. L. Rev.* 359, 376 (1951).

29. 2 F. Harper and F. James, *The Law of Torts* § 13.3, at 764–65 (1956).

30. Cooperrider, book review in 56 *Mich. L. Rev.* 1291 (1958).

31. *Ibid.*

32. For a discussion of this point, see J. O'Connell, *The Injury Industry and the Remedy of No-Fault Insurance* 125–26 (1971).

33. Prosser, *Law of Torts, supra* note 26, at 547.

34. *Supra,* ch. 2, notes 15–21, 49–53 and accompanying text.

35. *Supra* note 12 and accompanying text.

6

A Blind Alley or Two

PART I

No-fault automobile insurance seems finally to have come of age. No army of trial attorneys or timid insurance executives will likely stop it now.[1] After a decade of battling, the public widely recognizes that almost no idea is more intellectually inert than that of basing compensation for every auto accident on who was at fault in causing the collision.

The next crucial question facing the law of personal injury is how to adapt the no-fault principle to all kinds of accidents — those from manufactured products, medical malpractice, falls in stores, and many other causes.

Solving the problem of no-fault compensation of very large losses from auto accidents and, more generally, of losses from other accidents not covered by auto insurance reform is much more difficult than achieving no-fault compensation of smaller auto accident losses. No-fault auto insurance has been relatively easy to attain because of two interrelated factors: (1) a system of widespread fault liability insurance is readily and simply transferable into no-fault loss insurance without much fear that the transformation would impose new and unmanageable burdens on anyone, and (2) a sufficiently dangerous — or otherwise distinctive — activity (such as driving an automobile) means that the statute can readily identify who is to be required to pay for what loss.[2] But with other accidents — from medical malpractice or manufactured products, for example — no-fault insurance poses much greater problems because neither factor is generally applicable.

Notes on p. 80.

For example, consider injuries from, say, falls from ladders or burns from stoves. Unlike injuries from auto accidents, these commonplace injuries are not now covered by each of us with a separate insurance policy applicable especially to them. (It is true some losses from falls or burns would probably be covered by general health insurance policies applicable to any kind of illness or injury, but, as we have seen, that is not the same as no-fault insurance; true no-fault insurance involves the switch from fault to no-fault coverage.[3] It does not involve having health insurance applicable to injuries in addition to possible tort liability insurance. That is the situation that has long prevailed under accident law and that has long been a mess.)

So it turns out that there is no form of insurance applicable to nonauto accidents, whereby each of us is covering the other person based on fault, that can be switched over to no-fault insurance on ourselves. Indeed, even for auto accidents the fear of the high costs of providing unlimited — or even very high — no-fault benefits has caused reluctance to require such benefits, as we have seen.[4] Providing those benefits might conceivably drive costs substantially above present premiums. Nor can present product liability insurance carried by manufacturers be easily switched over to no-fault insurance. For example, if ladder manufacturers would be made liable for every fall from a ladder regardless of fault or any defect in the ladder and regardless of any negligence on the part of users of ladders, wouldn't this very likely expand their liability dramatically? Similarly, as suggested earlier, if stove manufacturers were forced to pay anyone burned by stoves — regardless of the lack of any defect in the stove or any carelessness on the part of the victim — wouldn't stove manufacturers insist that an unrealistic burden has been put on them?

Next, consider the second factor facilitating no-fault auto insurance, namely, that an activity is sufficiently dangerous that the statute can define readily who must pay for what loss. Would building a cement patio be considered sufficiently dangerous that the subcontractor laying the concrete, for example, should be automatically liable forever after whenever anyone falls on the concrete and injures himself? Or who pays for the resultant injuries when

Notes on p. 81.

someone trips over a book and falls down a flight of stairs — the publisher? the carpenters?[5]

Injuries inflicted in the course of medical treatment perhaps best illustrate the frustrations of trying to apply the no-fault principle to all kinds of accidents. Take the case of a person with a heart disease who consults a doctor. The doctor treats him, but subsequently the patient gets worse — even dies. Assuming the doctor did nothing wrong, can we honestly expect the doctor to pay for any additional medical expenses and wage losses incurred by the patient before his death or for any benefits to the victim's widow and children after his death? The problem is that people seeking medical attention in our society — especially those who undergo surgery — almost invariably have something wrong with them already. Trying to separate adverse results properly attributable to medical treatment from conditions more likely due to the complaint which led the patient to seek medical treatment in the first place (the presenting complaint) is particularly frustrating. Moreover, doctors interfere with our physical functioning in a pervasive and complex way (the same is true of manufacturers of pharmaceutical drugs, who in a way are both manufacturers of drugs and providers of health services). People are normally hurt by a simple, traumatic blow of one kind or another, but when a doctor begins prescribing drugs or rummaging around a patient's insides, infinitely greater possibilities of adverse effects arise. The origins of much ill health are so obscure that strictly non-negligent medical treatment may provoke untoward physiological responses. Indeed, any system of coverage or compensation for injury which moves beyond simple external traumatic impact is destined to encounter prodigious questions of causation. Witness the problem faced by many courts in trying to decide whether a cigarette manufacturer should be liable to a given lung cancer victim. Would that particular victim have developed cancer regardless of cigarette smoking?[6] Witness also the exasperating problems long facing the law of industrial accidents in its attempts to decide whether a slowly developing illness — or even a heart attack — was "caused by" the victim's employment and thus requires payment under workers' compensation.[7]

Notes on p. 81.

Professor Robert E. Keeton of the Harvard Law School has defined the legal problem which this scientific puzzle presents:

Perhaps the most troublesome problem facing those who propose to adopt a [no-fault] . . . insurance system for medical accidents in place of the existing malpractice liability insurance system is the causation issue. In the automobile accident context, [no-fault] . . . plans commonly employ the phrase "arising out of the maintenance or use" of a motor vehicle, or some variation on this basic theme, to identify the covered losses. The number of instances in which it may reasonably be disputed whether a particular loss fell within or outside the definition of the requisite causal relation will be few. The administrative cost of resolving disputes in those few instances would be only a minute percentage of the total cost of the system. In contrast, losses "arising from mistake or accident occurring during medical treatment" (or within some alternative definition of the required causal relation) would be more difficult to distinguish from losses resulting from the pre-existing condition for which medical treatment was given, and this difficult causation issue would be present usually rather than unusually. The resolution of these case-by-case disputes would involve substantial administrative costs in the [no-fault] . . . system. . . .[8]

One apparent solution to this problem is simply to abandon tort liability of any kind and pay everyone injured by accidents for his wage losses and medical expenses under social security. Indeed, won't impending national health insurance largely meet the needs of those suffering serious personal injury? Those who ask this question can point to recently enacted legislation in New Zealand which does, in fact, wipe out most tort liability and replace it with governmentally financed social insurance benefits covering wage loss and medical expense of accident victims.[9] Similar proposals have been made for the United States,[10] for Great Britain,[11] and, more seriously, for Australia.[12]

But the costs in the United States would be imposing indeed if we were to cover, under social security or some other form of social insurance, wage losses and medical expenses stemming from all accidental injuries. New Zealand already has a comprehensive system of national health insurance and generally much more social

Notes on p. 81.

insurance on which to build such a scheme. Even so, the potential costs of the plan have caused some unease there.[13] (Note that New Zealand is a homogeneous country — both economically and racially — with much less concern about the redistribution of income involved in social legislation than exists in the United States, with its deep mutual distrusts based on racial, economic, and geographic disparities.) In the United States, the costs of impending national health insurance — covering only medical bills but not wage losses — are causing much greater unease. Estimates, of course, vary widely, but even President Nixon's relatively modest new national health insurance proposal, which would not take effect until 1977, was estimated by the administration to entail costs of $40 billion annually. An administration cost estimate for Senator Edward Kennedy's earlier more ambitious bill was $80 billion annually.[14]

As a further indication of what funding medical services alone can cost — and of how uncertain costs can be — in 1971 Congress passed, and the president signed into law, social security legislation covering those suffering serious kidney ailments that require renal dialysis (to perform the kidney's functions). Coverage of all catastrophic illness had been considered by Congress earlier, but it had been cast aside as being too costly. An exception was made for dialysis because of the tremendously high cost of such treatment, which averages about $5,000 a year per patient but which can go as high as $20,000 a year. The dialysis provision alone was expected to cost $127 million in its first year, with eventual costs perhaps exceeding $500 million a year. And that is only a modest start. According to one official of the Department of Health, Education, and Welfare: "The dialysis provision is only the camel's nose under the tent. It means we are on the road to Federally-subsidized coverage of so-called catastrophic illnesses." According to another observer, in the coming years "every lobby will troop up to Congress to demand equal treatment for sufferers of cancer, leukemia, hemophilia, multiple sclerosis and any number of other diseases."[15] Certainly the spiraling and originally grossly underestimated costs of Medicare and Medicaid also give one pause when the costs of vast extensions of medical insurance are contemplated. Annual Medicaid costs in New York State, amounting to $1.99 billion, now exceed amounts spent there for welfare.[16]

Notes on pp. 81–83.

Keep in mind, too, that even if national health insurance is passed in the immediate future on a comprehensive scale, it would still meet only a relatively small portion of the total personal injury losses of accident victims. For serious auto accidents, for example, it is estimated that 79 percent of injury loss is for wage loss and only 18 percent for medical loss (with 3 percent for "other expenses").[17] But given the high costs that any national health insurance will be likely to impose, it will be a long time, indeed, before any national health insurance or social security is extended to cover wage loss as well. And one doubts that such protection will ever cover more than modest levels of subsistence income.

Nor should one overlook the tremendous competition for public — legislatively mandated — spending that coverage for accidental losses will face in coming years.[18] To give some idea of the impending dimensions of overall social need and the sources required to meet them, quite apart from further programs for medical and wage losses, Professor Lawrence Ritter of New York University calculates that during the rest of the 1970s public spending will have to average $46 billion *a year* above 1970 levels in just four areas: mass-transit systems, pollution control, law enforcement, and education.[19] This is, as Daniel Patrick Moynihan has pointed out, a world of "competing sorrows." As Moynihan's colleague Daniel Bell has observed in his brilliant book *The Coming of Post-Industrial Society*, there are therefore two racking problems impeding any plan for vast public spending for any given social need: lack of sufficient funds and lack of consensus on how to spend whatever is available, especially as more and more groups — blacks, the elderly, the poor, females — insist on more social focus on *their* problems.[20]

Nor are the problems limited to how public bodies will allocate more resources to competing needs. Future energy crises could portend fewer — not more — resources for *both* public and private needs. And if such an economic clime implies more and more centralized governmental decision making, it will apparently run against a widespread — and arguably worldwide — resistance to such decision making, especially if it involves more funds for public needs as opposed to market allocations for private needs.[21] Former Undersecretary of State and Yale Law School Dean Eugene Rostow has spoken of the trend "in Communist countries, developing na-

Notes on pp. 83–84.

tions and Western industrial states alike . . . toward greater decentralization, more reliance on market incentives, and more rapid growth in the private than in the nationalized sectors.[22]

To put all this in context, covering wage losses, as well as medical expenses, of *all* injury victims under social insurance, as is being tested in New Zealand, is going to have to face extremely cruel competition for public spending in coming years. One doubts very much that dismantling the tort liability system and replacing it with a vast scheme of social insurance to cover middle-class accidental wage loss will soon rank high in social priority. All the more reason, then, to think in terms of reforming tort law itself, as was done with no-fault auto insurance. Think for a moment about the European experience. Compared to the United States, all European countries have traditionally had much higher levels of social insurance and much lower levels of affluence with many fewer people in the prosperous middle or upper middle classes.[23] Thus, in Europe social insurance covers much more accident loss than in the United States, but the tort claim for losses above social insurance remains intact.[24] Both at the bottom and the top there is much less need for tort law in Europe than in the United States, but it remains. *A fortiori,* it will remain in the United States.

Even if we could cover all losses from all injuries under social security or general health insurance, economists specializing in loss allocation, such as Professor Guido Calabresi of the Yale Law School, tell us it would be unwise to have all injuries from whatever cause paid for out of a big, undifferentiated pool of "insurance" such as social security.[25] Rather, they argue, a given activity or industry should be made to pay for the particular losses it causes. Otherwise, the argument goes, there is less incentive to keep that activity or industry safe. Isn't your incentive to produce a safer product greatly lessened, it is asked, if persons injured by your product are paid exclusively from social security funded by assessments that make no distinctions between relatively safe products (like pillows) and unsafe ones (like power tools)? For Calabresi, what might be termed *market deterrence* is the best way for accident law to combine payment for loss with a reduction of accidents and accident costs.[26]

Notes on pp. 84–85.

Professor Leonard Ross has best summarized Calabresi's thesis:

[Market] ... deterrence operates by placing the costs of accidents on the activities which cause them; for example, by making power lawn mower manufacturers liable for all [personal injury] damage[s] caused by ... their mowers [regardless of anyone's fault or a defect]. In theory, mower prices would then rise and sales fall; some families would be induced to shift to manual mowers, the total amount of power mowing would be reduced, and the level of accidents would abate. Moreover, manufacturers might become choosy about customers, raising prices to non-institutional buyers or perhaps simply to obvious schlemiels. Finally, they would have an incentive to redesign mowers to improve safety features. A variety of market forces would be set in motion to lower the total loss through accidents.[27]

Obviously, a scheme of social insurance, private health insurance, or wage loss protection which pays out indiscriminately regardless of cause does not attempt to achieve any market deterrence. Social insurance or private health insurance pays the doctor when, say, an elderly victim is injured by an exploding bottle, but it does not normally turn around and claim against the bottler based on the latter's fault or a defective product. Even if it does, the amount of market deterrence achieved by such product liability suits is very minor, as we have seen,[28] especially when compared to the terrible waste that would result from reshifting losses once an efficient insurer like social insurance or health insurance has paid for the loss. Such an insurer pays out promptly and readily with relatively little overhead.[29] To then reshift the loss to a legal liability insurer means that all of us who pay for insurance would pay a lot more so that insurance institutions could spend vast sums to shift money back and forth, fighting over such often futile issues as whether someone made a split-second error in judgment in the course of an accident. Far better, once a loss has passed into the broad stream of insurance, to let it stay there rather than to pay extravagantly to relocate it from an efficient insurer to an inefficient insurer.[30] This is *especially* so where, as in the United States, there is so much loss from accidents not being met by *any* source of insurance.[31]

It might be possible to give social security some market deterrence

Notes on p. 85.

effect by having the social security agency institute large-scale proceedings to charge different industries or activities for the particular
risks and losses they create. For example, the social security agency
might try to accumulate data on how much of its total payout is
due to, say, stove injuries, and then make a corresponding assessment
against stove manufacturers. But such charge-back schemes are
even further off in the future than is much vaster social insurance.
They involve not only a giant bureaucracy paying out benefits, but
also a vast bureaucracy collecting benefits from myriad industries
and enterprises. This raises again the questions of how much more
governmental activity the body politic can be asked to accept in
coming years and what tasks are to be assigned to whatever level
of bureaucracy is acceptable. John Kenneth Galbraith and his
cohorts may be right: more and more public decision making — to
curb inflation and pollution, as just two examples — is probably
inevitable.[32] But that is all the more reason that unpopular but
essential institutions like governmental bureaucracies be rationed
to as few crucial tasks as possible. Leonard Ross and Peter Passell —
unabashed enthusiasts of more and more governmental control of
the economy — have recently spoken of an undeniably "growing
skepticism [even among liberals] about the notion of meeting social
problems with bureaucratic remedies."[33]

And in addition to the problems involved in having bureaucracies
do the collecting, one should not underestimate the cumbersomeness
of such charge-back schemes.[34] Presently we have no mechanism
for charging any given entity other than an individual enterprise.
No trade association, under present law or procedures, could be
readily charged for all the injuries from power mowers, say, with
authority to allocate the losses among the manufacturers.[35] And
even if that barrier could be overcome, allocations would have to
be individualized — and therefore to that extent made cumbersome
and inefficient — to identify high-risk and low-risk manufacturers.
(If both were to pay the same amount, market deterrence — or the
incentive to safety — would be greatly undercut, wouldn't it?)
Suppose, for example, that the social security agency relies, for
purposes of getting reimbursed, on a sample of hospital emergency
room records which indicate that a certain percentage of injury
victims suffered a certain average severity of injuries from, say,

Notes on pp. 85–86.

stove burns.[36] Each stove manufacturer is going to want to be heard, in extensive detail, on the validity and propriety of the overall data and then on the application of those data to the individual enterprise, is it not? Such procedures would be extremely cumbersome and expensive, perhaps rivaling present antitrust litigation.

To the extent, then, that losses from accidents loom very large, the multiple problems of covering such losses by social security loom even larger. But even to the extent that such losses turn out to be *not* so formidable — and thus, to a substantial extent, at least, absorbable by modestly expanding social security — it still might make sense, from the point of view of deterring unsafe products and services, to preserve some kind of separate system of accident law and insurance.[37]

In this connection, it is conceivable that swallowing up all accident losses under social insurance would *not* be all that intimidating.[38] Keep in mind the *relatively* small amounts presently being paid under various forms of liability insurance. The comparatively miniscule nature of liability insurance, excluding automobile insurance, as a proportion of other loss shifting systems is shown by the fact that benefits from nonauto liability insurance in 1969 equaled only $738 million annually.[39] This amounted to only 3.4 percent of private loss insurance benefits (health and life insurance and sick leave) of $22 billion,[40] and only 3 percent of pertinent social insurance benefits of $23 billion.[41] But the fact that currently so few losses under products liability and medical malpractice, at least, are in fact being paid makes one uneasy about what the costs will be once schemes of no-fault insurance, either government or private, guarantee much broader payment.[42] Covering such losses might well someday rival workers' compensation in amount, and workers' compensation benefits, which are universally conceded to be inadequately low, annually amount to $2.4 billion[43] (compared to $2.7 billion for automobile bodily injury liability insurance benefits).[44] Some idea of the costs of meeting all economic losses stemming from accidents is conveyed by figures concerning those who each suffer more than $25,000 of economic loss from auto accidents. A total of 45,153 persons annually were in that category in 1967,[45] constituting 8.8 percent of significantly injured traffic victims and 1.07 percent of the entire group of traffic injury victims.[46] These per-

Notes on pp. 86–87.

sons suffered present and future losses on the average of $76,341, totaling $3.48 billion. They recovered an average of $3,742 from tort liability insurance and $17,899 from collateral sources for an average aggregate of $21,641, leaving 72 percent of their losses — or $2.48 billion — unmet, and this in a category of a little over 1 percent of traffic victims.[47]

But even if we assume that losses from accidents will turn out to be so relatively small that they are readily absorbable by social security, it may make sense to preserve a separate system of accident law because, for relatively small aggregate amounts, one has a chance of achieving much more deterrence applicable to individual enterprise than a gigantic social insurance scheme could probably ever achieve or want to achieve.[48] In other words, to the extent that the loss amounts are small, the broader insurance scheme probably will not want to bother with a complicated charge-back scheme.[49] There is every indication that New Zealand legislators and officials are impatient with the need for doing so.[50] Similarly, health insurers in this country have never been anxious to get involved in elaborate schemes for charging back based on tort or surcharging based on risk. Workers' compensation does much more in surcharging based on risk, albeit not enough, but that is precisely because accidental losses constitute the great bulk of its business and are not dwarfed by other tasks.[51]

In summary, a separate accident law system for meeting losses beyond those met by social insurance is apparently going to be with us indefinitely. Perhaps one can envisage its ultimately being replaced one day by a vast scheme of social insurance supplemented by large-scale charge-backs against enterprises based on their risks, but at the very best that is a long way off, and in the indefinite meantime the need for a more sensible scheme of tort liability remains.

NOTES

1. See *supra,* ch. 2, note 4.
2. Driving a car is sufficiently a dangerous activity that we know without much confusion the types and extent of liability involved in paying for all the injuries caused by driving. In the case of any arguably dangerous activity, such as blasting, the same is true. That is one reason it has been so feasible

to impose liability without reference to any fault or defect on extrahazardous enterprises under the common law. Employment, it will be noted, is often not dangerous, but it is sufficiently severable in time and space that no-fault workmen's compensation statutes have been able to define in a manageable way who is to be required to pay for what loss (granted the vexing — but not insurmountable — problems in defining the phrase "arising out of and in the course of employment"). See also L. Fuller, *The Morality of Law* 75–76 (1964); Henderson, "Should Workmen's Compensation Be Expanded to Nonoccupational Injuries?" 48 *Tex. L. Rev.* 117, 126 (1969).

3. *Supra,* ch. 2, note 4 and accompanying text.

4. *Supra,* ch. 2, note 12 and accompanying text.

5. *Cf.* James, "General Products: Should Manufacturers Be Liable without Negligence?" 24 *Tenn. L. Rev.* 923, 925 (1957).

6. See, e.g., Lartigue v. R. J. Reynolds Tobacco Co., 317 F.2d 19 (5th Cir. 1963).

7. 1 A. Larson, *Law of Workmen's Compensation* § 38.83, at 622.20 (1967).

8. Keeton, "Compensation for Medical Accidents," 121 *U. Pa. L. Rev.* 590, 614–15 (1973).

9. Accident Compensation Act, 1972, No. 43, 1 N.Z. Stat. 521. For a discussion of the act, see Palmer, "Compensation for Personal Injury: A Requiem for the Common Law in New Zealand," 21 *Am. J. Comp. L.* 1 (1973); Palmer and Lemons, "Toward the Disappearance of Tort Law: New Zealand's New Compensation Plan," 1972 *U. Ill. L. Forum* 693; Palmer, "Abolishing the Personal Injury Tort System: The New Zealand Experience," 9 *Alberta L. Rev.* 169 (1971).

10. Franklin, "Replacing the Negligence Lottery: Compensation and Selective Reimbursement," 53 *Va. L. Rev.* 774 (1967).

11. T. Ison, *The Forensic Lottery: A Critique on Tort Liability as a System of Personal Injury Compensation* (1967). In December, 1972, a royal commission was established by Parliament under the chairmanship of Lord Pearson to study the entire area of compensation for personal injuries in the United Kingdom (338 Parl. Deb., H.L. [5th ser.] 1119–25 [Dec. 19, 1972]).

12. In January, 1973, a special three-member commission was established in Australia to report on a national compensation scheme similar to that enacted in New Zealand. Indeed, so interested is Australia in the New Zealand legislation that the unusual step was taken of appointing a New Zealander as one of the three committee members. He is Mr. Justice Woodhouse, the chairman of the New Zealand Royal Commission on Compensation for Personal Injury, the recommendations of which led to the New Zealand reform. The committee has just recommended even more sweeping reform than New Zealand's — covering illness as well as injury, concomitant to abolishing common law tort claims for personal injury. I *Report of the National Committee of Inquiry, Compensation and Rehabilitation in Australia* (1974).

13. "The cost of the plan will be met through levies on employers and the self-employed, and from payments by [motor] vehicle owners and from general taxation. Some groups see big problems ahead for the plan. For instance, medical organizations say that doctors will be under constant pressure to certify ailments as accident-connected. They assert that a large part of medical

practice will be taken up with contentious issues of this kind" (*N.Y. Times,* Dec. 30, 1973, p. 6, col. 1. See generally Palmer, "Compensation for Personal Injury," *supra* note 9).

14. *N.Y. Times,* Feb. 8, 1974, p. 12, cols. 1–8. But just what the costs under either proposal would be — and how effective either would be — is the subject of intense dispute. "The [Nixon] plan is so broad that it may well cover up to 80 percent of the personal health expenses of Americans for a total cost of $70 billion if the estimate of one senior Federal health official is correct. The amount is so large that it puts the Nixon Administration and Caspar W. Weinberger, the Secretary of Health, Education and Welfare, in some difficulty. The most liberal health insurance proposal before Congress, a plan introduced by Senator Edward M. Kennedy . . . , has repeatedly been criticized by the Administration as too expensive — from $70 billion to $80 billion. Now it appears that the Nixon version would cost roughly the same as the Kennedy version [although] . . . Administration officials had been saying for several months that the cost would be about $40 billion" (*ibid.*). Even under President Nixon's more modest national health insurance proposal of 1971, the Social Security Administration estimated that federal expenditures would amount to $34 billion of a total 1974 national health expenditure of about $107 billion (up from a total expenditure of $67 billion in 1970); the Social Security Administration then estimated that Senator Edward Kennedy's more ambitious bill would entail estimated federal expenditures of $91 billion (*N.Y. Times,* Aug. 6, 1971, p. 13, col. 1).

For a pessimistic appraisal of the pace and extent of national health insurance reform in the foreseeable future, see Hodgson, "The Politics of American Health Care," *The Atlantic,* Oct., 1973, p. 45. " 'If someone had asked me five years ago,' said Doctor Rashi Fein, 'to estimate when the United States would have some clearly universal and comprehensive system of national health insurance, I might have answered: in 15 years.' 'Three years ago,' he went on, 'my estimate would have been fifteen minus eight, or minus ten, or even minus twelve. But if someone would have asked me today when we will have national health insurance, my answer would be: many years more.' Dr. Fein, of the Harvard Medical School, is one of the most highly respected authorities on health policies in the country; the fact that both the Nixon Administration and Senator Edward Kennedy have consulted him gives some index of his standing" (*ibid.*). For a more optimistic appraisal of at least some greater guarantee of insurance for medical bills through a form of national health insurance, see *N.Y. Times,* Jan. 10, 1974, p. 27, cols. 1–3. But President Nixon's 1974 proposal in some measure confirms both pessimism and optimism. While it portends passage of some kind of national health insurance, the patchwork nature of the coverage may be problematic. While praising Nixon's plan as "a serious, carefully designed national health insurance proposal," Senator Kennedy pointed out that the plan's deductibles were so high that only one in four Americans would get any benefits in any given year (*N.Y. Times,* Feb. 7, 1974, p. 19, cols. 1–7). For a report on a revised proposal by Senator Kennedy, cosponsored by Representative Wilbur Mills (D., Ark.), more closely resembling President Nixon's proposal, see *N.Y. Times,* April 3, 1974, p. 1, col. 5.

15. *N.Y. Times,* Oct. 22, 1972, § E, p. 7, cols. 1–6; p. 69, cols. 1–6. See also *N.Y. Times,* Jan. 11, 1973, p. 1, cols. 2–3.

16. *N.Y. Times,* Nov. 30, 1972, p. 1, col. 1.

17. J. Volpe, *Motor Vehicle Crash Losses and Their Compensation in the United States: A Report to the Congress and the President* 6 (1971). These figures were computed from Table 2, Medical Expense, Wage Loss, and Other Expenses. Another Department of Transportation (DOT) study found that even when future lost earnings (beyond the date of settlement) were excluded, wage loss up to settlement constituted over 65 percent of victims' personal injury losses where the total of personal injury losses exceeded $5,000 (1 U.S. Department of Transportation, *Automobile Personal Injury Claims* 29 [1970]). "For the seriously and fatally injured, [still] another [DOT] study found future lost earnings to constitute 63% of their total economic loss exclusive of property damage" (*ibid.,* 28, citing 1 U.S. Department of Transportation, *Economic Consequences of Automobile Accident Injuries: Report of the Westat Research Corp.* 83–84, Table 7 FS [1970]).

18. Keep in mind that I am discussing political feasibility. The economist would point out that economically the losses — the real costs — have already been incurred. Argument that the expense of broader social insurance may be prohibitive has only political significance — unless, of course, expanded insurance coverage somehow increases accidents. For the economist the real issue is, Who bears the cost?

19. *Time,* Mar. 13, 1972, p. 68.

20. "The largest constraint [on vast public spending] is the very multiplicity of competing demands in the polity itself. A post-industrial society . . . is increasingly a communal society wherein public mechanisms rather than the market become the allocators of goods, and public choice, rather than individual demand, becomes the arbiter of services. A communal society by its very nature multiplies the definition of rights — the rights of children, of students, of the poor, of minorities — and translates them into claims of the community. The rise of externalities — the effects of private actions on the commonweal — turns clean air, clean water, and mass transit into public issues and increases the need for social regulations and controls. The demand for higher education and better health necessarily expands greatly the role of government as funder and setter of standards. The need for amenities, the cry for a better quality of life, brings government into the arena of environment, recreation, and culture.

"But all this involves two problems: we don't really know, given our lack of social-science knowledge, how to do many of these things effectively; equally important, since there may not be enough money to satisfy all or even most of the claims, how do we decide what to do first? . . .

". . . So the problem is one of priorities and choice.

"But how to achieve this? One of the facts of a communal society is the increased participation of individuals and groups in communal life. In fact, there is probably more participation today, at the city level, than at any other time in American history. But the very increase in participation leads to a paradox: the greater the number of groups, each seeking diverse or competing ends, the more likelihood that these groups will veto one another's interests, with the consequent sense of frustration and powerlessness as such stalemates incur. . . . Thus the problem of how to achieve consensus on political questions will become more difficult" (D. Bell, *The Coming of Post-Industrial Society* 159–60 [1973]).

"An ambitious society such as ours generates a fair number of political problems by continually adding new items to the political agenda which require the assembling of sufficient agreement. Lessons follow from this, of which the first is that a political structure in which it is difficult to aggregate power is not well adapted to clearing a heavy agenda of social issues. Hence, a prime inconsistency [of American reform] . . . in recent years has been the tendency to diffuse political power while lengthening the political agenda" D. P. Moynihan, *Coping* 25 [1973]).

21. Even Herbert Stein, then chairman of President Nixon's Council of Economic Advisers, suggested the need "of the United States to create a huge planning agency to coordinate and direct government economic policy. . . . It seemed ironic to some . . . that Mr. Stein, a Republican and a strong advocate of free-market processes, should suggest that the Government expand its role in economic policy matters" (*N.Y. Times*, Dec. 30, 1973, p. 1, col. 3).

The energy crisis has created more interest in the theories of Oskar Morgenstern concerning economic compression, which is significantly different from recession or depression. In 1966 Morgenstern published an article, "The Compressibility of Economic Systems and the Problem of Economic Constraints," in *Zeitschrift für Nationalökonomie*, setting forth his compressibility models. A compression, according to economist Leonard Silk, "is an orderly reduction in certain functions of the economy to prevent its collapse and to preserve those activities deemed most essential to the society. . . . [A] chief mechanism of compression is central planning and control, either by Government alone or by Government-business collaboration. Such control involves the use of production programs, priorities, quotas, rationing — and such new agencies as, say, the Federal Energy Office" (*N.Y. Times*, Jan. 30, 1974, pp. 43, 51, cols. 1–2, 3–4, respectively).

See Epstein, "The Big Freeze," *N.Y. Review*, Dec. 13, 1973, p. 32, for a short but extraordinarily lucid — and indeed chilling — summary of the conflict over the need for more and more public decision making in liberal democratic societies strongly resistant to widespread government controls. For an even more apocalyptic piece, see R. Heilbroner, *An Inquiry into the Human Prospect* (1974), a version of which appeared in *N.Y. Review*, Jan. 24, 1974, p. 21. On this subject of resistance to public spending, "polls show the ambiguity of public concern on [public] . . . spending. Ask the voters what they think of welfare mothers and the response is predictable. But ask whether the federal government has the responsibility to provide decent housing, education, medical care and food for everyone and the majority will say yes. For an even more dramatic response ask whether Medicare should be abolished" (Passal and Ross, "Taps for Liberals," *N.Y. Review*, Mar. 22, 1973, p. 26, col. 2, n. 1). But those responses will only confirm the point just made in the text concerning the cruel competition for public spending that compensation for accident loss victims is going to have to face in future years.

22. E. Rostow, book review, 72 *Colum. L. Rev.* 788, 792 (1972). Addi-

tional cause for concern about the lack of available resources to meet rising social needs lies in the resistance to wealth redistribution and centralization of authority not only *within* nations but also *between* them. Experts such as Lester Brown eloquently warn of the need for drastic redistribution of resources from richer to poorer nations and the need for more and more powerful and "enlightened" supranational institutions to cope with such phenomena as increasing hunger and illiteracy in many parts of the world (L. Brown, *World without Borders* [1972]). But see P. T. Bauer, *Dissent on Development,* for a view of the futility of foreign aid as a means of lessening the gap between rich and poor nations. See also McDowell, book review of *ibid.,* in *Wall St. J.,* June 21, 1973, p. 14, cols. 3–6. But see Epstein and Heilbroner, *supra* note 21.

23. "The per capita gross national product [in the United States] has pushed close to $6,200, still far and away the highest in the world. Japan and West Germany, especially, have been narrowing the living-standard gap in recent years, but both still have a long way to go" (*Wall St. J.,* Dec. 28, 1973, p. 1, col. 6).

24. For a discussion of the interaction of tort law and social insurance in Europe, see R. Keeton and J. O'Connell, *Basic Protection for the Traffic Victim: A Blueprint for Reforming Automobile Insurance* 189–218 (1965); U.S. Department of Transportation, *Comparative Studies in Automobile Accident Compensation* (1970).

25. G. Calabresi, *The Cost of Accidents: A Legal and Economic Analysis* (1970).

26. *Ibid.,* 26. Calabresi refers to market deterrence as "general deterrence," in contradistinction to "special deterrence," which is achieved by governmental or regulatory means. The difference is illustrated by having teenage driving curbed by the high cost of insurance for young people — that is, by what Calabresi calls "general deterrence" — as opposed to outlawing teenage driving, at least below a certain age, which is what he calls "special deterrence." I find the terms *market* deterrence and *regulatory* (or *governmental*) deterrence much more descriptive.

27. Ross, book review, 84 *Harv. L. Rev.* 1322, 1323 (1971).

28. *Supra,* ch. 2, notes 56–66 and accompanying text.

29. *Supra,* ch. 2, note 52 and accompanying text.

30. James, "Social Insurance and Tort Liability: The Problem of Alternative Remedies," 27 *N. Y. U. L. Rev.* 537 (1952); O'Connell, "Expanding No-Fault beyond Auto Insurance: Some Proposals," 59 *Va. L. Rev.* 749–781 (1973).

31. *Supra,* ch. 2, notes 13–17 and accompanying text.

32. J. K. Galbraith, *Economics and the Public Purpose* (1973). See also *supra* notes 20–21 and accompanying text. But, on the subject of the problem of the quality of centralized decision making by governmental bureaucrats, long a bugbear of conservatives but increasingly being recognized by liberals, one can have some rather grim fun with an academic like J. K. Galbraith, who calls for ever-increasing and powerful governmental bureaucracy on the one hand and yet brays as piteously as any businessman when called upon, under appointment to a high government post such as ambassador to India, to function himself under such bureaucrats (O'Connell, book reviews of J. K. Galbraith, *Economics, Peace and Laughter* and *The New Industrial State*

[2d ed.], *Wall St. J.,* Dec. 17, 1971, p. 8, cols. 3–5; 1971 *U. Ill. L. Forum* 540).

33. Passal and Ross, *supra* note 21, at 26.

34. Very little such ascription of responsibility is being done under the New Zealand act. For a discussion of the act in this regard, see Palmer, "Compensation for Personal Injury," *supra* note 9, at 23–31. The Australian proposal rejects any such variations in contributions to the insurance pool because of the attendant administrative difficulties (*supra* note 12 and accompanying text). For an indication of the complexities of charge-back schemes, see Franklin, *supra* note 10, at 802–8.

35. But *cf.* Chance v. E. I. Du Pont de Nemours & Co., 345 F. Supp. 353 (E.D.N.Y. 1972), in which the court refused to dismiss a complaint in a suit seeking recovery on a theory of negligence from the entire blasting cap industry for injuries to children caused by blasting caps.

36. See *infra,* ch. 7, note 5 and accompanying text.

37. As we shall see, that system need not necessarily be tied to a defendant's fault or product defect (*infra,* chs. 8 and 9).

38. If more and more government planning and control — and even ownership of enterprises — becomes commonplace, replacing the tort liability system might not seem very imposing. In national decision making the time could come when, thinking of Morgenstern's compression models (*supra* note 21), abolishing the tort system could look as easy as eliminating an army's band or a company's plane (*N.Y. Times,* Jan. 30, 1974, p. 51, col. 2). Of course there are constitutional problems (see *infra,* Appendix V), and those problems might mean that completely abolishing tort liability without much of a substitute simply would not be worth bothering with in a time of cataclysmic change.

39. *Best's Insurance Reports: Property-Liability* at xiii (1970). The figure is obtained from the Miscellaneous B.I. Liability table by multiplying premiums written ($1,025,000,000) by a loss ratio (72 percent). These are estimated figures for 1969.

40. This sum is a combination of various figures. Survivor benefits were $6,758,100,000 (Institute of Life Insurance, *Life Insurance Fact Book* 47 [1970]). Disability benefits were $1,572,000,000 (Health Insurance Institute, *Source Book of Health Insurance Data* 31 [1970]). Health insurance benefits were $14,000,000,000 (*ibid.,* 29). Thus, the total for 1969 was $22,330,000,000.

41. Department of Health, Education, and Welfare, *Social Security Bulletin* 28, Table 10 (Annual Statistical Supplement, 1969). The 1969 figures are obtained by combining disability benefits and survivor benefits. Disability benefits are obtained by combining benefits paid for Old Age, Survivors, Disability and Health Insurance (OASDHI), railroad retirement, public employee retirement, state temporary disability insurance, and railroad temporary disability insurance ($4,540,694,000). Survivor benefits are obtained by combining monthly benefits paid for OASDHI and railroad retirement ($7,139,-856,000) with lump-sum payments for OASDHI, railroad retirement, and public employee retirement ($476,422,000) to equal $7,616,278,000. See also *Statistical Abstract of the United States 1972,* Tables 452, 477, 486. Medicaid benefits (combining federal and state expenditures for public aid and vendor medical payments, $4,596,000,000), medicare benefits (combining benefits for hospital and medical insurance, $6,299,000,000), and Aid to the Blind

($94,000,000), when added to the earlier total of $7.6 billion, equal a grand total of $23,145,972,000.

42. *Supra,* ch. 2, notes 33 and 50 and accompanying text.

43. Skolnik and Price, "Another Look at Workmen's Compensation," in 33 *Social Security Bulletin,* no. 10, at 9–10 (1970). The 1968 total (approximately $2,364,000,000) is obtained from Table Four, which combines $165,-000,000 in survivor benefits, $1,369,000,000 in disability benefits, and $830,-000,000 in medical benefits.

44. *Best's Insurance Reports, supra* note 39. The figure is for 1968 and is obtained from the Auto B.I. Liability table by multiplying premiums written ($3,575,000,000) by the loss ratio (76.5 percent). The figures in notes 39–44 have been produced by updating the figures found in A. Conard *et al., Automobile Accident Costs and Payments: Studies in the Economics of Injury Reparation* 54–58, Table 1-3 (1964).

45. Figures derived from 1 U.S. Department of Transportation, *Economic Consequences, supra* note 17, at 277–78, Table 31 FS (1970). Unless otherwise noted, the figures in the remainder of the above paragraph in the text are obtained from this source.

46. This last figure is obtained by using 4,200,000 as the total number of traffic injury victims (U.S. Department of Commerce, *Statistical Abstract of the United States* 557 [1969]).

47. *Supra* note 45. (For comparable figures for permanently and totally disabled victims, see *supra,* ch. 2, note 13 and accompanying text.) Significantly injured traffic victims include those suffering death or serious injury. A serious injury is one involving "[m]edical costs (excluding hospital) of $500 or more, *or* two weeks or more of hospitalization, *or,* if working, three weeks or more of missed work, *or,* if not working, six weeks or more of missed normal activity" (1 U.S. Department of Transportation, *Economic Consequences, supra* note 17, at 9 [1970]). The study warns that these criteria are arbitrary and that one should expect some classification error. The seriously injured were classified by an initial screening questionnaire. If it was discovered during a subsequent detailed interview that a person did not meet the serious injury criteria, but had in fact suffered some injury, he was still included in the survey; the theory was that there would be a partial offset against persons who were in fact seriously injured but had underreported their injuries on the screening questionnaire (*ibid.*).

The existence of other significant uncertainties in the data, especially those due to the speculative nature of future economic losses, is also recognized by the study (*ibid.,* 19–24). The problems of truly estimating the costs of losses never before paid for are prodigious. When losses have been swallowed for generations, estimating what they amount to when they are out in the open is difficult indeed. There is, for example, the problem of increasing demand without increasing supply when rehabilitation services are guaranteed to every accident victim. One is reminded of the inflationary pressures of Medicare and Medicaid in increasing demand for medical services without increasing supply. And what happens to wage loss when it is paid for without work? Does it increase exponentially, even with deductibles, when the injured person does not *have* to go back to work? Keep in mind that, unlike those covered by workers' compensation, victims of nonindustrial accidents are not subject to the pressures of an employer who is paying the insurance bill. How much difference will that make?

48. This is not to say that basic accidental personal injury losses ought not be guaranteed by social insurance. For a further discussion of the possible happy eventuality after the expansion of social insurance so there will be almost no uninsured accident loss, see *infra.*, ch. 10, note 20.

49. Payments under Sweden's ambitious scheme of social insurance — termed general insurance — lessen the ultimate liability of the tortfeasor since there is no subrogation in favor of the social insurance scheme. "This is true even with respect to those who cause injury intentionally or with gross negligence. The reason is that when subrogation was in effect, the bother of investigating the victim's right to tort damages had not been worth the comparatively small sums collected. Moreover, since tort liability insurance is compulsory in Sweden, the group paying premiums for such insurance is largely the same as the group paying taxes and contributions to General Insurance, and thus 'it was considered unnecessary to move money from one of their pockets to another' " (Keeton and O'Connell, *supra* note 24, at 215–16, quoting from Hellner, "Reparation for Personal Injuries in Sweden," in Conard *et al.*, *supra* note 44, at 446). For a perceptive discussion of the varying roles of social insurance and tort law in allocating losses due to accident causes, see Hellner, "Social Insurance and Tort Liability in Sweden," in *Scandinavian Studies in Law* 189, 198–202 (1972).

50. *Supra* note 34 and accompanying text.

51. *Cf.* 2 F. Harper and F. James, *The Law of Torts* § 13.5, at 771–77 (1956). But see *infra,* ch. 10, notes 12–13 and accompanying text.

7

A Blind Alley or Two
PART II

Market deterrence of unsafe products and procedures is not achieved by social insurance or health insurance, neither of which pays sufficient attention to the causes of the accident. But neither is market deterrence achieved by those present tort liability systems, which pay too much attention to the causes. As Guido Calabresi has pointed out, the fault system (or its near-equivalent, a system requiring proof of a defect in a product) is not an effective system of market deterrence: "Fault uses the market in an expensive and unstable way to reduce fault-caused accidents, while from the standpoint of market deterrence, we want to use the market in an efficient and stable way to reduce accident costs whether they are fault-caused or not."[1] In other words, we want to deter to the greatest extent feasible *all* accidents, not just those caused by fault.

Accident victims, then, are left with (1) a tort liability system paying on the basis of who is at fault (or whose product is defective) and thereby paying too little, too late, too inefficiently, and without encouraging much safety, and (2) social and private insurance systems paying without reference to fault and thereby paying more, and paying more promptly and more efficiently, but still not paying enough and encouraging much less safety than does even the tort liability system. How can we restructure our accident insurance system to pay more, to pay promptly and efficiently, and still to encourage more safety?

Could we lump all injuries from other than auto or work accidents together under one general statute, creating a new no-fault

Note on p. 95.

law of "enterprise liability"? Such a law might provide that every enterprise entailing distinctive risks of personal injury (such as the production of ladders or power tools) must pay for the injuries it typically generates without regard to any fault or defect.[2] In that way when someone loses his eye because of a rock flung from a power mower he will be recompensed automatically without endless litigation over whether the mower was defectively constructed or whether he was careless in using it, just as he would be compensated under no-fault auto insurance without regard to anyone's fault for the loss of an eye in an auto accident. Under such a law — as under no-fault auto insurance — hugely expensive investigation and litigation over defects and fault would be eliminated. Also, as under no-fault auto insurance, in order to help finance payments for the more vital and measurable losses of medical expenses and lost wages, no payment would be made for so-called pain and suffering.[3]

Would this trade-off work? That is, would it be possible to assure payment for out-of-pocket loss, regardless of anyone's fault, merely on the happening of an accident, to replace the gamble of greater compensation dependent on proving who was at fault in the accident? Or put it this way: Would it work for nonauto accidents as it is obviously working for auto and employment accidents?

There is good reason to think that it would. In addition to ending payment for pain and suffering, such a law should provide — as many no-fault auto proposals have — that no payment be made for amounts already covered by other sources such as hospitalization insurance or sick leave — or even life insurance.[4] By such a provision, personal injury law would be made to serve a most worthwhile function: making payments tailored to large individual losses not met by other forms of payment such as social security or health insurance, which, though growing, are always going to remain inadequate to cover all losses. And enterprise liability would accomplish this payment in a way that would eliminate most of the expensive and often fruitless arguments over fault, defects, and the value of pain which dominate personal injury law today.

The crucial question in deciding whether to adopt a system of no-fault enterprise liability is this: Will the claims over which enterprise's risk created the loss end up just as, or more, cumbersome and technical than those over who was at fault?

Notes on p. 95.

One cannot be sure. One can argue that, statistically, serious accidents probably do not happen in many different ways. There seems to be, in other words, a pattern to accidents, so deciding what risks operated in most accidents will not be that difficult. Think again of the list of products in chapter 2 classified by the National Commission on Product Safety as especially dangerous. Enterprise liability might easily be invoked against:

¶ Those who manufacture and sell architectural glass when people are cut by it.

¶ Those who manufacture and sell fireworks when they explode prematurely and injure.

¶ Those who manufacture and sell floor furnaces when they cause burns.

¶ Those who manufacture and sell high-rise bicycles when people fall off.

¶ Those who manufacture and sell hot-water vaporizers when they cause burns.

¶ Those who manufacture or sell power tools when they mutilate.

Examination of accident data being compiled by the National Electronic Injury Surveillance System (NEISS)[5] of the federal government's Product Safety Commission will indicate, I venture, that as much as 30 percent and possibly 80 percent of all serious injuries being treated in hospital emergency rooms are readily attributable to certain obvious risks from clearly defined categories of products such as power mowers, hot-water vaporizers, or fireworks. We may well know from a simple examination of almost any accidental injury to what risk or what enterprise it should be charged.

Perhaps the best and calmest way to view this proposal of enterprise liability is as an altogether sensible extension of the no-fault principles presently applied to abnormally dangerous activities.[6] That doctrine is currently imposed by the courts only when "the activity is not a matter of common usage."[7] This limitation, as we have seen, largely emasculates the doctrine; to gain widespread effectiveness the doctrine should be applied whenever particularly dangerous activities are matters of common usage and when the injuries they cause are matters of great social concern, and thereby of prime concern for law and insurance. Enterprise liability in

Notes on p. 96.

effect would provide that no-fault liability may be imposed on any enterprise that systematically generates risks of personal injury whenever that imposition makes economic sense. The scheme subscribes to a principle in diametric opposition to the rule of current tort law; that is, the more common the usage, the greater the chance of no-fault liability. And as a tradeoff for the necessity of paying more claimants under enterprise liability, in each case the potential liability of the enterprise is delimited in the bargain made familiar first by workers' compensation and later by no-fault auto insurance; in the case of enterprise liability, the *quid pro quo* is exclusion of payment for pain and suffering and for items covered by collateral sources.[8]

It must be admitted though, as indicated earlier, that it is easy to pose difficult questions about the applicability of such enterprise liability. Take that guest who falls on his neighbor's cement patio and cracks his skull. Who pays if there are still losses once all the victim's own insurance has run out? Not the householder; generally speaking, he is in no better position to bear — or pass on — the loss than is his neighbor. How about the contractor who built the house? Or the subcontractor who built the patio? Or the seller of the cement? If all of them, in what proportion do they pay? Even more difficult conundrums present themselves. Take the case of a schoolboy football player suffering a serious head injury. Is the helmet maker to be required to pay, regardless of any defect in the helmet? Why him any more than the coach or the school?[9]

Similarly, under no-fault enterprise liability all the problems remain of deciding what are the proper risks of medical treatment attributable to the doctor or hospital. Recently it has been suggested that no-fault insurance be made applicable in the following way to injuries incurred in the course of medical treatment: a health care provider will compensate for

> any physical harm, bodily impairment, disfigurement, or delay in recovery which (I) is more probably associated in whole or in part with medical intervention rather than with the condition for which such intervention occurred, and (II) is not consistent with or reasonably to be expected as a consequence of such intervention or (III) is a result of medical intervention to which the patient has not given his informed consent.

Notes on p. 96.

Included within this offered definition are all medical injury situations which are currently compensated within the tort-liability system as well as a class of medical injuries which are relatable to unavoidable accidents and known risk treatments. The incorporation of this latter group of injuries provides the opportunity for compensating the medically-injured patient [and] removes the stigma from the possibly innocent health care provider....[10]

Such a proposal deems medical services, like manufactured products, as systematically generating irreducible risks — and deems losses from those risks as potentially transferable or distributable throughout the market for medical services. Indeed, to strengthen such a conclusion the medical profession often establishes its risks with remarkable precision. For example, reliable data have been collected showing that "the incidence of severe neurological complications from spinal anesthesia in San Diego County [California] in a series of 32,828 cases in a five-year period was 0.012 percent."[11]

The attempt is made, then, to divide surgical operations into two at least occasionally indistinct categories: those in which the patient's presenting complaint and the medical treatment administered combine to produce relatively expectable results, and those in which they produce quite unexpected consequences. The first category would include not only situations in which, in light of his condition and the treatment required, a patient would anticipate the expense and inconvenience of days, weeks, or months of recuperation, but also those cases in which, because either the procedure was very dangerous or the patient was particularly vulnerable, or a combination of the two, dire consequences might be expected, such as paralysis from a spinal fusion, or cardiac arrest of a patient with a severe cardiac condition during surgery. The second category would include consequences relatively unexpectable for a normal patient undergoing relatively safe surgery (for example, a patient without a heart condition who suffers cardiac arrest during a simple appendectomy). Clearly, enterprise liability is more logically applied to the second category than to the first; a rational presumption arises that the unusual complications found in the second group result from risks generated by medical processes rather than from conditions stemming from the presenting complaint.

Notes on p. 96.

But applying no-fault liability for harm sustained through medical treatment in this way broaches some racking factual and policy questions similar in complexity to those which have always plagued medical tort law. For example, if a patient gives informed consent to medical treatment, should a doctor be held liable without regard to fault for the consequences of his failure to discover an obscure idiosyncratic condition? Or should he be liable only to the extent he failed to exercise reasonable care in not discovering the condition? Should he be absolved of responsibility for risks which the patient had been warned to expect (with concomitant disputes about what *was* warned)? In this connection, in medical cases it is arguable that there is more ground for putting the burden of loss on an individual who voluntarily chooses to run a risk than is the case with those who choose to buy and use, say, a dangerous machine like a power tool. The risks of much medical treatment can perhaps be explained and appreciated and weighed more rationally by the individual patient in deciding whether to undergo a specified treatment than can the risk of injury from a manufactured product at the time the consumer decides to buy or use the product. A doctor, one hopes, is not as inclined as a seller of goods to lure and lull by advertising and other forms of puffing which trumpet the benefits and (either explicitly or implicitly) belittle the dangers of what is being provided.[12]

But even more fundamentally, is the line between expectable and unexpectable results from given medical treatments sufficiently definitive to serve as a generally nonlitigious criterion? And even if it is, does making a doctor accountable under enterprise no-fault liability for relatively unexpectable results enlarge his liability too much? Are the cases with unexpectable results properly attributable to medical malpractice so few that in trying to avoid having to identify medical misconduct we have swept in far too many other cases for doctors to pay for?

Obviously, then, as the foregoing suggests, a proposal of enterprise no-fault liability, if more modest than trying to cover all losses from all injury under social security, is still relatively revolutionary. It is extremely doubtful that firm data on the aggregate costs of the plan could be obtained. Business and professional men, fearful of the expense to their respective enterprises, would probably robustly

Note on p. 96.

— and successfully — resist passage of such comprehensive legislation on either a federal or a state level.

There is, in addition, the question whether legislation of the scope of enterprise no-fault liability ought to be enacted at one stroke, even if one could force it through. Immediate enactment is especially doubtful if intermediate steps or alternatives are available.[13] Even the most stouthearted liberals have been more than a little shaken by the unpredictable and inconsistent results often stemming in the 1960's from implementing ambitious but untried proposals for social reform as formulated by academics and civil servants. (It is not without significance, though, that no-fault auto insurance is one such proposal that seems to be working as well as the professors said it would.) Daniel Patrick Moynihan has pointed out that in view of this experience, "The nation can ill afford full scale social programs of unknown value that cost large amounts but have no [experimental] ... features — no way of genuinely assessing their contributions so that policy can be improved."[14] Feminist Ingrid Bengis has put it more pungently: "I am very wary," she said, "of conclusions that precede experience."[15] How, then, to experiment with no-fault insurance for various kinds of accidents beyond auto and workers' compensation insurance?

NOTES

1. Calabresi, "Views and Overviews," in *Crisis in Car Insurance* 240, 250 (ed. R. Keeton, J. O'Connell, and J. McCord, 1968); also printed in 1967 *U. Ill. L. Forum* 600, 610.

2. In order to be classified as a typical risk of an enterprise, the risk might be required to be not only typically and systematically generated by the enterprise, but a risk for which imposition of such enterprise no-fault liability would accomplish goals of (1) safety incentives, (2) resource allocation, or (3) loss spreading. For a discussion of the first two goals, see *infra*, ch. 10, notes 7–9 and accompanying text. For a discussion of such economic criteria in personal injury cases, see O'Connell, "Expanding No-Fault beyond Auto Insurance: Some Proposals," 59 *Va. L. Rev.* 749, 777–94, 815–21 (1973).

3. For a much more extensive discussion of this proposal, see *ibid*.

4. This should be true as long as the insurance proceeds exceed any savings or investment factor, which would mean that all proceeds from term insurance, for example, would be deductible, as would be those portions which represent excess over policy cash values in the case, say, of whole life or endowment policies. See Conard, "The Economic Treatment of Automobile

Injuries," 63 *U. Mich. L. Rev.* 279, 313–14 (1964); 2 F. Harper and F. James, *The Law of Torts* § 25.22, at 1350–52 (1956).

5. For a discussion of the National Electronic Injury Surveillance System (NEISS), see *Wall St. J.,* Oct. 30, 1972, p. 5, cols. 3–4; *N.Y. Times,* Nov. 19, 1972, § F, p. 4, cols. 3–8; Klein, "A Product-Injury Surveillance System," *Saturday Review,* Sept. 23, 1972, pp. 67–68.

6. Restatement (Second) of Torts, §§ 519–24a (Tent. Draft No. 10, 1964). See *supra,* ch. 5, notes 11–12 and 16 and accompanying text.

7. Restatement (Second) of Torts, § 520 (Tent. Draft No. 10, 1964).

8. Arguably, such enterprise liability might well be instituted by common law courts, without any need for legislation. See O'Connell, *supra* note 2, nn. 224–28, and accompanying text; but see Wights v. Staff Jennings, Inc., 241 Ore. 301, 309, 405 P.2d 624, 628–29 (1965), discussed *supra,* ch. 5, note 27.

9. See L. Fuller, *The Morality of Law* 75–76 (1964); Henderson, "Should Workmen's Compensation Be Expanded to Nonoccupational Injuries?" 48 *Tex. L. Rev.* 117, 126 (1969).

10. Ross and Rosenthal, "Non-Fault-Based Medical Injury Compensation Systems," in U.S. Department of Health, Education, and Welfare, *Appendix, Report of the Secretary's Commission on Medical Malpractice* 450, 460 (1973).

11. Mayor v. Dowsett, 240 Ore. 196, 211, 400 P.2d 234, 241 (1965).

12. But see *infra,* ch. 11, notes 17–23 and accompanying text.

13. On the merits and means of experimenting with social reform, see A. Rivlin, *Systematic Thinking for Social Action* (1971).

14. F. Mosteller and D. Moynihan, *On Equality of Educational Opportunity* 51–52 (1972).

15. *Newsweek,* Jan. 22, 1973, p. 89.

8

A Promising Approach or Two

PART I

As a solution to experimenting with no-fault insurance for all kinds of accidents, I suggest the following steps. Any enterprise should be allowed to elect, if it chooses, to pay from then on for injuries it causes on a no-fault basis, thereby foreclosing claims based on fault or a defect. Under such an option, payment would be made regardless not only of lack of fault or defect on the payer's part but also, as under no-fault auto insurance and workers' compensation, regardless of any fault on the victim's part.[1] In other words, elective no-fault liability would be true no-fault insurance, with the fault of neither the injurer nor the injured having a bearing on payment.[2] The enterprise would be allowed to select all or, if it chose, just certain risks of personal injury it typically creates, for which it could agree to pay for out-of-pocket losses when injury results from those risks. To the extent — and only to the extent — a guarantee of no-fault payment exists at the time of the accident, as under no-fault auto or workers' compensation insurance, no claim based on fault or a defect would be allowed against the party electing to be covered under no-fault liability insurance.

Obviously, such no-fault liability, not being tied to fault or a product defect, would entail a considerable broadening of liability for many, if not all, enterprises. In other words, just as no-fault auto insurance means that motoring insurance must stand ready to pay many more victims than the number paid when the motorist was at fault and the motoring victim free from fault, so no-fault

Notes on p. 106.

elective liability could mean potential payout to many more victims. Where, then, is the incentive for any enterprise to elect to be covered under no-fault? If the number of injured receiving payment will likely be increased, the amount of payment to each will be decreased; in contrast to tort liability, payment under elective no-fault liability would be limited to out-of-pocket losses above any amounts payable from collateral sources such as hospitalization insurance and sick leave. Neither would payment be made for pain and suffering. In return for electing no-fault liability, an enterprise would pay victims, for selected risks created by that enterprise, only amounts above and beyond other payments due from all other sources of coverage (including, perhaps, at least term life insurance).[3] And no-fault would not pay for psychic loss. In addition, the bargain for assuming more widespread liability might also be financed by a provision that although the medical benefits under elective no-fault liability would be unlimited, payment for wage loss would be limited to a maximum of, say, two hundred dollars each week for as long as total permanent disability should last, with correspondingly lesser amounts for lesser temporary or partial losses. Payments would be made periodically as losses accrue, and not in one lump sum.

Note the incentives on an enterprise to substitute such enterprise liability for traditional tort liability: although the enterprise might have to pay more people for injury, it would pay them much less in that it would not have to pay anything already covered by other insurance or anything for so-called pain and suffering. This would eliminate paying *anything* in most cases of smaller injuries;[4] it would also cut down substantially on what is to be paid in cases of larger injuries. In addition, the huge amounts now spent on legal fees and expert witnesses to determine that intractable question of whether there was fault or a defect in the causation of the accident would be saved.[5] Of great importance also to manufacturers and doctors, the stigma of liability would be substantially — and often totally — removed. One would no longer be paying because his product is defective or because he malpracticed, but rather on the morally neutral ground that the accident was just that — an "accident," actuarially inevitable in the course of the activity in question, without any fault necessarily being involved and without socially

Notes on p. 106.

futile blame being cast. Indeed, the need for payment in any case might as likely result from the fault of the user or the patient as from that of the enterprise. And so, despite the fact that the enterpriser was not at fault and his claimant was, the enterpriser would stand ready to pay, with payment casting him in a very different light than that at common law. Nevertheless, in one circumstance stigma could not be avoided: no one could preclude his regular tort liability for intentionally caused injuries. Similarly, a victim could not claim no-fault liability for an injury he intentionally inflicts on himself.[6]

As an example of the way elective no-fault liability would work, a manufacturer of a power tool could elect to take out a no-fault policy to pay for out-of-pocket losses — medical expense and wage loss — whenever an amputation results from use of the power tool. Just as no-fault auto insurance pays without regard to anyone's negligence, so payment would be made in this instance without regard to the victim's possible carelessness or to the lack of any defect in the tool. Similarly, a doctor, knowing the inevitable risks of, say, cardiac arrest in even normal patients regardless of anyone's fault in the course of a given surgical procedure, could agree to pay automatically for out-of-pocket losses stemming from such an adverse result of an operation. In both cases the prior agreement to make such no-fault payments would wipe out any claim based on fault, just as happens under no-fault auto insurance.*

Certainly an astute business or professional man, concerned about skyrocketing liability premiums under present law, would be inclined to check on what elective no-fault liability would cost him in comparison to regular tort liability. At least for some categories of injuries he might find it advantageous to pay only for out-of-pocket loss, albeit on a no-fault basis. The availability of such an option would certainly encourage many enterprises at least to develop data and focus on the question of which system of com-

---

* Note that under elective no-fault liability insurance the injured party would still claim against, say, a manufacturer or health care provider just as he does under regular tort liability law. Actually, most often, of course, the claim in both instances is against the defendant's insurance company. What is substituted is a claim based on liability without fault instead of liability based on fault.

Note on p. 107.

pensation would be to their advantage. Some enterprises might find the cost of no-fault to be much less, so wasteful is the regular tort system. This saving would be especially true for enterprises facing myriad regular tort nuisance claims such as claims for falls in stores or city streets,[7] irritatingly deleterious matter in food, and so on — that is, relatively trivial claims which greatly outnumber those for serious injury.

Others might find the costs closer to those of the regular system, but it is not inconceivable that humanitarian considerations would then operate to tip the scale in favor of no-fault liability. When the no-fault auto insurance controversy was reaching an early peak, a chief executive of a major car rental company read of the fantastic waste of the auto liability insurance system which resulted in so little of the premiums, despite their cost, being paid to traffic victims. Shocked and concerned by this waste, he called in his general counsel to investigate the matter further. The eventual result was that his company, along with other car rental companies, became an advocate of no-fault auto insurance even to the point of testifying and lobbying in various legislative forums, including the Congress. It is true that in this instance projected cost savings under no-fault served as an additional spur, but the businessman's outrage at the waste and cruelty of the tort liability system was a real catalyst.

It may be too much to hope that many businessmen would see a competitive advantage in being able to advertise their willingness to pay for injuries caused by their products, because businessmen, understandably perhaps, are reluctant to raise in their advertising the specter of possible injury. But a businessman's concern for the inevitable actuarial toll imposed by his products is not unimaginable, and elective no-fault liability will provide a beneficial outlet for that concern.[8]

Elective no-fault liability may thus make especially good sense for the medical profession as well as for pharmaceutical houses. Unquestionably, there are medical procedures which give rise to adverse but expectable results regardless of fault but which nonetheless often lead to medical malpractice claims. For many such procedures it would make sense to allow health care providers to elect to pay out-of-pocket loss automatically when those adverse results happen. Areas of anesthesia, neurosurgery, orthopedics, and

Notes on p. 107.

certain side effects from drugs, for example, come immediately to mind. It is not without significance that doctors — abhorring the stigma of malpractice suits — have already been advocating no-fault insurance payments covering medical injuries. Keep in mind, too, that the stunning success of no-fault auto insurance in allowing more people to be eligible for payment, while at the same time stabilizing and even reducing insurance premiums, is going to greatly increase the receptivity of all kinds of enterprises — medical and otherwise — to experimentation with no-fault insurance.

The wisdom of experimenting with no-fault insurance for injuries incurred in the course of medical treatment is echoed by the *Final Report* of the HEW Secretary's Commission on Medical Malpractice. The report states, "The principle of compensating for injury without the necessity of proving fault is an old one and growing ever more popular," but the report then cautions that there are "difficult problems we face in seeking to develop any effective medical injury compensation system which is not fault-based . . . [and] the Commission . . . does not believe that we should leap headlong from a system that works (with however many faults) into an untested one that may cause even more severe problems." In addition, the report recommends that various proposals "be developed, tested and demonstrated through both public and private initiatives. . . ."[9]

Actually, there is already strong precedent for an elective approach to no-fault accident law in the provisions of many state statutes which allow employers to elect to be covered by workers' compensation, thereby avoiding regular tort liability.[10] These laws were passed early in this century in light of such cases as the notorious *Ives* decision by the New York Court of Appeals, which declared compulsory workers' compensation unconstitutional.[11] Subsequent determinations that compulsory imposition of workers' compensation was in fact constitutional[12] subjected elective workers' compensation to the criticisms that it was unnecessary and that it frustrated the goal of universal compensation.[13] But such criticisms do not apply to elective no-fault liability: the political unfeasibility of compulsory no-fault liability immediately applicable to all enterprises has been pointed out in chapter 7. The *relative* unfeasibility of even a law imposing no-fault liability on comparatively hazardous

Notes on p. 108.

enterprises can be readily imagined in light of dispute over which enterprises ought to be singled out.[14]

Thus, an elective law seems the only politically feasible alternative to the present tort system, even if the elective approach has arguably outlived its usefulness for workers' compensation. But even the disadvantages of elective workers' compensation are relative: if passage of a compulsory workers' compensation law cannot be obtained in a state legislature, doesn't optional workers' compensation make sense? Indeed, until recently almost one-third of the states still had elective workers' compensation laws.[15] In those states, "most eligible employers . . . choose to be covered,[16] which would seem to augur well for businesses and professionals electing no-fault coverage. Of course, abrogation in regular tort suits of the "unholy trinity" of common law defenses to employment injuries based on an employee's fault has served as an additional incentive to election under workers' compensation statutes;[17] other incentives are the limitation to payment for only some out-of-pocket losses and the elimination of compensation for pain and suffering. Elective no-fault liability has not only the spur of abolishing payment for pain and suffering but also the additional spur of not paying when collateral sources already pay. In light of the social need for covering losses not covered by other sources, the latter incentive seems to be more socially useful than abrogation of the "unholy trinity."[18]

Of course, as Arthur Larson has pointed out regarding workers' compensation, there are problems with elective provisions, such as determining what constitutes "securing" compensation by an employer in order to foreclose a tort suit.[19] But against such frustrations two features must constantly be considered: (1) any scheme entails some frustrating factors of administration, and the scheme of elective no-fault liability absorbs them better than most in that it is reserved for large cases in which enough is at stake to justify such frustrations; and (2) such frustrations must be weighed against the appalling frustrations of regular tort liability. Trial lawyers constantly scorn workers' compensation and its administrative frustrations. But few objective observers would deny that workers' compensation, for all its problems, treats the typical seriously injured victim far better than does the regular tort system. It is not without significance that the principal controversy in personal injury law

Notes on pp. 108–9.

in recent years has not been about proposals to abandon a no-fault system such as workers' compensation in favor of a fault system, but vice-versa. The recent report of the National Commission on State Workmen's Compensation Laws, though highly critical of the way workers' compensation operates, states: "We have discussed the implications of abolishing workmen's compensation and reverting to the negligence suits, a remedy abandoned some fifty years ago. This option is still inferior to workmen's compensation. . . ."[20] The report characterizes tort "liability suits [as] a drawn-out, costly, and uncertain process that was dismissed long ago as a means of dealing with occupational injuries and diseases."[21]

It is important to note, too, that elective no-fault liability, in paying for out-of-pocket losses as they accrue without resorting to rigid, often outmoded scheduled benefits (for example, a set amount for any person's loss of use of his index finger, and so on), avoids what many consider among the principal administrative difficulties under workers' compensation.[22]

In effect, elective no-fault liability makes both factors which facilitate no-fault auto insurance applicable to many other kinds of accidents:[23] (1) those electing no-fault can decide for themselves if their fault liability insurance is readily and simply transferable into no-fault loss insurance without therefore fearing that the transformation will impose new and unmanageable burdens on them, and (2) similarly, the decision about who is to be required to pay for what loss is not left open-ended but is defined by the one electing in his own elective no-fault liability policy.[24]

The virtue of elective no-fault insurance is that it allows reform to be instituted piecemeal where and when it seems readily feasible. Some no-fault compensation for certain injuries can be expected to be instituted immediately, and then, based on experience, more and more will be instituted as time goes on. Note, too, that as traditional tort law expands — with ever-expanding bases of liability and larger and larger verdicts — the incentives to avoid such liability will increase the attractiveness of elective no-fault liability. And therein, to repeat, lies the virtue of elective no-fault — its gradual and pragmatic pace.

Regular tort liability can constitutionally — and fairly — be abandoned only to the extent a guarantee of no-fault payment is

Notes on p. 109.

substituted for it.[25] The overwhelming problems of providing no-fault benefits for all injuries — and thereby justifying the abolition of all tort liability — have been suggested in chapters 6 and 7. Some of the difficulties are well illustrated by the proposal for no-fault medical insurance contained in the report of the HEW Secretary's Commission on Medical Malpractice.[26] Under the proposal, no-fault insurance "will be compulsory in the sense that it abolishes relief for compensable medical injury through tort-liability."[27] The proposal calls for the establishment of a Medical Injury Compensation Commission (another bureaucracy, it will be noted),[28] which in time is to establish "schedules [of payment] for every conceivable medical injury, by type and severity," a truly monumental task which will be years in the doing, in the opinion of the authors of the proposal.[29] In the meantime, more subjective (and therefore arguably more disputable) judgments on the availability and amount of compensation are to be asserted by the commission and its hearing examiners in an elaborate, multitiered claims process that will ultimately lead to a hearing by a referee, with right of appeal to the commission review board and then to the courts.* Such a rigid bureaucratic nightmare can be contrasted with the self-executing nature of no-fault that simply allows anyone who wants to take out an insurance policy to cover on a no-fault basis those injuries defined in the policy. No new bureaucracy, no new hearings, no new appeals are called for. Both flexibility and experimentation are encouraged. Given the undeniable evils of the present system, certainly, at least experiment with reform makes sense.

Under elective no-fault liability, a businessman might be allowed to experiment further by limiting coverage to, for example, those products produced within a given calendar year. Similarly, he might be allowed to limit the application of no-fault liability to injuries incurred in a given geographical area in order to gain a control group to compare with the results of his experimentation. Obviously, too, a manufacturer might be nervous about indefinitely guaranteeing payment for injuries from his product regardless of its age. Thus, he could be allowed to limit paying for injuries caused by

* For a further evaluation of the cumbersomeness of a compulsory no-fault proposal, see *infra*, Appendix III.

Notes on p. 110.

his product to instances when the product is less than, say, ten years old, or any other appropriate age he chooses. He might also be allowed to limit the extent of no-fault benefits for which he is liable, perhaps to any multiple of $10,000. Enabling legislation would then require a corresponding tort exemption for claims above the no-fault benefits, precluding suit for pain and suffering amounting to less than, say, one-half of the multiple of $10,000. For example, if no-fault benefits of $20,000 were provided, no tort suit could be maintained for out-of-pocket losses of less than $20,000 or for pain and suffering totaling less than $10,000.[30]

In point of fact, there is no reason the law should limit elective no-fault liability to enterprises. Normally, it is true, individuals other than business or professional men probably will not find the shift to no-fault liability as advantageous as enterprises will since premium savings will be less likely. It is questionable whether savings would likely accrue from a switch in homeowner's coverage, for example. But motorists might well find it better and/or cheaper to elect no-fault liability to cover losses in a state without any no-fault auto insurance law or to cover their liability above the "threshold" for tort suits under limited no-fault auto laws.[31] Any motorist could thus insure to pay anyone injured in or by his car on a no-fault basis, just as an enterprise elects no-fault liability, in return for the abolition of tort claims against the insured. Allowing any and all to thus replace the cumbersome fault liability with no-fault liability will encourage further experimentation with no-fault coverage, with all the advantages therefrom.

The mechanics of such elective no-fault auto liability might be structured to preserve the advantage of no-fault auto insurance whereby the insured, his family, and the occupants of his car are paid by the insured's own insurance company without having to claim against a stranger's company. Thus, in a typical two-car collision between driver A and driver B, if both had elected no-fault liability A's insurer would pay the occupants of A's car (including A) on a no-fault basis, and B's insurer would pay the occupants of B's car (including B) on the same basis, with concomitant tort exemptions. If only A had elected no-fault liability, A's insurer would be required to pay the occupants of A's car as

Notes on p. 110.

well as the occupants of B's car (including B) on a no-fault basis, but A, as well as the occupants of both A's car and B's car, would then retain their right to sue B based on fault, and out of any proceeds of any payment from B they would be required to reimburse A's insurer for any amounts previously paid to them. As to accidents involving only one car insured for no-fault liability (whether the accident involved two cars or only one), any motorist could be offered optional no-fault coverage for himself. Perhaps, indeed, such coverage should be compulsory for anyone choosing no-fault liability coverage, just as it would probably be better to make no-fault coverage of one's own family compulsory even where the jurisdiction has a law of intrafamily immunity preventing one family member from suing another for regular tort liability.

Indeed, elective no-fault auto insurance could do much to alleviate the problems posed by inadequate no-fault auto insurance laws already enacted and those being urged by trial lawyers and some in the insurance industry. If, for example, the tort exemption threshold under a no-fault law is very low (as in Massachusetts) or even nonexistent (as in Delaware or Oregon), motorists could be expected to choose to initiate or greatly increase the exemption as it applies to them in return for agreeing to pay their victims' economic losses on a no-fault basis if all other insurance sources of payment for the accident victims are exhausted.[32]

NOTES

1. Fault would not be a barrier either in the form of contributory negligence or assumption of risk. For a definition of these terms, see *infra* note 17. For the germ of such an elective no-fault proposal, see M. Franklin, "Tort Liability for Hepatitis: An Analysis and a Proposal," 24 *Stan. L. Rev.* 439, 478–79 (1972). See also *infra* note 32.

2. See *infra,* ch. 9, notes 23–47 and accompanying text.

3. *Supra,* ch. 7, note 4 and accompanying text.

4. It might be that a "threshold" of, say, one hundred dollars or more of out-of-pocket loss would be necessary before a no-fault liability claim is allowed. Otherwise, relatively trivial claims for matters not covered by collateral sources — such as substitute help or babysitters — might overburden the no-fault liability insurance system.

5. For a discussion of the (fewer) issues that might have to be litigated under such no-fault insurance, see O'Connell, "Expanding No-Fault beyond Auto Insurance: Some Proposals," 59 *Va. L. Rev.* 749, 784–85 (1973) at text accompanying notes 110–12.

6. For a further discussion on this point, see *infra,* ch. 11, notes 6–16 and accompanying text.

7. Municipalities should, in particular, welcome a system of elective no-fault liability. For example, "Right now, the 78 lawyers in [the] Torts Division [of New York City's Law Department, known as the Office of the Corporation Counsel] are staggering under a caseload of 55,000 suits stemming [substantially] from defects in streets and sidewalks [and] malpractice in municipal hospitals. . . . 'It will take years to dispose of all those cases unless we have additional manpower,' says [Corporation Counsel Adrian P.] Burke" (*N.Y. Times,* Mar. 4, 1974, p. 31, col. 5).

8. For a discussion of the perhaps relevant theories of Nobel Prize winning economist Kenneth Arrow, formerly of Stanford and now at Harvard, see *Wall St. J.,* Feb. 14, 1974, p. 16, col. 3. Arrow, while not underestimating the difficulties involved, emphasizes the importance of developing and relying on ethical codes of behavior for business enterprises as a supplement and even to some extent a replacement of governmental regulation or other adversary proceedings, such as traditional civil litigation. "Government control is one way to create or enforce social responsibility on business, but Mr. Arrow finds this a slow and inflexible solution. Tax policy can deal with some problems — extra taxes on polluting firms, for example — but Mr. Arrow can't see its application to product safety or product quality. Damage suits and other legal actions tend to be costly control devices, often with all-or-nothing outcomes.

"So why not ethical codes — 'some generally understood definition of appropriate behavior?' Writing in *Public Policy,* Mr. Arrow admits 'this may seem to be a strange possibility for an economist to raise,' but argues that 'when there is a wide difference in knowledge between the two sides of the market, recognized ethical codes can be . . . a great contribution to economic efficiency.'

"For example, the medical profession's code of ethics may not be universally followed, but it is practiced widely enough to create a popular presumption that each doctor acts with the patient's welfare in mind — that he will not, say, order unnecessary tests or operations. The code protects patients, to be sure, but it also benefits doctors by maintaining the public's trust in the entire profession.

. . . .

"Mr. Arrow isn't so ivory-towered that he doesn't see all the hurdles — the public skepticism, the industry resistance, the unethical firm that doesn't abide by the code. But he doesn't think the scheme is so wildly impractical, either.

" 'A close look reveals that a great deal of economic life depends for its viability on a certain limited degree of ethical commitment,' he writes. 'There is almost invariably some element of trust and confidence.' Much business is still done verbally, without written contract; deliveries are made presently, with payment later" (*ibid.*).

As to the effect of the compensation system on deterrence of unsafe medical practice, one is reminded of the remark of Harvard sociologist Nathan Glazer (speaking of the comparative effect of prepaid versus fee-for-service systems on patient care, but equally applicable here): "In all systems, one must depend heavily on the professional ethic of the doctor to provide good and responsible care" (Glazer, "Perspectives on Health Care," 31 *The Public Interest* 110, 122 [1973]). See also *infra*, ch. 11, notes 6–16 and accompanying text.

9. U.S. Department of Health, Education, and Welfare, *Report of the Secretary's Commission on Medical Malpractice* 100–102 (1973) [hereinafter cited as HEW Secretary's Commission Report]. The report also states that "the Federal Government [should] fund one or more demonstration projects at the state or local level in order to test and evaluate the feasibility of possible alternative medical injury compensation systems" (*ibid.*, 107). But the problems of finding and funding even an experimental system for *imposing* no-fault liability on health care providers have already been alluded to (*supra*, ch. 6, note 8 and accompanying text). See also *infra* notes 26–29 and accompanying text. And so the advantages of experimenting through elective no-fault liability loom larger and larger the closer one gets to the problem.

10. 2 A. Larson, *Law of Workmen's Compensation* § 67, at 152.8–152.28 (1970). Of course, it is true that under elective workers' compensation, employees as well as employers are given an election to be covered under workers' compensation. (West Virginia allows the employer but not the employee to elect. W.Va. Code Ann. §§ 23-2-7, 23-2-8 [1970]). But see *infra*, ch. 9, note 17 and accompanying text.

11. Ives v. South Buffalo Ry., 201 N.Y. 271, 94 N.E. 431 (1911).

12. New York Cent. R.R. v. White, 243 U.S. 188 (1917); Hawkins v. Bleakly, 243 U.S. 210 (1917); Mountain Timber Co. v. Washington, 243 U.S. 219 (1917).

13. Larson, *supra* note 10, § 67.30, at 152.26–152.28.

14. *Infra*, ch. 9, notes 49–53 and accompanying text.

15. *Report of the National Commission on State Workmen's Compensation Laws* 44, 45, Table 2.3 (1972) [hereinafter cited as *Report on Compensation Laws*]. Recently, however, in an effort to head off federal intervention, state legislatures have enacted many improvements in their workers' compensation laws, including switching from elective to compulsory laws. As of January 1, 1974, "twelve states made workmen's compensation compulsory rather than elective. Thirty-eight states, or 78%, now comply with this 'essential element'" (*National Underwriter* [Property and Casualty ed.], Feb. 8, 1974, p. 18, col. 2, reporting on a survey by the American Mutual Insurance Alliance, listing the states wherein changes were made. For a report on the changes and the political controversies engendered thereby, see *Wall St. J.*, Feb. 25, 1974, p. 1, col. 6).

16. *Report on Compensation Laws*, *supra* note 15, at 44–45.

17. Larson, *supra* note 10, § 67.10, at 152.9–152.10. "[The employer] ... could always fall back on that 'unholy trinity of defenses': (1) *contributory negligence* — the worker could not recover if he himself had been negligent in any degree, regardless of the extent of the employer's negligence; (2) *the fellow-servant doctrine* — the employee could not recover if it could be shown that the injury had resulted from the negligence of a fellow worker; (3) *assumption of risk* — the injured man could not recover if injury was due to an inherent hazard of the job of which he had ... advance knowledge" (H. Somers and A. Somers, *Workmen's Compensation* 18 [1954]).

18. For a discussion of abrogating the defenses of contributory fault —

either alone or in conjunction with elective no-fault liability — see *infra,* ch. 9, notes 23–47 and accompanying text.

19. Larson, *supra* note 10, § 67.21, at 152.14–152.16.

20. *Report on Compensation Laws, supra* note 15, at 25. For a tongue-in-cheek illustration of the absurdity of abandoning a no-fault system of insurance for one based on fault, see Pedrick, "Tangential Introduction," in *Dollars Delay and the Automobile Victim: Studies in Reparation for Highway Injuries and Related Court Problems* at vii (1968).

21. *Report on Compensation Laws, supra* note 15, at 45.

22. R. Keeton and J. O'Connell, *Basic Protection for the Traffic Victim: A Blueprint for Reforming Automobile Insurance* 138–39 (1965).

23. *Supra,* ch. 6, note 2 and accompanying text.

24. Professors Walter Blum and Harry Kalven of the University of Chicago Law School have recently stated: "Many to-day favor broadening beyond the auto world the social goal of providing unconditional [i.e., no-fault] reparations for victims of accidents. It seems most unlikely that efforts to proliferate other *ad hoc* accident compensations will work. . . . There can be little doubt that the mood of society now favors legal intervention to shift accident losses off individual victims by one means or another. We think it likely that the auto accident has been singled out for legislative action not because auto accident victims have any special appeal as victims, but because of the high visibility of the auto accident problem and especially because of certain structural features of the auto accident world that make it feasible to rely heavily on first party insurance to compensate victims. These features include: the access to licensing as a way of enforcing the compulsory insurance; the existence, albeit in another form, of an insurance pool financed by motorists who are thoroughly accustomed to paying insurance premiums; the large overlap between actors who pay premiums and victims who receive reparations; the appeal of having first party insurance protect the motorist as a victim while erasing his legal obligations to others; and, finally, the ease of tracing the injury to the operation of an auto. The question for the next decade is whether some or all of these features, which seem to be special to the auto world, will prove to be limiting conditions on extending the auto plan strategy to other kinds of accidents" (Blum and Kalven, "Ceilings, Costs, and Compulsion in Auto Compensation Legislation" 3 *Utah L. Rev.* 341, 379 incl. n. 42 [1973]). But, for the reasons stated herein, it seems to me that elective no-fault insurance overrides the limiting conditions that constrict no-fault insurance to auto plans. Since it is not feasible to have us all take out separate policies covering different kinds of accidents (other than for auto accidents), such as a policy for falls from ladders, or a policy for each store in which one might fall, etc., the only feasible way extra insurance (beyond health insurance or sick leave) can be made to attach to those accidents from other than social security, in a way that traces the costs of those accidents with much precision back to the area of activity causing them, is through insurance attaching at the time of sale of a product or service. Such insurance is already in existence, but it is cumbersome "fault" (or "defect") insurance. Thus, switching such insurance to no-fault insurance means, contrary to Professors Blum and Kalven, that a variation of "the auto plan can be generalized as a solution for other accident problems" (*ibid.*).

25. *Supra* note 12, and accompanying text. See R. Keeton, *Venturing to Do Justice* 136 (1969).

26. *Supra*, ch. 7, notes 10–12.

27. Roth and Rosenthal, "Non-Fault-Based Medical Injury Compensation Systems," in *Appendix*, HEW Secretary's Commission Report, *supra* note 9, at 450, 481.

28. *Supra*, ch. 6, notes 32–33 and accompanying text.

29. Roth and Rosenthal, *supra* note 27, at 466. See also Havighurst and Tancredi, " 'Medical Adversity Insurance': A No-Fault Approach to Medical Malpractice and Quality Assurance," 51 *Milbank Memorial Fund Q.* 125 (1973), also printed in 1974 *Ins. L. J.* 69.

30. Alternatively, the enabling legislation could gauge the tort exemption as, say, one-half of the amount of no-fault benefits measured in medical bills (for example, if no-fault benefits of $30,000 are provided, no tort suit could be maintained unless medical bills exceed $15,000). The problem with any formula tied to medical bills is that it can encourage the padding of medical bills to exceed the tort exemption. But see J. O'Connell, *The Injury Industry and the Remedy of No-Fault Insurance* 118 (1971), indicating that fear of padded medical bills decreases with the seriousness of the injury.

Another problem of allowing a cutoff point for no-fault benefits, and preserving the tort action above it, is that the elector — who will be paying both fault and no-fault claims for some serious injuries — might well be tempted to use the availability of no-fault benefits in bargaining perhaps unfairly over the disposition of the tort claim, or vice-versa. See R. Keeton and J. O'Connell, *Basic Protection for the Traffic Victim: A Blueprint for Reforming Automobile Insurance* 350 (1965). But that disadvantage must be weighed against the flexibility of experimentation by allowing an elector to cut off the amount of no-fault benefits for which he assumes liability.

Note that elective no-fault insurance will mean that where workers' compensation benefits are inadequate, injured employees will have a much better chance to recover supplementary payment if those subject to third-party suits have elected no-fault coverage. To the extent workers' compensation laws are more and more adequate (see *supra* note 15), those subject to third-party actions will be induced to cover under elective no-fault insurance the relatively rare case in which workers' compensation benefits are inadequate. Also, employees covered by the Federal Employers' Liability Act who now face almost no-fault liability as well as common law damages will be very strongly encouraged to elect no-fault liability (see *infra*, ch. 9, note 43 and accompanying text). Similar incentives to opt no-fault liability will be felt by those liable to maritime workers under the Jones Act or the Merchant Marine Act and by all those liable under dram shop acts, scaffolding acts, or the Federal Safety Appliance Act. See W. Prosser, *The Law of Torts* § 80, at 534–40 (4th ed. 1971).

31. See *supra*, ch. 2, note 4 and accompanying text.

32. It is interesting to note that in 1954 Albert A. Ehrenzweig in effect proposed elective no-fault liability applicable to auto accidents (A. Ehrenzweig, *"Full Aid" Insurance for the Traffic Victim: A Voluntary Compensation Plan* 20, 31 [1954], also published in a slightly revised version in 43 *Calif. L. Rev.* 1, 24–25, 38 [1955]). Then ten years later he proposed *compul-*

sory no-fault liability for hospitals (Ehrenzweig, "Compulsory 'Hospital-Accident' Insurance: A Needed First Step toward the Displacement of Liability for 'Medical Malpractice,'" 31 *U. Chi. L. Rev.* 279, 284 [1964]). In our original proposal for no-fault auto insurance, Robert Keeton and I proposed compulsory no-fault insurance for auto accidents (Keeton and O'Connell, *supra* note 30, at 286–88), and I am in the present work proposing elective no-fault for, among other things, hospitals. Thus I am proposing the reverse of Ehrenzweig's ideas in both respects! (But to the extent no-fault auto insurance is not compulsory for unlimited losses, I do then propose elective no-fault liability for auto losses. On the other hand, to the extent that the legislative decision to limit the application of no-fault auto insurance is based on a conscious decision that the tort liability system should be preserved for some losses, then allowing elective no-fault liability to further extend the application of no-fault insurance for auto accidents — and correspondingly wipe out the tort action — should be rejected. But where the decision of the legislature is based on unease about the cost of no-fault, such elective experimentation to find the optimum point for no-fault coverage and a corresponding abandonment of tort liability makes sense.)

On another note, in light of the already extensive information required by doctors to be imparted to patients under the doctrine of "informed consent" (*infra,* ch. 11, notes 17–20 and accompanying text), might it not be feasible for doctors, even without enabling elective no-fault legislation, to offer to patients, prior to administering any treatment, the option of being paid for the adverse results discussed under no-fault insurance with its more certain if lesser payment? Indeed, isn't it at least worth speculating that a manufacturer, wholesaler, or retailer might, through an express warranty, bind the purchaser of its product to receive only such no-fault benefits for personal injury? The fairness of the bargain might well rebut the presumption of the Uniform Commercial Code (section 9-719[3]) against such limitation of personal injury liability. But see *infra,* ch. 9, notes 15–17 and accompanying text.

9

A Promising Approach or Two
PART II

As an indication of the balanced approach of elective no-fault insurance,[1] two questions of opposite import immediately come to mind in appraising the proposal. First, why should insurers be able to impose the bargain of no-fault compensation on the victims they injure? Second, why should the fault of the victim — or the risks he voluntarily undertakes — never be a factor in determining whether payment is due him under this new form of insurance?

In answer to the first question, it is important to examine just what is being taken away from a victim by no-fault liability. He first loses his right to be paid for pain and suffering if he was free from fault and his injurer was at fault. He also loses his right to receive from his injurer compensation for loss already paid from his own insurance (such as sick leave or hospitalization).

But several empirical studies have recently shown how little being paid from insurance under a fault criterion means to most people. Viewed after the accident, it must be admitted that there are some accident victims who will receive less under no-fault liability than they would under the regular tort system. But looking at the matter from the vantage of *before* an accident — that being the fairest way to measure various insurance options — the public seems strongly to favor relative certainty of payment for out-of-pocket loss over a gamble for payment of out-of-pocket loss plus pain and suffering.[2] A survey of Illinois residents asked the following question concerning automobile accidents:

Notes on p. 132.

Suppose you could buy either of the following types of automobile insurance for the same price, which would you choose?

Type A: If you are injured in a collision, Type A would pay you nothing if you were at fault or if you were unable to prove that someone else was at fault. But if you could prove the other person was at fault and you were not, this type of insurance would pay you full compensation, including not only the medical bills and wage losses, but also a reasonable amount to compensate you for your pain and suffering.

Type B: If you were injured in a collision, Type B would pay your medical loss and wage loss, but nothing for your pain and suffering. But it would pay you regardless of who was at fault in the accident.

Of those expressing an opinion, 71 percent preferred no-fault insurance with its certain, if smaller, payment, and only 29 percent preferred an uncertain, if larger, payment based on fault.[3]

Indeed, even after accidents, according to another survey conducted in Illinois, few of those who were successful in claiming for compensation based on who was at fault in the accident knew about, or learned about, or cared about being paid for pain and suffering by the so-called wrongdoer.[4] Fully 70 percent of accident victims had no knowledge or expectation of payment for pain and suffering at the time they were involved in the accident, nor did most of them ever learn about it. Furthermore, accident victims did not understand whether they had in fact been paid for pain and suffering. Only 34 percent of those who had been paid more than four times their out-of-pocket loss (and thus had clearly been paid — and paid quite well — for their pain and suffering) thought they had been paid for pain and suffering.[5] It was also found that there was no correlation between the amount of pain they suffered and the amount they were paid for that pain.

Startling, too, were the findings of what little difference being paid for pain and suffering apparently makes to accident victims. For example, very few victims ended up resenting the other drivers with whom they collided, and whether they were paid or how much they were paid for pain and suffering had no significant relationship in assuaging any feelings of resentment about the accident.[6] Indeed, payment for pain and suffering did not signifi-

Notes on p. 132.

cantly affect, in fact or amount, other pertinent attitudes toward the accident, including general feelings of satisfaction about how the victim was treated by the insurance company. Similarly, whether the victims *thought* they had been paid for pain and suffering had no significant effect on their attitudes toward the accident, including feelings of either resentment or satisfaction about it. Whether they thought they had been paid for pain and suffering neither affected the respondents' feeling about the rightness or wrongness of the situation nor served to assuage the amount of pain they experienced.[7]

To summarize the findings of the survey, for all the talk by lawyers and some insurance executives about the importance of blaming the "guilty" and paying the "innocent" for pain and suffering under the fault liability system, it appears that most accident victims are ignorant of — and indifferent to — payment for pain and suffering from the other party's insurance company under the fault criterion. Accident victims perceive what lawyers do not: "accidents" are just that, and what accident victims want is prompt payment for their real out-of-pocket losses with a minimum of fuss and argument.[8]

In this connection it must also be noted that no-fault insurance, in paying promptly for losses, including medical treatment to relieve pain, goes a long way toward alleviating pain and suffering. A dramatic increase has occurred since World War II in the development and use of medication to relieve pain, most often in the form of analgesics. And more sophisticated advances are likely. It is possible, for example, that a patient-operated device that applies electric signals to the nervous system to kill pain will be used more and more in the future.[9] In this age of medical innovation, a system of accident compensation paying, as no-fault does, for expenses which include medication and other medical devices may well be doing much more about an accident victim's pain than the present system does. Nor does payment under no-fault insurance stop with treatment for physical pain. Research demonstrates that deep depression can often accompany severe disabling injury. An insurance scheme that can assure prompt and sympathetic psychiatric and rehabilitation services is surely much more promising than a scheme that throws a large amount of money

Notes on pp. 132–33.

at a very occasional victim after years of acrimony and dispute. As I stated as coauthor in an earlier study:

> [I]n discussing payment for pain and suffering under the fault system and its curtailment under no-fault schemes, one should not overlook the "pain" imparted by the fault system in the uncertainty and delay attendant on whether any payment at all is to be made when the fault criterion is applied. When injury victims cannot know *when* they will be paid, *what* they will be paid, or *if* they will be paid, this can produce an anguish of its own. Professor Conard and his colleagues in their monumental study of auto accidents in Michigan devote a sobering section to the pained responses of many injury victims to the tort claims process, including their "reactions of disappointment and even bitterness" and "their dislike of 'uncertainty.' " In sum, Conard and his colleagues said their findings "painted an emphatic picture of anxiety, frustration, disappointment, and resentment felt by injury victims in the course of the adjustment and litigation processes."[10]

That no-fault insurance "has the benign effect of reducing the psychic shock, strain and subsequent 'traumatic neurosis' encountered by accident victims" is indicated by research conducted by Dr. Lester Keiser, chief of neuropsychiatry at Memorial Hospital, Hollywood, Florida, who has done extensive research on the subject of traumatic neurosis. Dr. Keiser confirms, according to a report on his research, that "under the old automobile insurance system, with its frequent and lengthy lawsuits, the nervous strain experienced by an accident victim is often intensified in the ensuing wrangles with claims adjustors and lawyers." The victim's rage often is aggravated by the protracted litigation, with some individuals becoming "so absorbed in nursing their symptoms and pressing their claims that they completely alter their lives. Dr. Keiser notes that no-fault insurance [enacted in his home state of Florida] obviously does not eliminate the inevitable emotional stress that follows an accident. But what it does do, he says, is eliminate many of the conditions that make such a trauma worse."[11]

Concerning no-fault's prohibition of multiple payments for the same loss, public preference may be less clear. Under a poll conducted by the University of Illinois Survey Research Laboratory, the general public was asked whether it would prefer to buy auto

Notes on p. 133.

insurance that would not duplicate payment from, say, Blue Cross but would cost correspondingly less. The response showed 54 percent in favor of no duplication. But a surprising result was that as many as 46 percent would seem to prefer more expensive insurance providing duplicate payment. In point of fact, many may have wanted the duplicate coverage out of fear — often based on experience — that one coverage, with its deductibles and limits, would not in fact completely cover all expenses. To that extent, no-fault insurance would resolve the dilemma by becoming payable when the first coverage, or "primary" coverage, as it is called, is exhausted.[12]

Even if the preference for multiple payment represents a desire to "profit" from an accident by getting an extra payment, that profit should not be allowed. Multiple payments for the same loss encourage the sad anomaly of the present tort liability system: overpayment of smaller, trivial losses chews up so much of the insurance dollar that underpayment of large losses is encouraged.[13] How ridiculous that accident victims should be induced to stay out of work or make an extra trip to the doctor in order to make an easy extra dollar by multiple reimbursement! Could anything lead to wasting precious medical and insurance resources more foolishly? Multiple insurance payable for the same property loss caused by fire or theft has long been forbidden for fear of the corrupt inducement of the "accidental" loss. The same ban makes sense for multiple insurance payable for the same personal injury loss.[14]

Some will certainly argue against the proposition that under elective no-fault insurance businesses or professionals are able to choose the form of insurance — fault or no-fault — applicable to the victim of the business or professional activity. Opponents will point out that elective workers' compensation laws commonly allow employees as well as employers to make the election concerning workers' compensation.[15] But election under workers' compensation is feasible because the employee is called upon to make his election before the accident — namely, at the time of employment. One could not allow election after an injury had occurred without confronting the employer with the dilemma of adverse selection — adverse selection, in other words, leaving the employer facing the worst of both worlds: tort claims for more money than would be

Notes on p. 133.

provided under no-fault by those who have reason to believe they have valid fault claims, and no-fault claims from those ineligible for payment under a fault claim. The only similar election time concerning the sale of goods is at the time of sale itself. But it is not feasible to ask businessmen — whether manufacturers or retailers — to require at the time of purchase that customers elect how they are to be paid in the event they are hurt by the product. The administrative — not to speak of the psychological — ramifications of such a procedure would be horrendous, and asking potential purchasers to sign forbidding legal forms covering potential injury would surely be a marketing disaster.[16] Actually, even the right of an employee to elect not to be covered under workers' compensation is highly theoretical. In Massachusetts, for example, where the employee retains the right not to be covered (although the act is compulsory for the employer), no employees ever elect not to be covered, and, as a practical matter, they would never be hired if they did.[17]

In effect, elective no-fault liability allows those potentially liable in tort to impose on accident victims the same bargain that the legislature imposes by enacting no-fault auto insurance. The reason the power to impose is delegated to individuals, as already pointed out in chapter 6, is that it is simply not feasible in the case of other kinds of accidents to impose, by widespread legislative command, the bargain that no-fault insurance entails.

Of course, the question will be raised why anyone should be allowed to elect to pay under no-fault liability a possible lesser total amount for injuries associated with his product or activity than he might pay under tort liability. The premise of no-fault liability is that the regular tort liability is often absurdly and unnecessarily wasteful, dilatory, and cruel. Far better, if necessary, to spend less and spend it wisely. Paying injured parties when their needs outstrip their resources, without the expense and delay of establishing fault or a defect in a product, is much wiser than funneling money through the regular tort liability system, where available funds so largely end up in the pockets of lawyers, expert witnesses, and insurance companies.[18] In addition, as elective no-fault liability proves feasible, on the basis of its success in given instances, com-

Notes on p. 133.

pulsory no-fault liability could be *imposed* on more and more enterprises for more and more injuries if society wishes to do so.[19]

Concerning the fairness of the bargain imposed by no-fault insurance, as suggested earlier, one should look at the options as they are presented before an accident. But viewed from either before or after the accident, one must start from the public's apparent preference for the relative certainty of prompt payment for out-of-pocket loss compared to a gamble for payment of out-of-pocket loss plus pain and suffering.[20]

When I first proposed this elective plan at a symposium on no-fault insurance in Louisville, Kentucky, in the fall of 1973, Leonard Ring, president of the Association of Trial Lawyers of America, asked this question from the floor: "Take the case of the retired person who loses an arm in the course of using a defective power tool of a manufacturer which has elected complete no-fault insurance. The victim suffers no wage loss (being retired) nor medical expenses (being covered by Medicare). What, then, does he receive under elective no-fault insurance?" The answer is, assuming that the victim actually suffers no medical expenses, as I admitted, "Nothing." Ring chortled, confident that he had scored a point, but my answer continued: If the victim suffers no economic loss, an insurance system designed to pay only economic loss is right to pay him nothing. Thus, the issue is, of course, Does an insurance system paying only for out-of-pocket loss make sense? I conclude that it does. Given the fact that there are only a limited number of insurance dollars to go around, which of the following should receive priority of payment: (1) the wage loss and medical expenses (including rehabilitation, as well as psychiatric services in the common event of depression) remaining after, say, a middle-aged house painter and breadwinner who has lost an arm has exhausted all his other sources of insurance payment, or (2) the noneconomic loss of a retired person who has lost an arm, all of whose economic losses (including, say, a prosthetic device) have been paid for?

Even viewed after the accident, if a choice has to be made (and constraints on costs always make such choices necessary), the former seems a wiser use of insurance dollars than the latter. This is especially the case when we remember that under the tort system (1) payment of the retired person's noneconomic loss will be highly

Notes on pp. 133–134.

speculative — even viewed after the accident — given the difficulties of proving that the power tool was defective and was properly used by the victim; (2) that any payment will be long delayed (indeed Ring's choice of a retired person was unfortunate from the point of view of us lawyers; by the time we lawyers got payment to a retired person, quite likely he would be dead); and (3) a third or more of any payment will go not to the retired person but to us lawyers. So, even viewed after the event the prospect for Ring's retired person is scarcely roseate.

But now look at his prospects from the vantage of *before* the accident. The elderly person who suffers grave injury is very likely to need extensive medical care — perhaps even temporary round-the-clock nursing care. Medicare does not cover *all* medical expenses — it certainly would not cover all those nurses — and, indeed, the pattern has been for more and more cutting of benefits in light of rising costs.[21] So the elderly person, with his limited and fixed retired income and his fear of unusual medical bills, perhaps above all will welcome certainty of reimbursement for out-of-pocket loss in return for giving up his right to fight with lawyers.

Here again, however, a legislator who disagrees with the complete denial of payment to an accident victim, such as a retired person, suffering little or no economic loss from the loss of a limb, could provide that elective no-fault insurance, like certain no-fault auto plans, can never preclude tort actions for certain defined serious injuries, including amputation. Alternatively, scheduled monetary benefits for nonmonetary losses could be provided for certain horrendous injuries like amputations. The problem with such provisions for noneconomic loss is that they clearly cost money and may well take away money that could be used for more compensation for genuine out-of-pocket loss.[22]

The second question at the beginning of this chapter asked, Why should the fault of the victim — or the risks he voluntarily undertakes — never be a factor in determining whether payment is due him under elective no-fault insurance? Not taking account of the victim's negligence is part of the no-fault bargain. Just as the injurer is asked to pay possibly more people (by paying regardless of his fault or a defect in his product) but to pay them less (nothing for pain and suffering or to duplicate collateral source payments),

Notes on p. 134.

so, conversely, by giving up his right to be paid for pain and suffering and for losses covered by collateral sources the injured earns the right to be paid regardless of fault.[23]

As a corollary, note that under elective no-fault liability, as well as under no-fault auto and workmen's compensation insurance, the law no longer focuses on isolated conduct by individuals as the cause of accidents. Speaking only of injuries to persons, not property, the basic premise is one accepted so long ago for work accidents and now being accepted for auto accidents: in a mechanical and complex age, where so often we are able to injure one another, unintentional lapses, along with attendant injuries, are inevitable. When those inevitable injuries occur, a sophisticated and sensitive society — especially one in which insurance plays a substantial role — ought to be cushioning and spreading those losses as effectively and efficiently as possible and, indeed, with a measure of courtesy and compassion. Given the literally accidental way fault arises in accidents, exhaustive attempts to analyze and prove individual fault are a fruitless business. Rather, considerations of (1) helping people who are hurt, and (2) doing so under efficient criteria ought to play the dominant part in constructing an insurance mechanism.

But what about the deterrent effect on *individuals* of no-fault payment? If, under market deterrence, forcing enterprises to bear the burden of personal injury losses will supposedly force them to be more careful,[24] won't relieving individual victims of the burden of their losses make them more careless? Winston Churchill, as the young home secretary helping, with Lloyd George, to push through the major social insurance programs of the Liberal government in the early 1900s, answered this question as well as possible. "Insurance," he said, "brought the miracle of averages to the rescue of . . . [the mass of mankind]."[25] As to punishing individuals for careless behavior by denying them insurance payments, Churchill said, "I do not like mixing up moralities and mathematics." One reason for not doing so, he said, is that "there is no proportion between [the] personal failings and the penalties exacted." Nor was there, he judged, any "reason to suppose that a mitigation of the extreme severities [visited upon the accident victim] will tend in any way to a diminution of personal responsibility, but . . . on

Notes on p. 134.

the contrary more will be gained by an increase of ability [of the victim] to fight than will be lost through an abatement of the extreme consequences of defeat."[26]

According to Guido Calabresi, apart from the "elusive" goal of "justice" (which, as suggested by chapters 1 through 5, the present tort system assuredly does *not* achieve), the "principal function of accident law is to reduce the sum of the costs of accidents and the costs of avoiding accidents." In the first place, we hope by imposing loss (whether by transferring it from the victim or leaving it with him) to influence conduct to lessen "the number and severity of accidents."[27] But speaking only of personal injuries, imposing losses on victims can never have much of a deterrent effect, because, unlike the case for the institutional defendant (such as a business or its insurance company), payment or nonpayment of insurance money can never begin to compare as a deterrent for the individual with the desire to avoid being hurt in the first place. Therefore, individuals, as a practical matter, whether they are driving a car or using a power tool — or deciding to do such things — will never be much influenced by fear that their conduct will deny them subsequent insurance payment (even in the unlikely event they understand the laws of contributory negligence or assumption of risk).[28] Moreover, not all insurance payments will be denied them; on the contrary, *only* liability insurance would be denied. Accident and health insurance, sick leave, fire insurance — even life insurance to their survivors — would be paid regardless of their fault. As a result, imposing economic loss from personal injury on the victim of an accident because he was at fault will virtually never contribute to reducing accidents and accident costs by making the potential victim more careful. The same is not true with reference to property damage. We may well be influenced in our treatment of property by fear of what it would cost to replace or repair it, precisely because property, unlike our person, can be so impersonally replaced or repaired. There, monetary cost *is* often paramount.[29]

And even to the extent one imagines that rules of law and insurance can induce more careful behavior on the part of the potential accident victim, a rule of law such as that under elective no-fault liability, denying payment for the victim's pain and suffering, imposes a substantial portion of the loss on him. (But the reason for not pay-

Notes on p. 134.

ing for the victim's pain and suffering is not so much to influence his behavior. Rather, it is because insurance dollars are precious; there are probably never going to be enough to go around. It would be better, then, to use those dollars to replace dollars lost than to use them to replace something essentially irreplaceable by dollars, namely, pain and suffering.) [30]

But for businesses or professionals, financial considerations — not fear of their own personal injury — are bound to predominate as a deterrent. The impersonal business or professional institution, by definition, cannot suffer personal injury. Of course, its officers — or the sole practitioner providing, say, medical services — for humanitarian reasons will most likely not want patrons to get hurt, but economic motives are also always going to be operating. Another way to think about this point is to recognize that the potential individual injury victim has only one personal injury to think about — that to himself — and the injury would be so awful to his person that he does not get around to thinking about its financial consequences. But for the business or professional person, personal injury losses caused by his activity mean losses to *others,* and he is inevitably going to be thinking about them in the aggregate and therefore about their financial repercussions on him. This explains why fear of paying damages may well influence a potential defendant to be more careful, whereas fear of not being paid damages will not influence a potential plaintiff to be more careful. [31] (The extent to which financial considerations predominate in a defendant-enterpriser's thinking about personal injury is illustrated by the true story of the general counsel to a corporation who recently complained, "We just got stuck for $450,000 verdict we had to pay out to a guy who fell and became a quadriplegic. That's twelve and a half cents a share!") The result is that who will bear the financial loss may well influence the care taken by the injurer but not that taken by the injured. [32]

This brings us to Calabresi's other principal aims of tort law in trying to reduce the costs of accidents. The first aim, just discussed, was "the reduction of the number and severity of accidents." [33] The second goal "concentrates instead on reducing the societal costs resulting from accidents" [34] by compensating accident victims through spreading the risk. In other words, society — and its members —

Notes on pp. 134–35.

suffer less when there is money to pay for medical expenses, including rehabilitation of accident victims, than when the individual and social devastation caused, for example, by uncompensated catastrophic loss to a breadwinner is ignored. The third goal "involves reducing the costs of administering our treatment of accidents,"[35] that is, achieving a suitably efficient system for administering claims (as opposed to spending too much on lawyers and insurance adjusters, for example).

Focus on a victim's negligent conduct not only has no effect on the primary goal of deterrence, but it also frustrates both the second and third goals. When a plaintiff's loss is not spread because he was at fault, he is denied maintenance and rehabilitation, and consequently the costs to him — and to society — of the injury he has suffered may well multiply. (In addition, to repeat another of Calabresi's points,[36] to the extent we base payment on anyone's fault, we spread the loss for fewer accidents, "externalizing" the costs of all the others.[37] In other words, we want to deter more than just accidents caused solely by the fault — or the defective product — of the defendant.) In addition, to dissect a plaintiff's conduct to ascertain whether or not it was faulty is to adopt the most expensive and inefficient aspect of current accident law. Like focusing on the defendant's fault or defect, this aspect is *hugely* expensive. Thus, neither deterrence nor compensation nor efficiency is served by a rule denying payment to negligent accident victims.

So it turns out that barring the injured victim from being paid because of his fault not only does not reduce the number and severity of accidents (by not adding significantly to his motive to avoid personal injury), but also subverts the other goals of (1) compensating accident victims and (2) administering claims efficiently.

Another way to say all this is to start again with Calabresi's point that a prime justification for imposing tort liability is to reduce accidents in number and severity. In his preceptive analysis: "Why is compensation for illness, even in highly welfaristic countries, much less complete than compensation for accident victims? . . . The answer is, of course, that accidents, unlike most diseases, can easily be reduced in number and severity, and that such . . . cost reduction can — indeed must — be an important aim of whatever system of law governs the field."[38] But conversely, once the law has found a

Notes on p. 135.

source (that is, a negligent defendant under the fault system or an employer under workers' compensation), payment from which will purportedly reduce the various costs of accidents, the only reason for *not* enforcing payment must be that *not* paying will also reduce the costs of accidents. But, at least where one is dealing with out-of-pocket losses from personal injury, not only is that *not* the case, but the opposite is also true.[39]

The question might be asked whether overlooking any contributory fault on the part of accident victims in paying them for their personal injury losses will not force the careful to underwrite the losses of the careless. In a measure, of course, it will. So does all insurance in a very substantial measure. No one can deny that such is the effect of fire insurance, disability insurance, workers' compensation, credit card loss insurance, and even, to a lesser but still substantial extent, health insurance and life insurance. To some extent, varying insurance rates according to one's safety record (under so-called merit rating) can alleviate the redistribution, but only moderately in practice, it turns out,[40] and precise merit rating is not at all feasible under most insurance which is sold on a group basis so that any individual's rate is not varied according to his own safety record. That need not disturb us. Because I, as an individual, never know when I am going to be unlucky and have an accident — whether I am careless or not — it is worth it to me to be assured of payment at the risk of subsidizing someone who may turn out to be "luckier" than I by having more accidents because he is more careless.

I know — or should know — that the price of dissecting every accident to see who is at fault includes (1) less money being available to pay those who are injured, (2) a risk of no payment to many (including, given the difficulties of truly re-creating the accident, some not in fact at fault), and (3) long delay in whatever payment is made. As a result, nowhere does one hear, for example, from employees that workers' compensation insurance should be abandoned because more careful employees are supposedly subsidizing less careful employees. And how far would any proposal get which purported to refuse — or reduce — payment from fire insurance based on whether one had been careless with a lighted cigarette?[41] It is true that railroad employees covered by the Federal

Notes on p. 135.

Employer's Liability Act (FELA) have resisted a switch to workers' compensation from the FELA, coverage under which purports to turn on the employer's negligence with a subtraction from the injured party's damages based on his comparative negligence,[42] but two special reasons explain that resistance to a switch to no-fault insurance. In the first place, railroad employees arguably have the best of both worlds — no-fault insurance, in fact, coupled with common law damages including payment for pain and suffering. A series of decisions, according to Prosser, has served "to reduce the extent of the negligence required [on the part of the employer], as well as the quantum of proof necessary to establish it, to the 'vanishing point.' "[43] This, coupled with the anachronistic level of workers' compensation benefits, which not only fails to pay for pain and suffering but which has not kept pace with inflation in paying even part of economic loss, may explain the reluctance of railroad employees and their representatives to switch to genuine no-fault insurance.

Actually, it also follows that the rule barring the guilty victim of personal injury from payment ought probably to be abolished under present tort liability regardless of any other reform. In other words, regardless whether any system of elective no-fault liability is instituted, the cumbersome rules of contributory negligence and assumption of risk, which, like rules concerning defendants' negligence, undermine all of Calabresi's goals of resource allocation, compensation, and efficiency, might well be abandoned forthwith in cases of personal injury. Abandoning any rule of contributory fault is especially valid for serious injuries, for which the discrepancy between the lapse and its consequence is so disproportionate, and therefore any achievement of "justice" by the application of such a rule is especially illusory. But because such a new rule would obviously add costs to the present system (already overly expensive in the eyes of many) without any attempt at compensatory savings, such a proposal may not be realistic. Of course, such a proposal to simply abandon contributory fault as a barrier to tort payment (while retaining a requirement of proving the defendant guilty of "faulty" conduct) could be coupled with compensatory savings by abandoning payment for pain and suffering in all cases. Alternatively, payment for pain and suffering could be eliminated or cut down (by

Notes on p. 135.

comparative negligence) by a finding of contributory fault although contributory fault would never be allowed to interfere with payment for out-of-pocket personal injury loss.[44] Another means of compensatory savings could stem from generally abolishing, for personal injury cases, the so-called collateral source rule whereby a tort defendant pays again for loss already paid from collateral sources such as sick leave or hospitalization insurance. All these proposals would seem to make more sense than the present tort system, but by maintaining bootless inquiries into the defendant's fault and, in some instances, into the victim's fault as well, they do not go far enough. An experiment with genuine no-fault insurance through elective no-fault liability would be better.[45]

Note, though, how a simple abolition of common law defenses of contributory fault in cases of personal injury could interlock with a proposal for elective no-fault. One would thereby take a leaf from the experience under early legislation dealing with industrial accidents and apply it to nonemployment injuries; before enactment of workers' compensation statutes, some early employers' liability statutes, while retaining a requirement of proof of negligence against an employer, nonetheless abrogated common law defenses for industrial accidents.[46] With common law defenses abolished, in a state allowing elective workers' compensation, an employer is under that much greater incentive to opt to be covered under elective workers' compensation. Similarly, in order to encourage any and all to opt to be covered under elective no-fault liability insurance, the defenses of assumption of risk and contributory negligence could be abolished against defendants in all personal injury actions. Such a move would have the additional advantage of eliminating at least part of the cumbersome arguments over fault — that is, the plaintiffs' fault — even when no-fault coverage is not elected.[47]

Nevertheless, one must reiterate that a concomitant proposal abolishing contributory fault in all personal injury cases might generate so much controversy that it would hinder passage of legislation allowing experimentation with a system of elective no-fault liability. In other words, a relatively modest law allowing elective no-fault liability might well be dwarfed in importance in the eyes of industry, the legislature, and perhaps even the public

Notes on p. 136.

by a concomitant abolition of assumption of risk and contributory negligence in all cases. On the other hand, maybe not; it's worth considering.*

Daniel Patrick Moynihan, in discussing the advantages of no-fault auto insurance, stated that the proponents of no-fault insurance "are right in the all important perception as to what it is Americans are good at. We are good at maintaining business relationships once a basis of mutual self interest is established. [No-fault insurance] . . . would establish one."[48] Elective no-fault liability, by allowing the businessman and his customer or a doctor and his patient to bypass the lawyers, with all their incredibly inappropriate and self-serving cumbersomeness, in the event of accidental injury in the course of using a product or service, is also surely an excellent example of establishing a relationship based on mutual self-interest.

Another device for initiating no-fault liability for other than auto accidents can be devised based on experience under limited workers' compensation schemes. In some states the compulsory imposition of workers' compensation has been limited to more hazardous employment. Similarly, no-fault liability might be limited to extrahazardous enterprises. Such a scheme, termed *extrahazardous no-fault liability,* might be initiated either in conjunction with, or as an alternative to, an elective no-fault scheme, or as a second step for extending it. In October, 1972, the president signed into law the Consumer Product Safety Act,[49] legislation stemming from the *Final Report* of the National Commission on Product Safety.[50] The law created an independent federal commission called the Product Safety Commission, composed of five commissioners, charged with establishing and enforcing safety standards on thousands of consumer products. Data for determining which products present "unreasonable risk of injury" are being provided by the National Electronic Injury Surveillance System (NEISS), a reporting system gathering data from 119 hospital emergency rooms on the frequency and severity of accidental injuries caused by household products.[51] The commission's mandate under the law is to set performance standards to assure the safety of products. For example, concerning architectural

---

* For a critique of economic theory that would retain the defenses of contributory fault, see *infra,* Appendix IV.

Notes on p. 137.

glass in patio and storm doors, long a source of serious injury, Malcom Jensen, then an official of the new commission, stated that the new act "would let us prohibit use of non-shatterproof glass" and impose substitutes of laminated, tempered, or wired glass or even plastics.[52]

To extend the new commission's responsibility to include setting no-fault liability standards would likely tax neither its resources nor its expertise. Amendments to the legislation could empower the commission to use the data which it gathers on dangerous products for the purpose of designating categories of products, and certain types of injuries therefrom, as appropriate subjects for the invocation of extrahazardous no-fault liability. The actual imposition of liability could be done by either the courts or the commission itself. Alternatively, the amending legislation itself could impose extrahazardous no-fault liability on certain categories of products and injuries on the basis of data gathered by the Product Safety Commission. For example, data previously gathered by the commission's predecessor, the National Commission on Product Safety, might justify the imposition of no-fault liability for typical injuries caused by specific types of products, such as power mowers, or broader categories of products, such as those made with glass, those that produce intense heat, those with engines, those using electricity, athletic equipment, and toys — a collection of categories which includes almost all the most dangerous items identified by the *Final Report* of the National Commission on Product Safety.[53] If such intervention of federal authority in tort law were deemed inappropriate, the commission could still develop standards to serve either as advisory guidelines or as minimum federal requirements for the implementation of extrahazardous no-fault liability by some state agency — for example, an insurance commission or a workers' compensation board — pursuant to state enabling legislation.[54]

Indeed, many economists would consider the commission's time much better spent in developing data and formulating more efficient rules for compensation than in mandating safety regulations; in their view there is a point at which prevention becomes unfeasible and the search for a cure must proceed apace. At a conference at the University of Rochester in the fall of 1972, some forty economists focused on consumerism, especially reports produced under

Notes on p. 137.

the aegis of Ralph Nader. Several conferees observed that from a cost-benefit viewpoint, "Nader's reports . . . tend to assign an excessively high value to safety. [Consider] . . . the hypothetical case of the exploding soda pop bottle, a classroom favorite for showing the economic limits of safety precautions. The riddle is this: Say one defective bottle in a million slips by the safety inspection on the assembly line. At twice the present cost, only one in two million will get by. And at four times the present cost, only one in three million bottles will pop. *When is it time to limit the outlay on safety, and settle for paying off the occasional consumer who gets hurt?*"[55]

But in fact, one place where Nader and his raiders seem to agree with Nader's economist critics is in the wisdom of imposing automatic no-fault liability as a means of achieving safety. In reply to the criticism quoted above, Nader associate Beverly C. Moore, Jr., wrote:

> If the soft drink industry were forced to compensate fully the victims of exploding bottles . . . or if the auto industry were obliged to pay out [billions] . . . annually in accident costs, I suspect not only that the optimum trade-off between accident and prevention costs would be realized without supplementary government safety standards but also that the new economic incentives would generate technological advantages which would in time substantially reduce the prevention costs.
>
> . . . The model of competitive capitalism, though, has . . . basic flaws, the correction of which is the fundamental purpose of the consumer movement. Specifically, this model contains no provision for . . . externalities such as . . . accidents (solution: cost internalization) . . . .[56]

Implicit in this formulation of the problem of compensating accident victims is the notion that from a purely economic viewpoint payment might be made automatically without regard to fault or defect.

Moore's point raises the possibility of another device for effectively combining safety regulation and accident compensation: Why not empower the Product Safety Commission to order a manufacturer, as an alternative or supplement, when appropriate, to other commission orders, to agree to pay no-fault benefits (with a corresponding tort exemption accruing to the manufacturer) to anyone injured by the hazard of the manufacturer's product identified by

Notes on p. 137.

the commission? Thus, in addition to, say, being ordered by the commission to notify known purchasers of the hazard or to offer to make repairs, the manufacturer could be obliged to pay no-fault benefits for pecuniary losses caused to personal injury accident victims by the hazard identified by the commission. Similar power to impose no-fault liability might be given to the National Highway Traffic Safety Administration of the Department of Transportation in ordering car manufacturers to recall defective cars. Note that such automatic no-fault liability would serve as an added incentive to the manufacturer to notify owners and expeditiously conduct the repairs. Similar power to order no-fault liability (accompanied again by a corresponding tort exemption) could be given to the Food and Drug Administration in authorizing the marketing of new drugs.

It might be thought that since the Product Safety Commission or the Highway Traffic Safety Administration has already identified a defect, it is not fair to take away the injured party's common law rights to sue on the basis of the defect in return for more limited no-fault benefits. But the finding of a defect by the agency is certainly not binding on a court in a subsequent tort suit against the manufacturer, and thus such a claim will entail all the cumbersomeness, expense, and delay of product liability suits.[57]

Note that the concept of extrahazardous no-fault liability is adaptable to injuries suffered in the course of medical treatment. Here, too, legislation or regulations, not an electing health care provider, would define the compensable injuries. The legislation or regulation would single out designated injuries from certain procedures. These would be procedures not only likely to produce the adverse results regardless of anyone's fault but also so likely to lead to medical malpractice claims that to pay automatically for out-of-pocket losses arising from such procedures, thereby avoiding frequent litigation, would represent a sensible step.[58] It may well be that just as the data gathered by NEISS for the Product Safety Commission would aid the process of formulating criteria for no-fault compensation,[59] so the standards for medical treatment under Professional Standards Review Organizations (PSROs) established under a new congressional enactment can be used. Under the statute, a network of regional review boards will be

Notes on p. 138.

established, each "charged with defining acceptable norms of medical aid and insuring that individual physicians and hospitals meet specified standards of performance."[60] Each PSRO will develop guidelines for a given illness, injury, or health condition specifying, for example, in the event hospitalization is necessary, the probable length of stay required in the course of proper care. Clearly, such data and standards might well be useful in formulating the norms required for no-fault liability insurance. Note, however, that the whole concept of PSROs and their functions has excited intense controversy in the medical profession because of what doctors fear will be rigid and unrealistic definitions of proper care which cannot possibly accurately apply to myriad individual cases.[61] Similar controversy about defining compulsory norms for the purpose of payment of compensation might be expected.

This leads back to a discussion of the two advantages that have made limited no-fault auto insurance so attractive: it is readily and simply developed from the existing fault liability insurance system, and the activity it insures is sufficiently dangerous or distinctive that the payer is readily identifiable.[62] Elective no-fault liability, as we have seen, makes both factors applicable to many other kinds of accidents.[63] Under extrahazardous enterprise liability (whether for medical treatment injuries or otherwise), the second advantage can be viewed as applicable since the legislation (or regulation under legislation) defines who is to pay for what loss. But the first advantage is not necessarily made applicable because there is no guarantee for any enterprise made subject to extrahazardous no-fault liability that its liability will not be greatly or, in the eyes of the applicable business or professional person, unfairly expanded. For that reason, enactment of extrahazardous enterprise liability will probably be resisted much more stoutly by businesses and health care professionals than will elective no-fault liability.

Extrahazardous no-fault liability, then, perhaps even more than its elective counterpart, would present problems; one could cite, in addition to those mentioned above, the general problems of confining some state workers' compensation laws to certain hazardous industries. But all these difficulties must be compared to those which plague the fault system or, at the other extreme, those confronting

Notes on p. 138.

a proposal for scrapping all tort liability for a system covering all injuries under social security.[64]

NOTES

1. *Cf.* O'Connell, "A Balanced Approach to Auto Insurance Reform," 41 *U. Colo. L. Rev.* 81 (1968).

2. For a comprehensive review of the public opinion surveys on this topic, see O'Connell and Wilson, "Public Opinion on No-Fault Auto Insurance: A Survey of the Surveys," 1970 *U. Ill. L. Forum* 307; also appearing in O'Connell and Wilson, "Public Opinion Polls on the Fault System: State Farm versus Other Surveys," 1970 *Ins. L. J.* 261; and O'Connell and Wilson, "The Department of Transportation and Market Facts Public Opinion Polls on No-Fault Auto Insurance," 1971 *Ins. L. J.* 239. But for a report on a statewide vote in Colorado rejecting a no-fault law under an initiative procedure, see *National Underwriter* (Property and Casualty ed.), Nov. 10, 1972, p. 1, col. 4. In that instance, the complications of trying to enact a complex statute by an initiative process render the vote doubtful as a reflection of public opinion on no-fault.

3. J. O'Connell and W. Wilson, *Car Insurance and Consumer Desires* 9 (1969).

4. J. O'Connell and R. Simon, *Payment for Pain and Suffering: Who Wants What, When and Why?* 29–34 (1972); also printed in 1972 *U. Ill. L. Forum* 1, 29–34.

5. *Ibid.*, 21, Table 3.2.

6. *Ibid.*, 26–27.

7. *Ibid.*, 25–28.

8. It might be noted that the occasion for resentment against a so-called tortfeasor is usually even greater for auto accidents than for other accidents. Individuals at least often *think* they know who caused an auto accident and have an immediate confrontation with him. For other accidents — such as product injuries or those from medical treatment — causation is often much more complex, remote, and confused. Also, in the case of such accidents, egregious conduct on the part of businesses or professionals is much more subject to deterrence in the form of peer review and/or adverse publicity, and so on, though not in the form of quasi-criminal proceedings such as traffic fines and the like.

On this subject of what people want from insurance, it is interesting to note that on a much broader scale Columbia University historian Robert Nesbit has recently criticized John Rawls's premise in *A Theory of Justice*, a first sentence of which ringingly declares, "Justice is the first virtue of social institutions, as truth is of systems of thought" (J. Rawls, *A Theory of Justice* 3 [1971]). "As a historian and social scientist," replies Nesbit, "I would not wish, myself, to declare any single virtue sovereign over all others, and capable of being intuitively arrived at. But if I were to speculate on what the majority of us would come up with 'intuitively' along these lines, I think it would not be justice, however defined. More likely it would be *protection* or *security* . . ." (Nesbit, "The Pursuit of Equality," *The Public In-*

terest 103, 110 [Spring, 1974]; see also *supra* chs. 1–5).

9. *Wall St. J.,* March 27, 1972, p. 1, col. 1.

10. O'Connell and Simon, *supra* note 4, at 53, quoting A. Conard *et al., Automobile Accident Costs and Payments: Studies in the Economics of Injury Reparation* 9, 280–81 (1964).

11. Burchard, "Newsletter: Social Science," in *Intellectual Digest,* Sept., 1973, p. 38, cols. 2–3, quoting 8 *Psychiatric News,* no. 1, p. 6, cols. 1–3.

12. Note that between the two coverages payment would be made to cover an entire loss subject to a possible deductible in the excess or secondary no-fault coverage. For example, if health insurance paid only $8,000 out of a $12,000 loss, then the no-fault insurance would pay the remaining $4,000, subject, perhaps, to a relatively miniscule deductible of, say, $100 (*supra,* ch. 8, note 4). See also R. Keeton and J. O'Connell, *Basic Protection for the Traffic Victim: A Blueprint for Reforming Automobile Insurance* 281–83 (1965). In point of fact, given the size of claims probably involved in no-fault liability, it might not be necessary to have any deductible applicable to it. In any event, the deductible would be so comparatively small that it would be insignificant in relation to large losses.

13. *Supra,* ch. 4, notes 6–11 and accompanying text.

14. J. O'Connell, *The Injury Industry and the Remedy of No-Fault Insurance* 97–104 (1971). Nor does it make sense to avoid duplication of payment by allowing an insurance company that has paid under a policy to claim for reimbursement against another insurance company also obligated to pay for the same loss. Such subrogation techniques, it is argued, at least prevent the person paid from collecting twice or more. But the flaw in this argument is that once an efficient loss bearer such as an insurance company has paid for the loss it has collected premiums to bear, it becomes wasteful, indeed, to reshift that loss to a second insurance company. The paper work, along with the costs of adjusters, arbitrators, and perhaps attorneys in reshifting losses, makes for great expense. When premium payers have paid an insurance company to shift the loss once (from us to them), they should not have to bear the expense (ultimately passed on to us) of having the loss shifted all over again to another insurance company. See *ibid.,* 103–4; *infra,* ch. 10, notes 16–27 and accompanying text. But see *infra,* ch. 11, note 1.

15. On the other hand, West Virginia allows the employer, but not the employee, to elect (W. Va. Code Ann. §§ 23-2-7, 23-2-8 [1970]).

16. Concerning this problem as it relates to injuries in the course of medical treatment, see *infra,* ch. 11, note 19 and accompanying text. See also *N.Y. Times,* June 24, 1974, p. 45, col. 3. But see *supra,* ch. 8, note 32.

17. Horovitz and Bear, "Would a Compulsory Workmen's Compensation Act without Trial by Jury Be Constitutional in Massachusetts?" 18 *Boston U. L. Rev.* 35–36 (1938).

18. Concerning the problem of possibly unfair bargains imposed on accident victims, see *infra,* ch. 11, notes 6–16 and accompanying text.

19. If at some point in the indefinite future a social insurance plan were deemed the preferable alternative to handling personal injuries (*supra,* ch. 6, notes 38–51 and accompanying text), experience under a regime of elective no-fault liability — with perhaps compulsory extensions — would offer insight into the broad economic effects of accident compensation and the prob-

lems of charge-back based on distinctive risks (*supra,* ch. 6, notes 34–36 and accompanying text) which would make that final transformation easier.

20. *Supra* note 3 and accompanying text.

21. HEW Secretary Caspar Weinberger, in speaking of the current expenditures for Medicare and Medicaid, amounting to $17 billion a year, stated, "[T]hat is $17 billion we were not spending prior to 1966. Yet older citizens now, seven years after those programs started, have to put up about the same percentage of their income for health costs as they did before — in effect, that $17 billion has disappeared and older Americans are in just about the same cost squeeze that led to the creation of those programs" (Iglehart, "Health Report," *National Journal Reports,* Nov. 10, 1973, 1684, 1685).

22. "If relief in the accident field is to be significantly extended, it may be that levels of compensation will have to be revised, and few would question that if damages have to be restrained non-pecuniary rather than pecuniary awards should be the first to be scrutinized" (Ogus, book review of J. O'Connell and R. Simon, *Payment for Pain and Suffering, supra* note 4, in 1974 *Mod. L. Rev.* 232).

23. O'Connell, "Auto Insurance Reform," *supra* note 1.

24. *Supra,* ch. 6, note 27 and accompanying text.

25. 2 R. Churchill, *Winston S. Churchill: Young Statesman, 1901–1914* 294 (1967).

26. As quoted in Gilbert, "Winston Churchill vs. the Webbs: The Origins of British Unemployment Insurance," *American Historical Rev.,* April, 1966, at 856, quoting, in turn, a document from Churchill to Llewellyn Smith, "Notes on Malingering," June 6, 1909, William H. Beveridge Papers, University of London. (Although I have adapted Churchill's quotation to apply to accidents rather than to unemployment, I believe no distortion of his message is conveyed.)

27. G. Calabresi, *The Costs of Accidents: A Legal and Economic Analysis* 26 (1970).

28. For an indication that between 40 percent and 50 percent of the public does not understand that contributory negligence bars recovery in tort claims, see U.S. Department of Transportation, *Public Attitudes toward Auto Insurance: A Report of the Survey Research Center, Institute for Social Research, the University of Michigan* 71 (1970); J. O'Connell and W. Wilson, *Car Insurance and Consumer Desires, supra* note 3, at 12–13.

29. For a more extensive discussion of why elective no-fault insurance is not extended to property damage, see *infra,* ch. 10, notes 1–6 and accompanying text.

30. See *supra* note 22. "What is the true accident cost including its 'pain and suffering' component? There is a bit of a dilemma. The individual himself is best able to gauge the psychic cost to him of losing a leg, an arm, or an eye. . . . In Calabresi's terminology, the individual worker [under workers' compensation] is the best avoider of these personal, psychic accident costs. Hence, by placing the burden of these costs on him (rather than transferring them to employers), society is likely to come closer to the socially optimal allocation of resources. This is not to imply that all of the accident costs should be borne by the worker, but only the personal 'pain and suffering' component" (Oi, "Workmen's Compensation and Industrial Safety," 1 *Sup-*

plemental Studies for the National Commission on State Workmen's Compensation Laws 41, 60 [1973]).

31. When, as in the case of auto accidents, one is dealing with two individuals (in that case as drivers), fear of higher insurance premiums *may* influence each of them to be more careful to avoid accidents. But to the extent they are thinking that way, they are not really thinking about getting seriously hurt. The minute *that* possibility enters their heads, it is not a financial consideration — such as a denial of payment for personal injury — that exerts much influence, but rather the horror of the specter of personal injury itself. Put another way, to the extent one is concerned about the effect on one's insurance rates of an accident, one is thinking like a business or professional man. In fact, one is thinking of oneself as part of a business enterprise, in this case an insurance company. And to the extent one is careful because of those considerations, one will continue to be so, even though one will be paid despite one's own negligence.

The view, incidentally, of the *individual* against whom a claim is made as an *institution* is reinforced by the fact that, as a practical matter, an individual tortfeasor faces no claim unless he is insured. *Cf.* James and Law, "Compensation for Auto Accident Victims: A Story of Too Little and Too Late," 26 *Conn. B. J.* 70, 78–79 (1952).

32. *Cf.* 2 F. Harper and F. James, *The Law of Torts* § 22.2, at 1204–5 (1956).

33. G. Calabresi, *The Costs of Accidents, supra* note 27, at 26.

34. *Ibid.,* 27.

35. *Ibid.,* 28.

36. Calabresi, "Views and Overviews," in *Crisis in Car Insurance* 240, 250 (ed. R. Keeton, J. O'Connell, and J. McCord, 1968); also printed in 1967 *U. Ill. L. Forum* 600, 610.

37. The costs of its accidents that are properly reflected in an enterprise's costs are, in the economists' argot, "internalized"; costs that are not thus reflected are "externalized."

38. G. Calabresi, *The Costs of Accidents, supra* note 27, at 43–44.

39. It may well be, though, that to the extent a reparation system is paying for pain and suffering and duplicating collateral sources, a rule of contributory fault may serve to reduce accident costs by cutting down on nuisance claims.

40. *Infra,* Appendix IV, note 10 and accompanying text.

41. See Pedrick, "Tangential Introduction," in *Dollars, Delay and the Automobile Victim: Studies in Reparation for Highway Injuries and Related Court Problems* at vii (1968). This is not to say that premium rates cannot be varied according to the risks of smoking. One home insurer, Hanover Insurance Company, a division of the American Group, now offers nonsmokers a 5 percent discount on home insurance premiums in three states — New York, Georgia, and Massachusetts. And the company has asked state regulatory authorities for permission to make the discount available in the rest of the United States (*Christian Science Monitor,* Nov. 9, 1973, p. 1).

42. W. Prosser, *The Law of Torts* § 81, at 534–37 (4th ed. 1971).

43. *Ibid.,* 536; Atlantic Coast Line R.T. Corp. v. Barrett, 101 So.2d 37 (Fla. 1958); Corso, "How FELA Became Liability without Fault," 15 *Clev.-Mar. L. Rev.* 344 (1966).

44. One problem with abolishing payment for pain and suffering while preserving the necessity of proving the defendant or his product faulty or defective is that the latter often makes a lawyer necessary, and it is from amounts paid for pain and suffering that the claimants' lawyers are in fact paid (J. O'Connell and R. Simon, *supra* note 4, at 51; Morris, "Liability for Pain and Suffering," 59 *Colum. L. Rev.* 476, 477 [1959]; Jaffe, "Damages for Personal Injury: The Impact of Insurance," 18 *Law and Temporary Problems* 219, 223 [1953]). But for a proposal calling at least for payment of one-half of the lawyers' fees by the defending insurance company, in addition to payment for the claimants' actual losses, see Keeton and O'Connell, *supra* note 12, at 293–94.

45. Note that if payment for pain and suffering and for collateral sources were generally abandoned in all tort cases, the advantages of not paying would, of course, disappear as incentives to adopt elective no-fault liability. But if elective no-fault liability is not forthcoming — and proposals for it clearly face hurdles and difficulties — the alternatives sketched above might be worth pursuing. Of course, it must be admitted that the abolition of contributory fault will present problems. To some extent, the problems stem from the interaction of the defenses of contributory fault with the concept of proximate cause (Prosser, *supra* note 42, § 66, at 427; Bohlen, "Contributory Negligence," 21 *Harv. L. Rev.* 233 [1908]). Is the manufacturer's product "defective" when it is misused and thereby causes injury? Granted these problems, abolishing the defenses of contributory fault will clearly mean recovery in many cases where recovery is not now allowed. As Prosser puts it, "contributory negligence is not the same thing as abnormal use; and although the two frequently coincide, one may exist without the other" (Prosser, *supra* note 42, § 102, at 670). Second, a manufacturer, for example, might well be justifiably held liable for failure to anticipate general misuse of his product in many more cases if his defense of the plaintiff's particular misuse is abolished. Finally, that the abolition of the defenses of contributory fault can be efficacious is illustrated by the abolition of contributory fault (along with the defense of a fellow servant's negligence) under Employer's Liability Acts. "Such legislation," says Prosser, "has done a great deal to palliate the rigors of the common law ..." (Prosser, *supra* note 42, § 80, at 534). For a discussion of the special problems of abolishing assumption of risk with relation to injuries incurred in the course of medical treatment, see *infra*, ch. 11, notes 17–23 and accompanying text. But for a discussion of generally abolishing in tort law the defenses of contributory fault while retaining under traditional tort suits damages for pain and suffering and the obligation to duplicate collateral sources, see *infra* note 46 and accompanying text.

46. Prosser, *supra* note 42.

47. When an accident concerns two private, noncommercial individuals — as opposed to, say, an individual claiming against a manufacturer or other business or professional enterprise — the question might be asked, Why shouldn't the negligence of the victim count as much as the negligence of the other private party to the accident? In the case, for example, of two motorists colliding, or one neighbor carelessly falling down the carelessly maintained steps of a second neighbor's house, there are several answers. First, as a practical matter accident claims are rarely actually made by one individual against

another. Only when the potential defendant is insured is a claim in fact pursued (*cf.* James and Law, *supra* note 31). As a result, tort claims for personal injuries as a practical matter always entail an individual claiming, in form or in fact, against an enterprise. Conceivably, to take care of the rare case when an individual accident victim actually claims for personal injury losses against another individual, with no insurance involved, one might provide by law that the defense of contributory fault be abolished only when the defendant is insured (or is a corporate self-insurer). Would such a provision encourage people *not* to carry insurance? Hardly. In the case of motorists, insurance is as a practical matter required by law. For others — such as homeowners — the same instinct that prompts people to insure under present tort liability will continue to operate, and, as a practical matter to the same extent — namely, the necessity of preserving one's assets. The fact that some defenses would be available to the uninsured homeowner would scarcely cause a homeowner to go uninsured, given his inability to know in advance whether he would be lucky enough to face only a claim by a careless victim.

48. Moynihan, "Next: A New Auto Insurance Policy," *N.Y. Times,* Aug. 27, 1967, § 6, pp. 26, 82.

49. Pub. L. No. 92-573, 86 Stat. 1207 (1972); 15 U.S.C.A. § 2051 *et seq.* (Supp. 1973).

50. *Supra,* ch. 2, note 1.

51. For a discussion of the NEISS, see *Wall St. J.,* Oct. 30, 1972, p. 5, cols. 3–4; *N.Y. Times,* Nov. 19, 1972, § F, p. 4, cols. 3–8; Klein, "A Product-Injury Surveillance System," *Saturday Review,* Sept. 23, 1972, pp. 67–68; Kelman, "Regulation by the Numbers — the Consumer Product Safety Commission," 36 *The Public Interest* 83 (1974).

52. *Wall St. J.,* Oct. 13, 1972, p. 5, col. 3.

53. *Supra,* ch. 2, note 34 and accompanying text. For a possible means of expediting no-fault payments through the use of health insurers under extrahazardous enterprise liability, see O'Connell, "Expanding No-Fault beyond Auto Insurance: Some Proposals," 59 *Va. L. Rev.* 749, 779–80 n. 102 (1973).

54. If the fear is too great that irresponsible manufacturers will act unfairly in imposing the no-fault bargain on those injured by their products, only those products meeting the safety standards as promulgated by the Product Safety Commission might be allowed to elect no-fault coverage. At least initially, this might be a means of allaying fears in inaugurating elective no-fault insurance (but see *infra,* ch. 11, notes 6–16 and accompanying text). For a similar use of government-sponsored standards under medical elective no-fault, see *infra* note 58 and accompanying text. See also *infra* note 57 and accompanying text for another approach.

55. *Wall St. J.,* Nov. 24, 1972, p. 6, cols. 4–6 [emphasis supplied].

56. *Wall St. J.,* Dec. 12, 1972, p. 22, col. 5. Concerning "internalization," see *supra* note 37. A relatively painless — and economically efficient — way to get "internalization" of injuries is to get the relevant entrepreneur to insure at the point of sale against possible injury costs by the product. This is better than, say, having a health or social insurer pay for all the losses (even assuming the latter is economically feasible; *supra,* ch. 6, notes 13–17 and

accompanying text) in that the latter achieves so little deterrence (*supra,* ch. 6, notes 25–29, 48–51, and accompanying text).

57. Concerning the impossible situation now prevailing in drug cases, see *infra,* ch. 11, notes 24–27. The no-fault compensation to victims stemming from orders of the Product Safety Commission or the Highway Traffic Safety Administration would be made, I suggest, regardless of whether the repairs had in fact been effectuated. And notice to purchasers would indicate the availability of the no-fault benefits. But it need not be feared that this combination would deter those notified from having the repairs made. It would be made clear that compensation would not extend to property damage and thus the normal pressure to avoid that loss would operate (see *supra* note 29). And, in the case of personal injury, insurance of another source of compensation (beyond, say, health insurance) would not seem to induce a lack of care (see *supra* notes 23–32 and accompanying text).

58. For an extensive discussion of a proposal for imposing no-fault liability for injuries in the course of medical treatment, with such injuries and liability being designated by law, see Havighurst and Tancredi, " 'Medical Adversity Insurance': A No-Fault Approach to Medical Malpractice and Quality Assurance," 51 *Milbank Memorial Fund Q.* 125 (1973), also printed in 1974 *Ins. L. J.* 69.

59. *Supra* note 51 and accompanying text.

60. Winsten, "Imposing Controls on Doctors," *Wall St. J.,* Dec. 6, 1973, p. 14, cols. 3–6.

61. *Ibid.; N.Y. Times,* Dec. 6, 1973, p. 1, col. 3.

62. *Supra,* ch. 6, note 2 and accompanying text.

63. But as to insurance for large or catastrophic losses after auto accidents, there, too, uncertainty about the first factor has deterred reform (see *supra,* ch. 2, notes 12–14 and accompanying text). Thus, elective no-fault auto insurance would be one possible way of providing quick coverage for those losses. At the least, meaningful experimentation could be expected (see *supra,* ch. 8, notes 31–32).

64. *Supra,* ch. 6., notes 13–51 and accompanying text.

10

A Question or Two

PART I

Even a lengthy book could not purport to answer all the questions raised by this proposal for elective no-fault liability and the concomitant or alternate proposal for extrahazardous no-fault liability. In a separate work I propose to present a draft statute along with extensive commentary on each section. Suffice it here to present a discussion of some of the more pressing questions about the proposals outlined in this work.*

Why does elective or extrahazardous no-fault liability not extend to property damage?

In the first place, tort liability for property damage does not entail payment for an amorphous item (pain and suffering), the elimination of which can be used to finance paying more victims. Thus, the incentive to any enterprise to agree to pay on a no-fault basis in order to avoid paying for pain and suffering simply does not exist. In other words, the payer cannot agree to pay for less loss by paying automatically on a no-fault basis and still thereby cover the victim's out-of-pocket loss.

Second, although *amorphous* items are not enough a part of tort property damages to encourage potentially liable persons to choose no-fault liability to avoid paying for them, *tangible* items present the

* For a discussion of the constitutionality of the elective proposal, see *infra,* Appendix V.

opposite problem. They are already so commonly covered on a no-fault basis by potential victims' own property insurance that the other part of the no-fault bargain — covering only losses not already covered by the victim's own insurance — is *too* attractive to the potential defendant. It is already possible, and indeed commonplace, to obtain relatively complete insurance coverage for large and expensive items of one's own property (houses, commercial realty, and cars).[1] Thus, a person potentially able to damage others' property is not benefiting his potential victims that much — as is the case concerning their personal injury — when he agrees to pay on a no-fault basis for loss not already covered by the victims' own insurance. Consequently, he should not be allowed to impose that bargain on others. Also, as a practical matter, much property damage involves large commercial items — factory equipment, large generators, and the like — where the damage is caused by one company in a contractual relationship with another company such that the ultimate bearer of the loss is or can readily be the subject of bargaining between commercial parties against the background of sophisticated commercial law under the Uniform Commercial Code.[2] Even with respect to individually owned large items like cars, commonly one insurance company paying under no-fault (collision) benefits will expeditiously settle any claim against the tort liability insurer of the other car involved in the accident under procedures worked out for intercompany arbitration. There is less need, then, at least at the moment, to change these commercial and industry practices with a new and radical law applicable to property damage.[3] It is only with personal injury that massive losses beyond any coverage — and beyond any realistic hope of coverage soon being available — are commonplace. Of course, it is true that natural disasters such as floods and hurricanes can cause such large-scale property damage, but there is no one to surcharge for such "acts of God" — no one there to bargain with, if you will. As to manmade catastrophic disasters such as those from what are so euphemistically called nuclear "incidents,"[4] it is not without significance that, in effect, limited no-fault liability has long been substituted for common law liability under an amendment to the Atomic Energy Act based on an ingenious proposal by Professor David Cavers of the Harvard Law School.[5] But, generally speaking, it makes sense to separate

Notes on pp. 147–48.

compensation schemes for large-scale property damage from those for personal injury.[6]

Won't the fact that elective no-fault liability only pays for losses above those covered by collateral sources mean that those electing no-fault will be paying for fewer losses they cause, thus undermining the aims of market deterrence?

Under so-called market deterrence, it will be recalled, the theory is that having enterprises or activities pay for losses they cause will ultimately reduce the number and severity of accidents.[7] The parameters of the operation of this principle have been suggested by Professor Marc Franklin of the Stanford Law School. Safety incentives are served, says Franklin, when the person marketing a product or providing a service is forced to take into account the accident costs associated with that product or service when deciding whether and how to make or provide it. The basis of this rationale is the defendant's knowledge of, and access to, the intricacies of other product designs, production techniques, and service procedures. If he is forced to bear all accident costs, the businessman or professional will have an incentive to find the optimal accident level for his product or service. In the case of a producer of a product, for example, "[h]e may seek to minimize accident costs by shifting to a slightly more expensive, but much safer, component, or by redesigning his product altogether. He will make such shifts as long as the potential saving in accident liability is at least as great as the added costs associated with the shift. If the producer concludes that it is cheaper for him to pay all accident claims than to alter his production techniques, he will act accordingly and tort law would do little more than compensate the victims. At least, however, to the extent that the law has imposed additional costs on his activity, he has increased financial incentive to search for safer alternatives."[8]

Market deterrence is also served, says Franklin, when consumers are informed of the true costs of products and services in the market price and when the price charged by the producer or professional includes not only the costs, for example, of labor and materials but social costs as well. If social costs are not reflected in price — externalized — then there will be excessive demands for underpriced

Notes on p. 148.

products or services, and the overall allocation of resources throughout society will be distorted. According to Franklin, "In the . . .
product [liability] cases, this argument would require that if two
products appear similar in function and cost of manufacture, but
one causes users or bystanders many more personal injuries, their
prices would reflect this differential so that consumers can be aware
of the actual social costs of the products."[9] And so, to the extent
enterprises are able under elective no-fault liability to reduce their
accident insurance costs, "externalities" would seem to be increased.
Their increases will arguably thereby further distort the economic
indices by which the price system operates.

But several factors must be kept in mind here. In the first place,
generally speaking, the whole problem of externalities is as vexing
and intractable as any facing the study of economics.[10] In one measure, it is true, achieving effective internalization might seem easier
when dealing with personal injury losses, since one is largely dealing
with medical bills and wage loss where one already has a measure
of amounts, as opposed to trying to measure externalities for "amorphous" items like air pollution.[11] But even with reference to personal
injuries, achieving internalization has proved most intractable.

It may well be that the cost of accidents is simply too small,
compared to other costs of doing business, to induce manufacturers
to change their *modus operandi* in the interest of safety or to influence the price of goods and consumer demand for them. The recent
report of the National Commission on State Workmen's Compensation Laws indicates, for example, that for the average employer
"workmen's compensation costs represent only about one percent of
payroll, a relatively unimportant charge compared to wages or to
other fringe benefits which add about 25 percent to straight-time
wages."[12] The commission concedes that "[a]lthough the procedure
used to set workmen's compensation insurance rates should substantially affect the safety records of industries and firms, especially
large firms, it is difficult to demonstrate this relationship statistically. . . . Data suggest again that workmen's compensation insurance rates are not the strongest force affecting the frequency of
accidents."[13]

Patrick Atiyah of Great Britain has similarly expressed doubt

Notes on p. 148.

about the ability of market deterrence to affect resource allocation because of the comparative unimportance of insurance costs:

[A] ... presupposition that is made by [market] ... deterrence is that the market is in fact operating smoothly so that consumer preference is correctly reflected in the prices at which goods are sold. It would be a mistake to underestimate the extent to which the price mechanism still operates in our mixed economy, but there are great distortions produced by government decisions to tax or subsidize this or that activity. Besides these distortions the cost of accidents, or even of disease, pales into insignificance. . . . The total premium for industrial injury insurance in the United Kingdom is 1s 9d. [or about 21 cents] per employed adult male per week, whereas the selective employment tax (levied on service but not manufacturing industry) is now 48s [or about $12.00] per employed adult male per week. The effect of this tax is substantially to increase the cost of services relative to goods with the deliberate purpose of changing the allocation of our resources and so encouraging our export industries. Here therefore the whole policy of the government is to distort the effects of the market mechanism simply because the market has the disastrous effect of encouraging people to buy too many imported goods.

Or again, there is the immense burden of taxation imposed on the motorist in the form of purchase tax on vehicles, excise licence on vehicles, and excise duty on petrol, a burden which amounted to nearly £1,200 million [or about $3 billion] in 1967. There is some doubt whether the motorist pays the total social cost of road accidents in insurance premiums at the moment but even if the entire cost were placed on motorists it could hardly be more than about £300 or £400 million [or about $750 million to $1 billion] per annum. This sounds a large sum and could certainly lead to a substantial misallocation of resources, but when set against the figure of £1,200 million in annual taxation it begins to look less significant. In the face of figures of this kind it is indeed hard to assert with any confidence that placing more costs on the motorist would lead to an improvement in the allocation of national resources, which implies that there is at present "too much" motoring, i.e. that the activity does not pay its full social cost.[14]

Dean Richard Roddis of the University of Washington Law School has noted the additional difficulty of determining with any

Note on p. 149.

precision the optimal level of internalization of the costs of personal injury since multiple causes of injury so often interact:

> Internalization of Accident Costs to [for example] the Motor Vehicle Economy . . . is an economic doctrine which has gained considerable fashion in recent years and particularly so among advocates of "no-fault" automobile insurance. As a general principle of broad economic planning it is a useful idea with which we are all more or less in sympathy. It is not, however, a doctrine which is susceptible to rigid enforcement throughout the economy. From a practical standpoint, it is a goal which is unattainable in a pure sense if for no other reason than that our society does not consist of a series of clearly identifiable separate spheres of activity for economic purposes. The characterization of the "automobile economy" as a subject of internalization is at least partly artificial. Suppose I am employed as an executive of an insurance company with offices in a downtown location and am injured while driving to the office from my suburban home. One could just as well say that the societal sphere to which the accident cost should be internalized is that of conducting an insurance business or that of having office buildings located downtown with employees living in distant suburbs as to say that it is the sphere of transportation or of motor vehicle transportation. Internalization certainly is not a doctrine for the perfection of which a sensible society should pay a great deal. Apart from all academic considerations, as an insurance consumer, my thought would be that internalization is a nice idea but I would rather you did not charge me too much for it.[15]

Perhaps, then, we should be content to know only that a significant portion of personal injury costs are being internalized.

One must grant, though, that not paying when collateral sources pay would likely be a reason for the reduced cost of elective no-fault liability. One must grant, too, that if enterprises were required to reimburse collateral sources through subrogation, internalization of accident costs would be increased. But thereupon a big incentive to elect no-fault — not having to pay to the extent collateral sources pay — would be lost. In addition, subrogation — with its trading of money back and forth between insurers — is extremely wasteful.[16] Better, as under elective no-fault liability, to provide enterprises with an incentive to pay for losses *not* being paid for by other sources — the crucial need — and risk some externalities.

Notes on p. 149.

Granted that several sources of insurance reimbursement should not be paid for the same loss, which insurance system should have primary responsibility for payment?

For years the casualty insurance industry has been insisting on the necessity for it to be the primary payer of accident losses to the point of paying for "loss" regardless of the fact that the loss has already been paid for.[17] But the health insurance industry also stoutly insists that, with its greater efficiency, it should be the primary payer, with casualty insurance paying only to the extent that health insurance does not pay.[18] It is unseemly for these two parts of the insurance industry to be battling to be primary payers to the point that both often pay in smaller cases while the real tragedy of accident compensation is that often neither pays in cases of severe injury. Obviously what ought to happen, in light of health insurance's much greater efficiency in its ability to return so much more of the insurance dollar to victims, is that casualty insurance, less efficient but more experienced in dealing with larger, individualized losses, ought to pay for larger losses to the extent they are not dealt with by other coverages. A problem has been, though, that the casualty insurance industry has doubted that paying only for large losses would support its empire, and thus it has resisted being consigned to an excess insurer status and to paying when other coverages are exhausted. The fear has been especially effective in light of expanding noncasualty coverages in the form of social insurance, health insurance, sick leave, and so on. The casualty insurance industry has feared that being consigned to excess insurer status is to face a continuing rising floor which will ever more displace it.[19] It has also feared being consigned to pay for losses that, as a practical matter, are not now insured by *any* source — either by the victim himself or by the other party to the accident. It is not atypical, for example, for liability insurance to have limits of $20,000. Given the remote possibility of any given potential defendant to face liability of hundreds of thousands of dollars in any given accident, many insureds resist investing in even the relatively modest additional premium to cover catastrophic losses. That reason helps explain why the casualty insurance industry so fears being caught in the squeeze of having someone else insure smaller personal injury losses

Notes on p. 149.

while it is left to cover the catastrophic losses where there is now relatively little market for coverage.[20]

A corollary here is the relatively little casualty loss from personal injury currently being paid from casualty insurance — or from *any* source. Study after study has shown that the really seriously injured accident victim falls into desperate economic straits. As we have seen, among those seriously injured or killed in traffic accidents who suffer $25,000 or more of economic loss, on the average their total loss is $76,341. But the average payment from all sources — tort and non-tort — is only around $23,000, or 30 percent of their losses. According to a Department of Transportation study, "70 percent of those with losses over $10,000 received less than a half their losses," including 6 percent who got nothing from *any* source.[21] And this for traffic victims who, on the whole, fare much better than victims of other kinds of accidents.[22] At the same time, study after study has shown that while the tragically injured are pathetically underpaid, the relatively slightly injured have a much better chance of generous — and often extravagant — payment. Those suffering losses of $500 or under were, on the average, receiving more than twice their losses.[23] Nor is the tragic phenomenon of gross underpayment from a person's own insurance or social insurance for large losses likely to change; witness the pathetically inadequate levels of coverages today under life insurance, health insurance, sick leave, pensions, and the like.[24] Witness, too, how few personal injury losses will be met even by national health insurance (assuming, once again, it ever comes). And with prosperity reaching more and more people (surely the long-range pattern for our society and others), the need for coverage beyond other coverages will be increasingly felt. *That* is the role for casualty insurance as far as personal injuries are concerned.[25]

Far from using casualty insurance dollars to compete with — and often duplicate — the payment of small losses where it is at a disadvantage, and far from using so many of its dollars fighting over mundane matters of fault and contributory fault, elective and/or extrahazardous no-fault liability allows those dollars to be used to meet the great unmet societal need here: paying expeditiously for large losses where there are no other coverages. Elective no-fault liability opens up much greater opportunity for — and experimentation with — this most proper and effective role for casualty insur-

Notes on pp. 149–50.

ance covering personal injury. Elective and/or extrahazardous no-fault liability, along with no-fault auto insurance and workers' compensation, means, then, a worthy and intelligent role for the casualty insurance industry in covering personal injury.[26] Unless it finds such a role, the future of casualty insurance, at least as it applies to personal injury, looks grim indeed. How long will society tolerate the present tort liability system as it applies to products, medical practice, and general liability?

In sum, elective and/or extrahazardous no-fault liability will probably expand and certainly make more sense of the function of casualty insurance as applied to personal injury. If there ever was an industry in need of finding a sensible mission, it is the casualty insurance industry in its treatment of personal injury.[27]

In another practical respect, too, no-fault liability may mean a great advantage to the casualty insurance industry. Trying to predict loss experience under present tort liability is a nightmare. Among other things, an insurer must try to predict under what circumstances a product will be ruled defective or a medical procedure negligent, he must try to predict how much will be awarded for pain and suffering, and he must try to extrapolate present experience into the future with a time lag of many years between claim and settlement or verdict in light of the prolonged arguments over fault, defect, or contributory fault. All this means a horrendous task for underwriters and actuaries in a rapidly changing legal climate.[28] The experience under no-fault coverages is much more stable: claim frequencies and losses (without in the latter case having to pay for the vague variable of pain and suffering) are much more predictable, and the time lag in payment is usually much smaller. Elective and/or extrahazardous no-fault liability will make personal injury coverage more manageable than it can ever be under the highly unpredictable tort liability system that operates today.

NOTES

1. But see Keeton and O'Connell, "Alternative Paths toward Nonfault Automobile Insurance," 71 *Colum. L. Rev.* 241, 260–62 (1971), for a discussion of the no-fault system as applied to car damage. The article is also printed in J. O'Connell, *The Injury Industry and the Remedy of No-Fault Insurance* 157–60 (1971).

2. One can overstate the sophistication of the commercial law here. The Uniform Commercial Code would seem to allow such matters to be handled by bargaining, but the courts, in interpreting the code, are not always so realistic. For example, assume that a manufacturer making a multimillion-dollar piece of equipment is asked to produce spare parts for it. He *may* fear that a forty-five-cent part could malfunction and lead to millions of dollars of damage, but he should be readily able to bargain with the large purchaser (who else buys multimillion-dollar equipment?) to disclaim such liability. Clearly, this would be an arm's-length transaction between sufficiently equal parties. But in the eyes of some the courts have been too prone to interpret such contracts with the precedents of contracts of adhesion and so on (*cf.* Wilson Trading Corp. v. David Furgeson, Ltd., 23 N.Y.2d 398, 244 N.E.2d 685 [1968]), so the manufacturer might well refuse to build the part for fear of the disclaimer or indemnity clause being held invalid. Still, property damage is a severable problem from personal injury. Besides, I can't solve everything!

3. It may be that eventually, for reasons pertaining to "externalities" or charging enterprises with the damage they cause (see *supra,* ch. 9, note 37), enterprise liability might be applied to property damage. But enterprises that are strangers to each other, as indicated above, do not normally inflict vast property damage on one another. As a result, the bargaining of which I speak normally operates to force enterprises to pay for property damage they generate. As to occasions when that is not the case, see *infra* note 4 and accompanying text.

4. A key problem with reference to property damage is that relatively rare but stupendous losses, even compared to losses from serious injury, are overwhelmingly formidable. Compared even to the large damages which can be involved in personal injury cases, writes Patrick Atiyah, "it is still much easier to cause vast losses (in terms of money) by damaging property than by injuring or killing people. . . . [T]he ingenuity of man is constantly devising novel methods of causing widespread property damage — such as spreading oil over the beaches of fishing or holiday resorts — which may cost millions to put right. But it would be a very unusual disaster which caused anything like this liability in terms of personal injury or damage" (P. Atiyah, *Accidents, Compensation and the Law* 144–45 [1970]).

5. Pub. L. No. 89-210, 79 Stat. 855 (1965); Cavers, "Improving Financial Protection of the Public against the Hazards of Nuclear Power," 77 *Harv. L. Rev.* 644 (1964).

6. See *supra,* ch. 9, note 29 and accompanying text.

7. *Supra,* ch. 6, note 27 and accompanying text.

8. Franklin, "Tort Liability for Hepatitis: An Analysis and a Proposal," 24 *Stan. L. Rev.* 439, 462 (1972).

9. *Ibid.,* 463.

10. B. Ward, *What's Wrong with Economics?* 90 (1972).

11. O'Connell, book review of *ibid.,* 1973 *U. Ill. L. Forum* 604, 610.

12. *Report of the National Commission on State Workmen's Compensation Laws,* 124 (1972).

13. *Ibid.,* 96–97. But a close examination of the data used to support the above conclusions indicates that those data might well obscure through the

operation of extraneous variables the effect of workmen's compensation liability on safety. Indeed, it is interesting to note that the data to which the commission refers do not dissuade it from following its intuitive judgment that proper loss allocation *can* have a substantial impact. The commission ends by making the assertion: "We are not prepared to abandon the basic principles of merit rating [whereby an employer's premiums vary with his accident record]. Indeed, we think that the theory of the present procedure [of variation in rates] is basically sound and that merit-rating is a virtue which distinguishes workmen's compensation from other programs providing benefits to disabled workers, such as the Disability Insurance Program of Social Security" (*ibid.*, 98).

14. Atiyah, *supra* note 4, at 596–97. But see G. Calabresi, *The Costs of Accidents: A Legal and Economic Analysis* 86–87 (1971).

15. R. Roddis, "Memorandum to Special Committee to Draft a Uniform Motor Vehicle Accident Reparation Act for the National Commissioners on Uniform State Laws," June 15, 1972. See also Hellner, "Social Insurance and Tort Liability in Sweden," in *Scandinavian Studies in Law* 189 (1972).

16. See *supra*, ch. 6, notes 28–30 and accompanying text. Procaccia, "The Effect and Validity of Subrogation Clauses in Insurance Policies," 1973 *Ins. L. J.* 573.

17. Jones, "The Case for Making Auto Insurance Payments 'Primary,'" 23 *Washington Insurance Newsletter,* No. 46 (1972).

18. McNerney, "No-Fault Auto Insurance Reform: The Blue Cross View," 23 *Washington Insurance Newsletter,* No. 40 (1972).

19. *Cf.* O'Connell, "The Automobile Insurance Industry and Federal Takeover," 36 *U. Chi. L. Rev.* 734 (1969).

20. To the extent losses not eventually being covered by social insurance are very small, incentive to elect no-fault (because paying only for those losses will be relatively inexpensive) will be that much greater. If we ever reach the happy situation where the bargain of elective no-fault liability is too good (keeping in mind that there will be internal limits such as reimbursement of only $200 a week for wage loss and so on), then the legislation could adjust elective no-fault liability by having it become a primary payer — to some extent, at least — when its benefits overlap those of other insurance (*infra* note 25). Also, any no-fault insurance could include scheduled amounts for pain and suffering, as under New Zealand's new scheme (Palmer and Lemons, "Toward the Disappearance of Tort Law: New Zealand's New Compensation Plan," 1972 *U. Ill. L. Forum* 693, 711–12). The incentives to elect no-fault — avoidance of paying for (1) common law damages for pain and suffering and (2) lawyers to make common law factual determinations of fault and/or defects, as well as avoidance of the stigma of tort liability — would still be substantial.

21. 1 U.S. Department of Transportation, *Economic Consequences of Automobile Accident Injuries: Report of the Westat Research Corp.* 41–42 (1970). See also *supra,* ch. 6, note 47 and accompanying text.

22. *Supra,* ch. 2, notes 15–17 and accompanying text.

23. *Supra* note 21.

24. *Supra* notes 21–23 and accompanying text. Concerning life insurance, "[a]n insurance industry survey of widows published in 1970 showed that the

husbands of 92 per cent of those surveyed had carried some kind of life insurance. Yet more than half the widows were left with less than $5,000 in insurance money and only 8 per cent of them received as much as $25,000 from their husbands' insurance. Another study, conducted at the University of Minnesota, suggests that at least 45 per cent of American families are 'seriously' underinsured" (*Consumer Reports,* Jan., 1974, p. 35).

25. Indeed, in order to assure this role a statute enacting elective or extrahazardous no-fault insurance might well preclude other insurers from making themselves co-insurers or excess insurers with respect to such no-fault insurance. As suggested above (note 20), that law might be altered if we ever reached the point where so much loss from accidents is being paid from collateral sources — both governmental and nongovernmental — that a specified percentage of the collateral sources, say one-half, could be repaid by the no-fault insurer as a way of achieving more market deterrence. But concerning the possible encouragement of first-party insurance along with extrahazardous no-fault liability insurance, see O'Connell, "Expanding No-Fault beyond Auto Insurance: Some Proposals," 59 *Va. L. Rev.* 749, 779–80 n. 102 (1973).

Note that there is no need to fear that individuals will buy less life or health insurance, for example, because of the abolition of the collateral source rule with respect to no-fault liability insurance. Their motives for purchasing such life and health coverage are unlikely to be decreased by no-fault liability, given the range of motives that influence such purchases and the myriad sources of ill health and injury not covered by no-fault liability insurance.

26. Another "enterprise" which would find its functions enhanced by no-fault liability insurance would be the Product Safety Commission if extrahazardous no-fault liability were to be imposed based on the commission's determinations (see *supra,* ch. 9, notes 49–56 and accompanying text). Such no-fault product insurance could greatly show to the commission's advantage because the beneficial results of its activity could be so readily seen and measured in lower insurance costs and more money being paid to the injured. These advantages are highly measurable, indeed, whereas the avoidance of accidents as a result of the commission's activity is harder to demonstrate, and its impact is more diffused. People who do not have accidents do not realize it, but when people who are injured are paid more money and paid more promptly, *that* is demonstrable and manifestly heartening.

27. It is true that deducting collateral sources means penalizing people for having them. In other words, the more collateral sources a person has available, the less he will be paid under no-fault liability. On the other hand, there is a rough correlation between one's wealth and the number and amount of one's collateral sources, which means that the more collateral sources one has, the greater are one's medical expenses and especially one's wage loss. Thus, the two often even out in the sense that wealthier people may have more collateral sources deducted, but they claim for larger losses.

28. "In making rates, the actuary relies on an interpretation of a large volume of past experience to indicate what he should expect. If the loss cost per case and the frequencies are relatively stable, and continue so, it is not a difficult task. The volume of business provides the creditability of reliance on past indications as a guide within reasonable narrow limits to the future. But when the basic ingredients of rates — the frequency and average claim

costs — are accelerating rapidly and violently, the ratemaker's problem becomes extremely difficult; the valuations and the projections for the future become unreliable and, as we have learned [in the case of medical malpractice], fall far short of the premium levels necessary to cover the loss and expense ultimately experienced" (Hazam, "Actuary Eyes Rating, Other Problems of Professional Liability on Doctors," *National Underwriter* [Property and Casualty ed.], Nov. 17, 1972, pp. 46, 47, col. 1). See also U.S. Department of Health, Education, and Welfare, *Report of the Secretary's Commission on Medical Malpractice* 41–42 (1973).

11

A Question or Two

PART II

How will these new forms of no-fault liability handle the problem of multiple causes of injury and/or multiple enterprises being liable for injury?

Assume that a power-tool manufacturer, A, has elected to pay no-fault liability for certain injuries, including electric shock, caused by his power tool. Assume further that the electric shock caused to B, who is using the tool, was in fact "caused" not only by A's tool but by a defective extension cord, marketed by C, who had not elected no-fault liability.

The enabling statute will have required those electing no-fault insurance to pay for all or selected injuries "arising out of or in the course of" use of the product or service (or similar terminology). Thus, just as neither the workers' compensation insured nor the no-fault auto insured can normally defend against a no-fault claim on the ground that a proximate cause of the industrial or auto accident was the tort of a third person, so A cannot defeat B's claim on the ground that C's tort was the proximate cause of B's injury. But just as under no-fault auto and workers' compensation insurance the no-fault insurer could be reimbursed from its payee's tort claim, so the no-fault elector and its insurer could be reimbursed from any tort claim against a nonelecting tortfeasor.[1]

Note that occasionally, and perhaps often, one enterprise in a chain of commerce, but not others, may elect no-fault liability. Thus, a retailer might elect to cover on a no-fault basis certain injuries

Note on p. 163.

from a given manufactured product although neither the manufacturer nor the wholesaler has elected to do so. Or, from the other end, a pharmaceutical house may elect to cover for a certain drug's side effects on a no-fault basis, but the doctor prescribing the drug may not. In such situations, any right of the retailer, for example, for indemnity against the manufacturer of a defective product would remain.[2] Note, however, that very often these matters would be handled by bargaining between the parties. Oftentimes such parties will have an incentive to work out the ultimate burden for losses by contract — and often in gross, by standard contract provisions, arranged through trade associations and otherwise. Professor Leonard Ross of the Columbia University Law School, in speaking of the difficulty of implementing a scheme such as no-fault enterprise liability caused by "the need to allocate the cost among various activities responsible for the accident," states that the parties will "recognize the risk and allocate it by contract," especially where enterprises and trade associations are involved.[3] Similarly, under present liability law the courts have been confident that, as between various enterprises in the chain of marketing, such enterprises will be readily able to adjust costs of liability among themselves, regardless of which enterprise is singled out for initial liability.[4] And even where the matter is not handled by such adjustment, note that the placement of any ultimate burden will be fought out between large institutions — insurers and self-insurers — which can afford the time, expense, and expertise required for such bargaining, in contrast to the plight of the injured victim waiting to be paid for his wage loss and medical bills.

When two or more parties, both or all of whom have elected no-fault liability (or who have had it imposed on them by extrahazardous no-fault liability), are liable for the same injury, very often they, too, will be in a commercial chain so that they can easily bargain with each other on the ultimate burden to be shouldered by each. But, as in the case of no-fault auto insurance, the statute will provide that any no-fault insurer paying benefits can recover on a pro rata basis from other applicable no-fault insurers, based on the number of such insurers.[5] Here again, such claims will involve negotiation between insurers or self-insurers.

Notes on p. 163.

If businesses or professionals are to have the option of electing whether to assume no-fault liability and for what injuries to assume it, what guarantee is there that the "bargain" they strike will be fair to their potential victim?

In the first place, substitution of the chance of enforcing liability based on fault by expeditious payment of no-fault benefits is generally not only greatly to the advantage of accident victims but also perceived by them to be so, both before they get involved in accidents and after.[6] It is, of course, conceivable that a given business or professional might try to impose an unfair bargain in substituting no-fault benefits for tort liability. For example, a doctor might try to assume no-fault liability only in cases of obvious tort liability, such as leaving foreign substances like sponges or surgical needles in patients' bodies after surgery. But even there, several safeguards against abuse exist. In the first place, even in such cases, would patients, both as a group and individually, not be better off being guaranteed prompt payment for their economic losses if their resources run out rather than pursuing a right to fight? Keep in mind, too, that doctors would be precluded from exempting themselves from regular tort liability for intentionally inflicted injuries. True, intentional infliction of injuries would be narrowly defined, as under some no-fault proposals, to exclude from the definition of intentional conduct instances of gross negligence or its equivalent.[7] But note that, as under some no-fault auto insurance laws, a person guilty of intentionally injuring another would remain liable for no-fault benefits as well as being liable under regular tort liability.[8] Given the exceedingly difficult job of distinguishing oftentimes gross from ordinary negligence, the danger of retaining regular tort liability for gross negligence is that many claims will be made alleging it in order to gain greater compensation.[9] Certainly those instances in which the law has drawn the distinction (as in allowing the guest passenger in a motor vehicle to recover for his host's gross but not ordinary negligence) have proved to be a nightmare of illogical and tenuous distinctions.[10] On the other hand, a legislature that disagrees could provide that those guilty of gross negligence remain liable both for no-fault benefits and for regular tort liability benefits.[11] The disadvantage of such a provision would be that it would create less incentive to elect no-fault liability since the possibility

Notes on pp. 163–64.

would remain greater of being liable for both no-fault and regular tort liability benefits.

A corollary provision under elective or extrahazardous no-fault liability would provide that although the accident victim who intentionally injures himself is not eligible for no-fault benefits, here, too, "intentionally" is defined to permit payment to the grossly negligent victim.[12] Problems of distinguishing between ordinarily negligent and grossly negligent conduct are thereby avoided here as well. In addition, punishment by the total denial of compensation for further wage loss and medical expenses when the destitute victim's resources have been exhausted is simply too disproportionate even to acts of gross negligence. Granted, for example, that the victim of the power-tool accident had been drinking at the time of the accident: Does it really make sense to deny him expenses for a prosthetic device and rehabilitation if no other insurance is available? Note that no other form of insurance — including workers' compensation, health insurance, or fire insurance — would be denied to the grossly negligent victim.[13] But here, too, a legislature that disagrees could provide that the grossly negligent victim be barred from no-fault payments.[14]

Let us go back to the question of a doctor trying to assume no-fault liability only in cases of obvious tort liability, such as leaving a foreign substance like a sponge or surgical needle in a patient's body after surgery. There are other safeguards against abuse. It would probably not be worthwhile for businesses or professionals, or their insurers, to get approval from an insurance commissioner of an elective no-fault policy which tightly restricts application of the coverage to a very few situations, since the narrower the application of the no-fault policy, the greater the continuation of regular tort liability. Second, a manifestly unfair policy would not be approved by an insurance commissioner.[15] (It might well be that advisory committees of business or professional persons should be established to assist an insurance commissioner in approving given types of elective no-fault policies.) And finally, even if an unfair policy made it by these safeguards, a court would be empowered to invalidate an elective no-fault policy under familiar legal doctrines such as those invalidating unconscionable contracts. In such a case

Notes on p. 164.

the business or professional would be held liable for both no-fault and regular tort liability benefits.[16]

How does elective no-fault affect the patient's "informed consent," traditionally required for medical treatment?

An interesting aspect of the bargain between the potential injurer and his victim is presented by the concept of "informed consent" in medical cases. The HEW secretary's report on medical malpractice describes the doctrine as follows:

> In the absence of [express or implied] . . . consent [from a patient to a doctor for any given medical procedure], liability may be imposed [on the doctor] solely because there was a touching of the patient. In legal theory, it is of no consequence that a medical procedure constituting [an unauthorized touching and therefore] a battery was performed skillfully and improved the patient's health.
>
> Where a patient gives his express consent to a surgical procedure or particular course of therapy, the physician may nevertheless be held liable if the patient can show that he was not adequately informed of the risks and consequences of the operative procedure or course of therapy. In short, the law requires that the consent be an effective or "informed" one, so that the patient can make an intelligent choice from among the various courses of possible treatment, or to refuse treatment altogether.[17]

One should not, however, overlook the complexities of the extent to which the law ought to be encouraging enforced "informed consent" to medical procedures. The American Hospital Association recently approved a so-called Patient's Bill of Rights, which includes the following: "The patient has the right to receive from his physician information necessary to give informed consent prior to the start of any procedure and/or treatment. Except in emergencies, such information for informed consent should include but not necessarily be limited to the specific procedure and/or treatment, the medically significant risks involved, and the probable duration of incapacitation. . . ."[18] Being against such a provision seems a little like being against motherhood (except that in these days of "sexist" charges, the invulnerability of even motherhood as an institution seems no longer to be taken for granted). But Dr. Michael Halber-

Notes on p. 164.

stam (brother of writer David and himself a gifted writer on medical affairs) has written of the difficulties presented by "informed consent":

> Since about 10 percent of claims arise from the patient's contention that he was not adequately advised of the risks of surgery, the "consent forms" used in hospitals have become more and more elaborate. Patients now often sign two forms, one after they have heard an explanation of the risks of surgery in general, the other after the risks of the specific operation have been explained. A parody of these forms recently circulated among the surgeons I know, with the patient acknowledging that "I am aware that after a _____, adhesions may form, clots can develop, sutures may be infected, I.V.'s can infiltrate, aspiration might occur, E.K.G.'s could electrocute me and my wife might run off with my neighbor in my absence."
>
> Behind the parody lurks a real bitterness. Almost every part of a surgical procedure has some attendant risk. There seems to be a tendency by the courts to ignore the general preoperative briefing given in the past by conscientious surgeons (the death rate with this kind of surgery is 1 percent — another 5 percent have serious complications — 15 percent have "no benefit at all") in favor of an explicit warning about the *kind* of complication at issue. Since almost every surgical procedure encompasses a multitude of places where things can go wrong, from pre-op medicines to the recovery room, only a fool would consent to surgery after each hazard had been spelled out in detail. Furthermore, even when the patient does consent, the psychological principle of motivated perception is at work. Told they may develop certain problems, many susceptible people promptly do.[19]

According to the HEW Secretary's Commission on Medical Malpractice:

> Recent judicial decisions in the area of informed consent have imposed an affirmative duty of disclosure upon physicians, whether or not the patient inquires as to specific risks. The Commission notes that the number of cases in which the doctrine of informed consent has been asserted is not large, but further notes that the number is steadily increasing. Moreover, there is some evidence that courts are beginning to apply the doctrine unevenly in order to

Note on p. 164.

hold a physician liable when the patient's injury is severe but he lacks sufficient evidence to prove the physician was negligent.[20]

Arguably, a doctor should remain liable under traditional tort liability for an adverse result which he elects to cover under elective no-fault liability and for which he fails to give the patient adequate warning of the risk. On the other hand, because elective no-fault liability will delineate the risks covered — and specify for whom they are covered — it will likely encourage better focusing on both the risks and information about the risks. If, for example, a doctor knows his no-fault insurance will pay for an adverse result from a given procedure regardless of how it happens, he will be more likely to make sure the patient is in an appropriate condition for the procedure, and he will probably be more likely to discuss those risks with the patient.

On the other hand, given the real problems about the extent to which informed consent should be sought, if litigation over informed consent mushrooms and proves to be cumbersome and wasteful on the scale of other traditional medical malpractice litigation, a case might be made for abolishing the tort action based on lack of informed consent once the doctor agrees to cover the adverse result on a no-fault basis.[21] It might be better to rely only on the burden of having to pay for the adverse result, regardless of fault, and on medical peer group review (which might well be more aggressive with the specter of much-resented malpractice litigation removed)[22] to encourage medical propriety rather than also to continue to rely on civil litigation insulated by impersonal insurance payment, especially where reliance on civil litigation diverts funds from other — and arguably better — uses, namely, payment for out-of-pocket losses.

In any event, health care providers should be required to spell out clearly in their no-fault liability insurance policies the adverse results to be covered by no-fault liability; they might also be allowed to exempt from payment certain categories of patients, also clearly delineated, who are overly susceptible to such adverse results. Generally speaking, a doctor might be required at least to have on file, available for inspection, the terms of his no-fault liability insurance policy, written in language comprehensible to a typical patient,

Notes on pp. 164–65.

explaining which procedures and results are covered by no-fault liability. The extent to which an additional duty of communication of the adverse results covered by elective liability should be required (and the extent to which that duty should differ, if at all, from the normal rules of disclosure of medical risks) should be the subject of further exploration in drafting the enabling legislation. But if a doctor is allowed to include a patient within the exemption from no-fault liability because of the patient's peculiarly susceptible condition, he should probably be required to certify in advance that the patient comes within the terms of the exemption and reveal that to the patient.[23] In the event a patient is thereby exempted from claiming under no-fault liability, any right to claim under regular tort liability would naturally be preserved. Unless such provisions for exemptions are made, it could be argued that health care providers such as doctors and hospitals would be overly inhibited in administering and developing certain procedures or in including as many procedures under their election of no-fault liability.

What is the effect on pharmaceutical houses of rules relating to health care providers?

Manufacturers of pharmaceutical drugs overlap the categories of manufacturers of products and producers of health services. For them, too, no-fault liability based on the calculated risks to some users of their drugs makes much more sense than do the tortuous ratiocinations presently dominating drug cases. Those cases currently abound with unreal exegeses on whether a warning was properly given, to whom it was proper to give it, and whether the victim could be expected to appreciate or honor it, if he knew of it. For example, in March, 1963, one Glynn Davis, aged thirty-nine and in good health, the father of young children, took polio vaccine manufactured by Wyeth Laboratories at a mass immunization clinic; within thirty days he suffered paralysis and other symptoms of polio, and he has remained paralyzed from the waist down ever since. He sued Wyeth Laboratories and, after losing in the trial court, appealed to the Court of Appeals for the Ninth Circuit. The appeals court speculated (*speculated* indeed, as will be seen in the following discussion) whether "means of communication such as

Note on p. 165.

advertising, posters, releases to be read and signed by recipients of the vaccine, or oral warnings (of the dangers of the vaccine)" would have reached Davis, and if reaching him would have affected his behavior.

A special report of the surgeon general, published in 1962, stated: "Present data indicate that for 1962 the paralytic poliomyelitis rate for those under 20 will be approximately 7.6 per million; for those over 20, about 0.9 per million." A further report stated later in 1962: "Because the need for immunization diminishes with advancing age and because potential risks of vaccine are believed by some to exist in adults, especially above the age of 30, vaccination should be used for adults only with the full recognition of this very small risk[!]. Vaccination is especially recommended for those adults who are at higher risk of naturally occurring disease; for example, parents of young children [and Davis fell in this class]...."[24] Said the court of appeals: "While appellant [Davis] was the father of two young children, he resided in an area that not only was not epidemic, but whose immediate past history of incidence was extremely low. We have no way of knowing the extent to which either factor would effect the critical statistics. Thus, appellant's risk of contracting the disease without immunization was about as great (or small) as his risk of contracting it from the vaccine."

Ordering a new trial, the appellate court said that Wyeth Laboratories had "a duty to warn the consumer (or make adequate provision for his being warned) as to the risks involved, [and that] ...failure to meet this duty rendered the drug unfit in the sense that it was thereby rendered unreasonably dangerous."[25]

The negative pregnant of this is that if Wyeth had used means of communication such as "advertising, posters, releases to be read ...or oral warnings" so that Davis might be expected to know of them, liability might not be imposed.

Surely this is an instance in which the consumer is put in an impossible situation. Even assuming that he learns of the warning, how can he rationally weigh the risks when the court itself, after the fact and after exhaustive evidence and exhibits and arguments before it, has "no way of knowing" how those risks would affect him? Better, is it not, in such a case, to identify the risk in gross and indemnify for their out-of-pocket loss the hapless few who are

Notes on p. 165.

struck down rather than litigating endlessly the adequacy of the warning and its possible effect on such individuals, with the attendant possibility of denying them any payment if it is determined they made a wrong choice among choices which are, as the court has to admit, impossible to make very rationally anyway?[26]

Should pharmaceutical houses, like other health care providers, be allowed to exempt certain overly susceptible persons from no-fault benefits? As the situation in the *Davis* v. *Wyeth* case indicates, arguably not. What, though, is the distinction between pharmaceutical houses and, say, doctors in this regard? Doctors must certify the individual patient ineligible for benefits, which a pharmaceutical house is scarcely in a position to do. If it is thought that development of new drugs and/or election of no-fault insurance by pharmaceutical houses would be unduly hindered by the inability to invoke some exemptions from no-fault liability, pharmaceutical houses should not only be restricted to exempting persons susceptible to the adverse results as clearly delineated in their policies, but also should be restricted to exemptions only for drugs used by prescription, and even then only when the doctor, in prescribing the drug, certifies the application of the exemption and reveals that to the patient.[27] One could expect the bargaining relationship between the doctor and pharmaceutical houses to adjust their respective shares of responsibility.

Should elective or extrahazardous no-fault liability be instituted by state or federal government?

This question has no clear answer. Tort law applicable to personal injury is such a mess that any jurisdiction inclined to institute such no-fault liability should be strongly encouraged to do so.

It would seem best if some state could be induced to pass a law permitting elective no-fault liability. That would be a relatively quick and easy way to get significant experimentation, making use of Brandeis' "laboratories" of the states.[28] But given the intransigence of the states in enacting significant no-fault auto insurance reform (often because of the inordinate power of the trial bar in and before state legislatures),[29] federal law might well be resorted to. Given the manifestly interstate nature of insurance,[30] a federal law could allow the substitution of no-fault liability insurance for

Notes on p. 165.

any injuries subject to regular tort liability.[31] Such a federal law, like the federal no-fault auto insurance bill, could provide flexible standards — including variable levels of income replacement, dependent on the average income within the individual state — permitting the states to accommodate the law to their own needs. It could also, as does the principal federal no-fault bill, leave the regulation of insurance in state hands.[32]

A statute mandating the new federal Product Safety Commission to implement extrahazardous no-fault liability on the basis of its injury surveillance system (NEISS) must manifestly be passed at the federal level.[33] But, as to products, a state could set up its own commission to impose no-fault liability on certain dangerous enterprises, perhaps drawing its data from the federal government's injury surveillance system. A state could similarly define the adverse results from medical services to be covered by no-fault liability.[34] It might be that state-mandated extrahazardous no-fault liability would be so disruptive of interstate commerce, in creating such very different burdens depending on which state one operates in, that a federal bill would be best — but not necessarily. A price of our federal system is a wide variety of common and statutory law applicable to many enterprises, and there seems little in personal injury law to render it peculiarly susceptible to a federal rationale.

Nor would the conflict of laws problems presented by state elective or extrahazardous no-fault liability be insurmountable.* Already there is often a multitude of possibilities of law applicable to an accident. Obviously, a defendant liable under a new state no-fault law would face the adverse selection of some victims' "forum shopping."[35] But the terms of any no-fault payment could readily provide that acceptance of no-fault benefits precludes any tort action against the no-fault elector anywhere (other than for common law damages authorized to be brought by a no-fault beneficiary in the no-fault state).[36] Comprehending the difficulties of pursuing a tort claim, most victims will probably be happy to accept automatic no-fault benefits as opposed to pursuing their right to fight. But if the problems of adverse selection seem too forbidding, the party

* When the differing laws of two or more jurisdictions can be seen as rationally applicable to a given case, the issue of which law to apply is said to be one of "conflict of laws."

Notes on pp. 165–66.

electing to pay no-fault benefits could confine eligibility for no-fault benefits to domiciliaries of the enacting state.

NOTES

1. Concerning these rights to reimbursement in a no-fault insurer, see National Conference of Commissioners on Uniform State Laws, *Uniform Motor Vehicle Accident Reparation Act* (*UMVARA*) § 6 and commentary at 30–32 (1972) [hereinafter cited as *UMVARA*]. It is more understandable that a no-fault insurer, such as an elective no-fault insurer or workers' compensation insurer, will and should pursue rights of reimbursement more than a social or health insurer would. See *supra*, ch. 6, note 51.

2. Concerning rights of indemnity, see W. Prosser, *The Law of Torts* § 51 (4th ed. 1971).

3. Ross, book review, 84 *Harv. L. Rev.* 1322, 1325 (1971). Note that trade associations, and, in the case of health care providers, boards of specialties as well as state and county medical societies, etc., would probably aid in formulating and recommending elective no-fault coverages for their members.

4. See R. Keeton, *Venturing to Do Justice* 106–7 (1969).

5. See *UMVARA*, *supra* note 1, § 4(c)(3).

6. See *supra*, ch. 9, notes 3–8 and accompanying text.

7. See *UMVARA*, *supra* note 1, § 5(b) and commentary at 25–26, 30; see also R. Keeton and J. O'Connell, *Basic Protection for the Traffic Victim: A Blueprint for Reforming Automobile Insurance* 276–77, 304, 394–95 (1965).

8. This is the rule, for example, in Hawaii (Hawaii Rev. Stat. § 294-6[c] [2][1973]) and Michigan (Mich. Stat. Ann. § 24.13135[2][a] [Cumm. Supp. 1974]). See also *UMVARA*, *supra* note 1, § 5(a)(3) and commentary at 25, 28; Keeton and O'Connell, *supra* note 7, at 395–96. A doctor guilty of gross negligence would be subject to criminal prosecution. An Illinois statute, for example, which makes reckless conduct criminal, could be applied to a doctor (Ill. Rev. Stat., ch. 38, § 12-5 [1973]). Admittedly, though, a review of the cases illustrates few such prosecutions, and then only where death has ensued (45 A.L.R.3d 114 [1972]). But perhaps the lack of criminal prosecutions tells us something about how rare heinous medical conduct is. If the object of the victim and his family is retribution, a criminal sanction seems better suited than a civil action for damages. If compensation is the aim, no-fault liability seems a better avenue.

9. Of course, a form of tort fines could be instituted for reckless conduct, payable over and above no-fault benefits for pecuniary loss, but if a health care provider remains liable for damages over and above no-fault benefits in an accusatory proceeding, the attractions of electing no-fault liability are diminished. Concerning any fear that freeing doctors from liability will lessen deterrence of unsafe medical practices, one must consider the sorry state of the deterrent effect of traditional malpractice liability (*supra*, ch. 3, notes 32–45 and accompanying text. See also Glazer, "Perspectives on Health Care," 31 *The Public Interest* 110, 122 [1973]). No-fault workers' compensation, it is generally conceded, led not to less but to more incentives for safer prac-

tices (G. Calabresi, *The Cost of Accidents: A Legal and Economic Analysis* 245–46 [1970]; 2 F. Harper and F. James, *The Law of Torts* § 13.5, at 773–75 [1956]). Concerning no-fault insurance and deterrence of unsafe medical practices, see also O'Connell, "Expanding No-Fault beyond Auto Insurance: Some Proposals," 59 *Va. L. Rev.* 749, 793 n. 127 (1973).

10. Prosser, *supra* note 2, § 34.

11. Generally speaking, under no-fault auto insurance laws the drunken driver, or the driver otherwise guilty of gross negligence, is not liable under traditional tort liability, but only for no-fault benefits, as are other drivers. E.g., see Mass. Ann. Laws, ch. 90, § 34A (Cumm. Supp. 1972) as amended ch. 599 (1973) Mass. Laws; Mich. Stat. Ann. § 24.13105(4) (Cumm. Supp. 1974).

12. *UMVARA, supra* note 1, § 22 and commentary at 54–55; see Keeton and O'Connell, *supra* note 7, at 394–98.

13. J. O'Connell, *The Injury Industry and the Remedy of No-Fault Insurance* 130–35 (1971); Keeton and O'Connell, *supra* note 7, at 396–97.

14. Generally speaking, no-fault auto insurance laws have split on this question. Several states indicate that policies can be drawn to bar the grossly negligent victim from being paid. E.g., see Fla. Stat. Ann. § 627.736(2) (1972); N.Y. Ins. Law § 672 (McKinney 1973). Other states do not permit such a bar. E.g., see Mich. Stat. Ann. § 24.13105(4) (Cumm. Supp. 1974); Keeton and O'Connell, *supra* note 7, at 396–97.

15. See R. Keeton, *Basic Text on Insurance Law* § 2.10(b) (1971).

16. Such doctrines, preventing unfair advantage to an insurer under an insurance policy, are many and varied (*ibid.,* ch. 6).

17. U.S. Department of Health, Education, and Welfare, *Report of the Secretary's Commission on Medical Malpractice* 29 (1973) [hereinafter cited as HEW Secretary's Commission Report]. For a discussion of the battery theory plus a theory of negligent failure to disclose the risks of the medical procedure, see Wilson v. Scott, 412 S.W.2d 299 (Tex. 1967).

18. American Hospital Association, *A Patient's Bill of Rights* (1972).

19. M. Halberstam, "The Doctor's New Dilemma — 'Will I Be Sued?' " *N.Y. Times,* Feb. 14, 1971, § 6, pp. 8, 34–35. Dr. Henry Greenberg, a staff cardiologist at New York's Roosevelt Hospital, has commented on the general ignorance of and indifference to medical information on the part of the public, both generally and as it applies to a patient's given condition: "There is little public cry for medical information and no demand for appropriate education, and few patients ask for meaningful explanations of illness" (Greenberg, "℞ for Conciliation," *N.Y. Times,* Feb. 20, 1974, p. 35, cols. 2–3).

20. HEW Secretary's Commission Report, *supra* note 17, at 29.

21. See *ibid.* Speaking of a similarly complex issue of "permission," Robert E. Keeton writes: "Applying the criterion of 'permission' under the omnibus clause of an automobile insurance policy typically involves disputed issues of both fact (*e.g.,* what was said or otherwise communicated by the named insured to the driver about the use of the car, and what was the use that was going on when the accident occurred?) and evaluation (*e.g.,* was the use within the scope of the permission express or implied in the communication between the named insured and the driver?). This interrelation between fact

issues and evaluative issues commonly leads courts to submit the entire mix to a jury rather than treating the evaluative issue as one for the courts. As is well illustrated by the issue of permission under the omnibus clause of automobile policies, the interrelation between fact issues and evaluative issues also tends to breed litigation" (R. Keeton, *supra* note 15 § 1.6, at 24). For a criticism of American law as involving too many such complex "decision points," see J. Frank, *American Law: The Case for Radical Reform* 85–110 (1969); on this point, see also O'Connell, *supra* note 13, at 154.

22. See *supra,* ch. 3, note 45 and accompanying text.

23. In other words, it might be sensible — in light of the dangers of wholesale revelation of risks — to allow a doctor simply to inform the patient of the availability of a list of risks covered by his no-fault insurance for examination by an interested patient (followed by a discussion, if the patient desires). But in the relatively rare case when the risk is so great the doctor does not wish to assume it, the patient would have to be told in order for him to be able to decide whether he wishes to assume it.

24. Davis v. Wyeth Laboratories, Inc., 399 S.2d 121 (9th Cir. 1968).

25. *Ibid.,* 124.

26. *Ibid.,* 130. Making the question turn on the adequacy of the warning, in the eyes of most courts, moves the issue back to one of negligence as opposed to strict liability (Basko v. Sterling Drug Inc., 416 F.2d 417 [2d Cir. 1969]).

27. See Merrill, "Compensation for Prescription Drug Injuries," 59 *Va. L. Rev.* 1 (1973).

28. The states, said Brandeis, should serve as "laboratories" to "try novel social and economic experiments without risk to the rest of the country" (New State Ice Co. v. Liebmann, 285 U.S. 262, 311 [1932] [dissenting opinion]).

29. "[No-Fault Automobile Reform] ... has run into a stone wall in state legislatures across the country.... In state after state, the plan has been defeated or bottled up in committees, often through the efforts of powerful lobbies of lawyers' groups and insurance companies, both of which are heavily represented among members of state legislature" (*N.Y. Times,* Nov. 15, 1970, p. 70, cols. 4–5; see also *N.Y. Times,* May 9, 1971, p. 60, cols. 1–3).

30. U.S. v. South-eastern Underwriters Assoc., 322 U.S. 533 (1944).

31. See Griswold, *Hearings on S.354 before the Senate Committee on the Judiciary,* 93d Cong., 1st and 2d Sess. 747–69 (1974).

32. S. 354, 93d Cong., 2d Sess.

33. *Supra,* ch. 9, note 51 and accompanying text.

34. *Supra,* ch. 9, note 60 and accompanying text.

35. Assume that State X enacts an elective no-fault law and that A, a domiciliary of State Y (which has not enacted such a no-fault law) is injured by the product of B Co., an X corporation electing no-fault coverage for the type of injury suffered by A. If A had no valid tort claim he would claim no-fault benefits, perhaps coming into State X to improve his likelihood of gaining them (though the courts of State Y might be as inclined to award them to him). But if A had a valid tort claim and sued B in State Y, the courts of State Y would most likely allow that claim (as indeed might the

courts of State X). Thus, B Co. faces "adverse selection" by victims from outside State X — no-fault claims by those without valid tort claims and tort claims by others.

36. It will be recalled that a no-fault elector might be allowed to cover multiples of $10,000 on a no-fault basis, preserving tort suits above that amount (*supra,* ch. 8, note 30 and accompanying text).

Coda

Start from the premise that everywhere in the world, even after extensive private and social insurance programs have paid for personal injury losses, large losses remain uncompensated for at least some accident victims. Even in Sweden, with its model (and hugely expensive) programs of social insurance, according to Jan Hellner, "even for those entitled to full protection [from the systems of public and private protection] there are important gaps in the reparation. No existing kind of insurance [for example] gives sufficient protection when an injured person is in need of expensive permanent care."[1] If that is true for Sweden, to that much greater an extent is it true everywhere else in the world — and especially in the United States, with its relatively niggardly programs of social insurance.

Start, too, from the premise that, worldwide, programs of health insurance or social insurance are relatively weak in achieving market deterrence of accidents. To use Sweden as an example once again, provisions allowing the general health insurance scheme subrogation against tortfeasors have been abolished. According to Hellner: "Subrogation against those who had acted intentionally or with gross negligence [the only instances where subrogation was allowed] had proved absolutely worthless. With respect to accidents due to motor traffic, the earlier subrogation rested on the idea that motor traffic should help to carry the burden of acute illness caused by motor accidents. But the sums received were never great . . . and social insurance had no wish to spend time on investigating the injured victim's right to tort damages in order to get these comparatively small sums."[2] And even where such subrogation rights are preserved, they are often fraught with many procedural difficulties,[3]

Notes on p. 170.

and, even more basically, they entail the waste of insurance money being used to transfer losses already paid by a more efficient insurer to a less efficient insurer.[4]

Start finally from the premise that tort liability, as imposed everywhere in the industrialized world, is extremely cumbersome, calling for extensive, expensive argument over who was at fault. Generally speaking, in Europe neither a presumption of liability nor rules of comparative negligence alter the basic need to dissect individual accidents, as in the United States, in order to base payment on precise appraisal of supposed human error.[5]

Under either elective or extrahazardous no-fault liability, once the insured event is simplified to eliminate, wherever feasible, arguments over who or what is to be paid by virtue of no-fault insurance, tort law can more readily perform two essential functions: it can concentrate on providing compensation in those cases of large losses where all other sources of payment have been exhausted, and it can, by providing a mechanism for surcharges based on risk creation, help to lessen accidents and accident costs through market deterrence without the waste of subrogation claims.

Note that to the extent uncompensated losses loom very large for many people (as in the United States), a scheme of tort liability that calls for those creating risks of loss to pay automatically for economic losses not met by other (so-called collateral) sources achieves all three goals of (1) simplifying the insured event, (2) covering crucial unmet losses, and (3) achieving with some efficiency some market deterrence of accidents.

Actually, the need to structure tort law so that it pays this way on a genuine no-fault basis, wherever feasible, is great all over the world — whether the amount of loss not being met by other sources of payment is large or small. To the extent that the total amount is relatively small, tragic cases presenting great social need can be solved for relatively little money. (Nor is a better answer to simply expand social insurance to cover all losses. To cover all losses from *all* injuries or illnesses might well be prodigiously expensive anywhere in the world.[6] Recent elections in Sweden have been seen as a rebuke to plans for ever more social insurance there.)[7] All the more sense, then, in taking money now being paid for liability insurance — and often mispaid to determine precise accident causa-

Notes on p. 170.

tion, to cover losses already covered from other (more efficient) sources, or to pay for noneconomic losses (pain and suffering)[8] — and to allow such money to be used as efficiently as possible to pay for unmet losses.

In other words, to the extent those unmet losses are relatively small, the task of using liability insurance money to pay a significant portion of them is all the more manageable. On the other hand, to the extent those unmet economic losses are vast, the need to at least use liability insurance dollars to pay as many of them as possible — to use this ready source of money to meet as much as possible of that great social need — is all the greater. When unmet losses are vast, it is all the more tragic to be misspending precious insurance dollars on lawyers to determine precise accident causation, to cover losses already paid from other (more efficient) sources, or to pay for noneconomic losses.

To view all this another way, there are three sources of savings in the United States from no-fault insurance compared to regular tort liability, one or more of which (and more likely at least two of which) are applicable in other countries as well: (1) eliminating determinations — usually by lawyers or, at the least, insurance personnel — of precise questions of fault, (2) eliminating duplicate payments for losses covered by collateral sources, and (3) eliminating payments for pain and suffering. All countries in varying but substantial degrees suffer from determining precise questions of fault. A few do not have tort damages duplicate — even with subrogation — payments from other sources, and some do not allow large payments for noneconomic loss (though increased payment for pain and suffering seems a growing phenomenon almost everywhere in the developed world).[9] As a result, any country will likely be able to utilize one or more of the above savings under no-fault insurance.

Since, therefore, any nation that examines its experience will find that there are significant personal injury accident losses not being met by other sources of payment and that its tort law can be simplified so that money can be found to meet more of those losses, either elective or extrahazardous no-fault liability insurance — or both — makes sense (1) for a country like Sweden which has a high level of both tort damages and social insurance, (2) for a

Notes on p. 170.

country like the United States which has a high level of tort damages but a low level of social insurance, (3) for a country like Spain which has a low level of both tort damages and social insurance, and (4) even for a country like the Netherlands which has a high level of social insurance and a low level of tort damages (although admittedly less is relatively available from tort law to fill gaps in social insurance in such a country; still, what is available ought to be used).

The United States — along with many other industrialized countries — began to apply genuine no-fault insurance to work accidents shortly after the turn of the last century. It would be ironic in the extreme — with all the changes that have taken place in the developed world since the early 1900s — if we were all to wait to attempt to apply it to all kinds of accidents until the turn of the *next* century.

NOTES

1. Hellner, "Analysis of the Swedish Auto Accident Compensation System," in U.S. Department of Transportation, *Comparative Studies in Automobile Accident Compensation* 115, 131 (1970).

2. *Ibid.*, 124–25.

3. See Durin, "Sources of Reparation for Automobile Accident Victims in France," in A. Conard *et al., Automobile Accident Costs and Payments: Studies in the Economics of Injury Reparation* 455, 466 (1964); 1 H. Mazeaud and A. Tunc, *Traité théorique et pratique de la responsabilité civile* [Practical and theoretical treatise of civil liability] §§ 232–71 (5th ed. Paris: Éditions Montchrestien, 1958); D. Durin, *Des recours des caisses de sécurité sociale en matière d'accidents* [On the recourses of the social security funds in cases of accident] (Paris: Librairie générale de droit et de jurisprudence, 1962); M. Dahan, *Sécurité sociale et responsabilité* [Social security and liability] (Paris: Librairie générale de droit et de jurisprudence, 1963).

4. See *supra,* ch. 6, notes 28–30.

5. For a description of French, German, British, and Swedish law, see U.S. Department of Transportation, *supra* note 1; see also R. Keeton and J. O'Connell, *Basic Protection for the Traffic Victim: A Blueprint for Reforming Automobile Insurance* 189–219 (1965); A. Conard *et al., supra* note 3, at 415–83.

6. See *supra,* ch. 6, notes 14, 17, 21–24.

7. Nossiter, Washington Post–Outlook News Service, week of Oct. 7, 1973.

8. Although payment for pain and suffering is not as extensive in Europe as in the United States, it is apparently escalating all over the world. J. O'Connell and R. Simon, *Payment for Pain and Suffering* 5 (1972), also printed in 1972 *U. Ill. L. Forum* 1, 5.

9. *Ibid.*

Summary

The passage of quite limited plans of no-fault auto insurance does nothing to aid victims of non-automobile-related accidents — for example, people injured by other manufactured products or through medical malpractice — nor does it help those who sustain large losses in traffic accidents. These less fortunate victims must resort to traditional tort litigation, where the delay and expense of proving fault or a defective product and the pecuniary value of nonpecuniary loss operate to oppose their interests and needs and often only add insult to injury.

The problems of these other losses are both different from and similar to those for small and medium-sized auto claims. In both cases, it makes sense to eliminate, if possible, an overly cumbersome insured event that makes so likely case-by-case disputes over payment after an accident. In both cases the issues of fault (or its analogue, a product defect) and the payment for pain and suffering contribute most heavily to the cumbersomeness of the insured event.

The difference is often in the existence of nuisance claims. And cases other than small and medium-sized auto claims are often both better and worse than such auto claims in this regard: better in the sense that nuisance claims are much less likely, with therefore less overpayment of small claims, and worse in the sense that any payment at all is much less likely. Proof of fault or defect is so cumbersome in such cases (especially product liability and medical malpractice cases) that they tend, unless the claim is very large, simply not to be worth pursuing.

But in both auto and non-auto accident cases, arguably the worst

problem stemming from the tort liability system lies in the underpayment of large losses. In auto cases this problem is especially
compounded by the reverse tragedy of overpayment of small losses.
That dual phenomenon, indeed, made no-fault insurance applicable
to small and medium-sized losses so sensible because one could
thereby eliminate much of the waste applicable to small losses and
apply the funds thereby saved to large ones (or to lower premiums
— less desirable, from a social viewpoint, perhaps, but *so* politically
palatable). But one reason some reformers of auto insurance have
shied from trying to solve the problem of the catastrophically injured
traffic victim has been uncertainty about what that solution would
cost.

As another way of looking at all this, much of the auto problem —
that relating to small and medium-sized losses — was relatively susceptible to solution because for such losses everybody was already
mutually insured, albeit for tort liability. It was thus relatively easy
to shift around and force everyone to insure himself under efficient
no-fault auto coverage rather than forcing him to insure the other
fellow under inefficient fault coverage. But for massive losses — and
for losses not related to auto accidents — such mutual coverage was
not by any means universally available, and thus the switch could
not so readily be imposed. As a result, limited no-fault auto insurance
leaves us not only with a lack of coverage for the more seriously
injured traffic victim but even much less assured compensation for
other accident victims. How to apply the virtues of no-fault reform
to this remainder?

In the first place, keep in mind that the key problem is compensating for losses not now being met. Keep in mind, too, that with
expanding sources of coverage from both social and private insurance, more and more losses are being paid for — although progress
in expanding coverages is exasperatingly slow. Also keep in mind
that it probably will not be financially or politically feasible in the
foreseeable future to simply abolish the tort system and substitute
compensation for accident victims from social insurance. Thus, a
separate system of casualty insurance will most likely remain with
us indefinitely, no matter how slowly or speedily we expand other
forms of insurance.

How, then, to make (more) sense of the rest of tort liability remaining after the passage of no-fault auto insurance? It does not seem immediately — or perhaps even ultimately — feasible to have tort law payable for all injuries without regard to fault, given the new and perhaps unmanageable burdens this will impose on many, and given the difficulties of deciding, once fault is no longer a factor, who should pay for what. But one workable experimental scheme would be to allow anyone in a position to do so to shift all or part of his tort liability for personal injury based on fault to liability not based on fault. Elective no-fault liability, taking a leaf from elective workers' compensation, allows anyone to elect to be covered up to any multiple of $10,000 or for unlimited pecuniary losses by no-fault liability for all or designated risks he chooses that stem from his activity. Neither contributory negligence nor assumption of risk would be a defense to elective no-fault liability. But such liability would be limited to payment for out-of-pocket losses in excess of all collateral sources, subject also to modest wage loss limitations. Neither would payment be made for pain and suffering.

Upon electing no-fault liability coverage, the electing party would be exempt from regular tort liability for pecuniary losses thus covered plus corollary nonpecuniary losses.

Note the incentives for an insured to substitute elective no-fault liability for common law tort liability: he would thereby eliminate paying for (1) pain and suffering, (2) collateral sources, and (3) expenses of determining both fault (or the existence of a product defect) and the value of pain and suffering. Also, of great importance to manufacturers and doctors, for example, the *stigma* of liability would be substantially — and most often, totally — removed. (No one, however, could preclude his own common law tort liability for intentionally caused injuries, nor could any victim claim elective no-fault benefits for an injury intentionally inflicted on himself.)

In effect, elective no-fault liability allows anyone in a position to do so to adopt the advantages of no-fault insurance. With other than auto accidents smaller than, say, $10,000 there has been no mutual and universal fault liability insurance covering others' losses that is switchable to no-fault insurance covering the insured's own losses. But under elective no-fault liability, anyone carrying fault liability insurance covering others' losses may find it feasible to substitute no-fault liability for those losses, subject to possible selections by the insured of limitations on risks and amounts to be covered by no-fault.

As an alternative or as a supplement to elective no-fault liability, extrahazardous no-fault liability, taking a leaf from workers' compensation imposed for only certain hazardous employment, imposes such no-fault liability, for named risks only, on enterprises designated by law as especially risky.

Accidents from medical malpractice or manufactured products, for example, pose great problems for conversion to universal or compulsory no-fault insurance because there is neither: (1) an already extant system of widespread fault liability insurance readily and simply transferable into no-fault loss insurance without, therefore, much fear that the transformation would impose new and unmanageable burdens on anyone, nor, generally speaking, (2) a sufficiently dangerous and defined activity (for example, driving) that a statute can readily identify who is to pay for what loss. Note, however, that elective no-fault liability makes both these parameters applicable to many kinds of accidents other than small auto accidents because: (1) electors can decide for themselves if their fault liability insurance is readily and simply transferable into no-fault loss insurance, without thereby fearing that the transformation will impose new and unmanageable burdens on them, and (2) similarly, the decision as to who is to be required to pay for what loss is not left open-ended but is defined by the elector in his own elective no-fault liability policy.

Under extrahazardous no-fault liability, the second parameter is made applicable since the legislation (or regulation under the legislation) defines who is to pay for what loss. But the first parameter is not necessarily made applicable because there is no guarantee for any enterprise made subject to extrahazardous no-fault liability that its liability will not be *greatly*, or, in the eyes of the business or professional, unfairly expanded. For that reason, enactment of extrahazardous no-fault liability might well be much more stoutly resisted by businesses and health care professionals than will elective no-fault liability.

In sum, no-fault liability (elective and/or extrahazardous) accomplishes the following:

1. It helps tort liability for personal injury (of which such no-fault liability will be a part) accomplish a goal peculiarly appropriate for it — relatively individualized payments for large losses not met by other more efficient but generalized forms of payment, such as social security or health insurance, which, though growing, will continue to remain inadequate, especially for coverage of wage loss.

2. It accomplishes this in a way that eliminates, where feasible, the wasteful arguments about fault and the pecuniary value of non-pecuniary loss that dominate tort liability today.

I

More Sly Tricks

To illustrate the slippery, treacherous slopes involved in personal injury trial tactics, consider the following example from an actual case in California. On June 25, 1954, Mrs. Paula Daggett and her two children were killed in a collision between their automobile and an Atchison, Topeka, and Santa Fe Railroad train operated by engineman Glenn H. Benton. The accident took place on the Plaza Street crossing in Solano Beach, California. As a result of the accident, John Daggett, husband and father of the dead woman and children, brought suit against the railroad and Benton on the grounds of the engineman's negligence in operating the train.

At the time of the accident, the speed limit for trains in this district was generally ninety miles per hour, although it was less in certain places such as curves. After the accident, in the interests of greater caution, the railroad changed the speed limit at the accident site to fifty miles per hour. Now the rule of law is that such a change cannot be admitted in evidence as tending to show that the first practice was unsafe. Allowing such evidence of a change would obviously discourage the institution of safe practices, since the defendant would always fear that his change for the better was an admission of his earlier dereliction, when in fact both before and after he may have been acting in a safe and proper way, with the later precaution being just that much safer.[1]

There is also another rule of law, however, that allows a cross-examiner to use contradictory evidence to show that what has been testified to is wrong — to "impeach" the witness in the language of the law. Thus, if, for example, the engineman on his own testified that the speed at the accident site was *now* ninety miles per hour,

Note on p. 182.

it might be proper to show that in fact it was now fifty miles per hour. This would be admitted in evidence not for the purpose of establishing the subsequent precaution in order, in turn, to show the inadequacy of the earlier speed limit, but *only* for the purpose for undermining the witness's credibility.[2] In other words, the jury would be asked to consider the evidence only as it affects the engineman's veracity as a witness but would be supposed to shut its mind to the more dramatic meaning of the evidence — namely, that the railroad had been unsure enough of its earlier speed limit to revise it downward, thus indicating that the former speed may have been too high (and therefore negligent) in the first place. There is obviously some doubt whether the jury can be expected to consider the evidence only for the less dramatic reason, but, at any rate, that is the theory behind its admission.

Note that since the rule allows the evidence to be admitted for the one purpose and not the other, and since there is doubt whether the jury can really keep the scope of the evidence confined in its mind, a lawyer is under a tremendous temptation to pretend to want to introduce the change in speed limit supposedly for the purpose of impeachment but actually to get before the jury the all-important fact of change which seems to suggest the crucial factor of negligence. In the case of *Daggett* v. *The Atchison, Topeka, and Santa Fe Railroad,* there was some indication that the engineman did testify that the speed limit was now ninety miles an hour, and Melvin Belli, representing the plaintiff, seized upon this to show that the speed had been changed to fifty miles per hour — and thus Belli got this crucial fact before the jury.

In order to understand how Belli got himself into the fortunate position of having the engineman apparently make the mistake of saying the speed limit was now ninety miles per hour, it is important to note that there were two speed limits in question: the general speed limit of ninety miles per hour was in effect in the so-called fourth district, which ran between Fullerton and San Diego, California, and included the Plaza Street area of Solano Beach, the site of the accident in question. But *within* the fourth district, as suggested earlier, there were slower speed limits on curves and in other places. Before the accident, then, the Plaza Street area of Solano

Note on p. 182.

Beach was not a place with a slower limit, but it became one after the accident.

Read the following transcript of Belli's cross-examination of Benton, the engineman. To what extent are any confusions concerning speeds, times, and districts invited or brought about by Belli himself? Keep in mind how much Belli is tempted to seize upon any such confusion (to the extent that it exists or that he can get it to exist) to get before the jury the otherwise inadmissible evidence of the change in speed limit after the accident. (All italics have been added to the original transcript.)

"[By counsel for plaintiff] What *was* [at the time of the accident] that crossing posted for as far as the railroad was concerned? A. 90 miles an hour. * * *

"Q. Now, with reference to whether you were early or late, were you late on that run, on that day? A. We were. We were late. * * *

"Q. And where was the place to the Los Angeles side of Solano Beach where you had last attempted to pick up some time? A. The speed restriction down *at the district* is 90 miles per hour, *with the exception of where there is curve restrictions or restrictions otherwise.* * * *

"Q. Well, how fast *did* you usually go across that intersection in Solano Beach? A. Between 80 — between 80 and 90 miles per hour. * * *

"Q. But across this intersection your speed varies [note present tense used by counsel for plaintiff] between 80 and 90 miles an hour. Right? A. Yes, sir. * * *

"Q. Could you go as fast as 90 miles an hour around this curve that comes into Solano Beach or *is* [note the present tense] that restricted to less? A. That is 90 miles an hour.

"Q. And do I understand that you could go 90 miles an hour all the way from Los Angeles to San Diego? A. No, sir, because *there is restrictions, curve restrictions, and other forms of restrictions.*

"Q. How about that curve from Cardiff into the place of the accident; isn't [note present tense] that curve restricted to 85? A. That's a 90 mile an hour curve. * * *

"Q. * * * Now, you have driven these diesels similar to the one you were driving on that day for some time, haven't you? A. Yes, sir.

"Q. And in driving those diesels, have you gone over 90 miles an hour with them? * * * A. I have. Those diesels are a hundred-mile-an-hour diesel, but *that* particular *district is 90 mile restriction* down there. *That's known as the fourth district.* * * *

"Q. What does fourth district mean; can you tell us? A. Well, that's the district from one station to the other.

"Q. That has nothing to do with the type of speed, does it? A. No.

"Q. Merely nomenclature of the area, merely geographically a description or appellation of the area, what it is called; is that right? A. What the company, what particular restriction they put on that particular district, why [the reason why] I don't know.

"Q. *Is* [note present tense employed by counsel for plaintiff] that put on the whole district from Los Angeles all the way to San Diego? A. That just runs from Fullerton to San Diego, but from Los Angeles to Fullerton is a portion of the third district.

"Q. And then you *have* [note present tense] to go slower in that area? A. That's right.

"Q. What speed *do you go* [note present tense] in the area between Fullerton and Los Angeles? * * * A. The speed *restriction on* all *districts* in the Santa Fe Los Angeles Division *is 90 miles* an hour.

"Q. So there *is* no more restriction there than is down here? A. Not at this time. I don't recall whether — it was a hundred on all districts but the third and the fourth districts it was less, but it is the same all over now, with the exception of the third district. That *is* 80.

"Q. You are not speaking of what it is now, are you? A. No. It *is 90 now* on the first, second, and *fourth districts.*

"Q. Well, Mr. Benton, the *restriction now is 50 miles an hour, isn't it?*

"Mr. Nielsen [Counsel for defendants]: I will object to that, your Honor, on the ground that has no materiality in the case.

"The Court: I don't know what district you refer to.

Mr. Belli [Counsel for plaintiffs]: He is referring to the fourth. He says that the restriction *in the fourth district now is 90* miles an hour. *We are prepared to show* that the *restriction* in this district *at this crossing now,* rather than being 90 miles an hour, *is 50* miles an hour.

"Mr. Nielsen: Just a moment, your Honor. Let's take this up outside the presence of the jury. * * * I cite the statement of counsel as misconduct in attempting to bring before the jury a totally immaterial issue.

The Court: Counsel is simply stating his theory of the case, what he expects to prove. Proceed sir.

"Mr. Belli: Q. Mr. Benton, you say that the speeds *in these areas then* and *now* are 90 miles an hour?

"Mr. Nielsen: I will object to that —

"The Court: That is compound. Then and now.

"Mr. Belli: Q. You have told us that the speed *in the area* right *now* is 90 miles an hour.

"Mr. Knowlton [Counsel for defendants]: Your Honor, I object to that question as being immaterial. The only critical factor there is the speed at the time of this accident.

"The Court: I thought — now, if you mean the entire area from Los Angeles to San Diego —

"Mr. Belli: *First that and then at Plaza Street.*

"The Court: Well, I don't know yet. You say first and then Plaza Street. *I don't know whether you mean there at Solano Beach at the intersection* in question *or whether you mean an entire area between Los Angeles and San Diego. It is vague and indefinite* to me, sir.

"Mr. Belli: May I withdraw that and put it this way, your Honor?

"Q. Mr. Benton, is it your testimony that the speed area at this *Plaza Street now is 90* miles an hour?

"Mr. Knowlton: I object to that question, your Honor, on the grounds it is immaterial to any issue in this case.

"The Court: Objection overruled. You may answer.

"Q. *The speed now at the plaza area.* A. *50 miles.*

"Mr. Belli: Q. It is 50 miles now? A. *Yes,* sir.

"Q. Do you know when that was changed to 50 miles an hour?

"Mr. Knowlton: The same objection, your Honor.

"The Court: Objection sustained.

"Mr. Belli: A. *At the time of the accident, the speed at the Plaza crossing was 90* miles an hour?

"Mr. Knowlton: Objection to that question, your Honor, on the grounds it has been asked and answered four times.

The Court: Objection sustained.[3]

The reader will note, as Mr. Justice Schauer pointed out in his dissenting opinion on appeal of this case,[4] how Belli swings back and

Notes on p. 182.

forth between the past and the present tenses; more precisely, the reader will note how Belli, by talking about speed restrictions without specifically indicating whether he is referring to restrictions within the entire railroad district or to restrictions in a small area (such as the Plaza Street crossing), succeeds in confusing the court. He then seizes on this confusion — which he himself has engendered — not only to bring before the jury the fact the speed limit had been changed to fifty miles per hour, but to emphasize that the change had been instituted after the accident. But the admission of such evidence did not — and could not — impeach Benton, who had *never* said that this speed limit at the Plaza Street intersection had remained at ninety miles per hour unto the time of trial. He only said that the *general* speed limit remained at ninety miles per hour. Thus, the subsequent change of speed limit should never have been admitted to impeach the witness for saying something he had not said, and thus, in turn, the change should never have been brought before the jury.

How important all this was to Belli is illustrated by the fact that he evidently emphasized the change of speed and its timing in his closing argument to the jury. Also, it is important to note that the case was sufficiently close that the admission of the change of the speed and timing may very well have been crucial in allowing Belli's client to win.

All this is not to imply that all personal injury trial lawyers skirt the limits of propriety in their tasks. It is simply to illustrate how tricky the work can be and how skillful and shrewd lawyers often are in exploiting every opportunity, deserved or undeserved, on questions of fault.

NOTES

1. McCormick, *Evidence* § 275, at 666 (ed. E. Cleary, 2d ed. 1972).
2. Daggett v. Atchison, Topeka and Santa Fe, 313 P.2d 557, 561 (1957).
3. *Ibid.*, 565–67.
4. This discussion is closely based on the dissenting opinion of Schauer, J., *ibid.*, 564–67.

II

An Expert's Testimony

The following is a small portion of the transcript of the *relatively* simple testimony of one expert, among several, in the actual case of *Smith* v. *Wire Rope Corporation of America, Inc.*[1] In that case the defendant supplied wire cable or rope to the plaintiff's employer. The wire rope was used as a cable on a crane. After being in use for about five days, the rope broke, causing a concrete piling that was being carried by the crane to swing free, resulting, in the words of the court, in "very severe personal injuries" to the plaintiff.

The plaintiff, of course, had the burden of proving that the wire rope was defectively manufactured. Put yourself in the position of a typical juror and try to follow the examination and cross-examination of the plaintiff's expert witness — keeping in mind the fact that the jury is exposed to all this through the quick and elusive spoken word. Isaac Stewart, a consulting engineer, testified (in small part) as follows:

Q. ... I believe you examined the individual wire rope that is involved in this case, marked Plaintiffs' Exhibits 1 and 1-A, did you not?

A. Yes, I did, sir.

Q. And could you give us the condition of the individual wires that constituted this one half inch cable?

A. Well, when I received the specimens they were well lubricated. There was a pretty good quantity of lubricant present on the wires, and I went into a study of the failure of this particular

Note on p. 188.

exhibit. I noted that the outer wires, the nineteen main wires that I illustrated in the diagram on the board as comprising the load-bearing wires of this rope per strand, were of a thirty-two thousandth of an inch in diameter and the six little filler wires were a thirteenth thousandth of an inch in diameter, and, as I indicated, there was a regular Lay construction on those strands and a 7 × 7 independent wire rope center in a Lang lay direction. I noted that this particular type of rope has a load carrying capacity of eleven and a half tons or twenty-three thousand pounds, and that the reserve strength which I indicated earlier was forty-four per cent for this particular type of construction. I found evidence of severe abrasion on the wires and I found a great many fractures and cracks, both in the area of the failure itself and remote from the area of failure farther down along the length of the wires comprising the specimen.

Q. Mr. Stewart, what do you mean by abrasions and fractures and cracks?

A. Well, a fracture, of course, is a crack or a break. An abrasion is a wearing away that has occurred from contact with the sheaves over which the equipment operated, over which the wires operated, and those conditions were evident to me on examination, both visually and by the aid of optical magnifying equipment that I used.

Q. Did this condition exist in the independent wire rope center?

A. Yes, sir, I found the same condition to exist in the independent wire rope center which normally is in a protected location within the construction of this rope.

Q. Did you make a microscopic study of these wires?

A. Yes, I did, sir.

Q. What did they indicate?

A. Well, first of all, there were a large number of transverse breaks and cracks. At the very end of the wires right where the failure actually had occurred and the wires themselves had separated, there were flat transverse breaks with no reduction of area of the wire. Now, this condition is a typical condition of what is known as a fatigue type failure. In other words, these wires did not break because they were overloaded or pulled or stressed to a point beyond which they could normally sustain — the nature of the break was that known as fatigue. In other words, the loads that this wire rope was subjected to was substantially below its normal capacity and yet it did fail because of this fatigue characteristic.[2]

The defendant wire company did not strenuously dispute that fatigue failure had caused the wire rope to break. Rather, it contended that the wire rope was properly manufactured and the break was caused by the use of a very small pulley by the plaintiff's employer on its crane. That, in turn, supposedly subjected the wire rope to a degree of flexing and bending beyond that considered safe in the trade. After extensively pursuing this theory on cross-examination, the defendant then recalled as a witness the operator of the crane, who testified the pulley in question was *six or eight inches in diameter,* with grooves in the pulley of less than an inch. Thereupon defendant continued its cross-examination of Mr. Stewart as follows:

Q. You have brought a couple of books down here with you?
A. Yes, I did.
Q. What are those books?
A. Metal sign [design?] book and the Robling Wire Rope Manual.
Q. Are both of them standard and recognized authorities in their field?
A. Yes, sir.
Q. Do you recognize them as such?
A. I do.
Q. May I have the Robling book, please?
A. Yes, sir.
Q. I refer you to page 52 of the Robling Handbook, which is a handbook on wire rope?
A. Yes, sir.
Q. There is a chapter there "Factors which influence equipment design"?
A. Yes.
Q. You have read this, I take it?
A. Yes, I have.
Q. Would you tell us what it says about proper sheave diameter?
A. Under the heading of "Sheaves and Rollers" and sub-heading "Proper Sheave Diameter," the manual reads as follows: "The effect of sheave diameter on the ultimate service received from operating ropes often is greatly underestimated. This is a sub-

Note on p. 188.

ject which should receive careful consideration, since not only is sheave diameter reflected in the rate of fatigue in the wires of the rope, but it is also reflected in the rate of wearing, or cutting, of the sheave grooves, which results in non-productive work and shortened service for the rope. It is of utmost importance that sheave and drum diameters be set as large as possible, in order that the most economical rope service can be obtained. It is not possible, of course, to maintain the same ratio of sheave diameter to rope diameter for all classes of wire rope installations, and, by the same token, neither is it possible to secure the same amount of work from a given size and construction of wire rope operating on these different installations. It is true that a difference in sheave diameter can be partially compensated for by the use of another construction of rope, but such a step often means a sacrifice of other desirable and necessary qualities in the rope itself for the particular duty under consideration. In general, it is advisable to design sheave equipment so that the tread diameters are approximately in accordance with the average values given in Table A. By referring to Figure 1, it will be seen that the tread diameter is measured at the bottom of the groove."

Q. All right, now, what is the average diameter recommended for a 6 × 19 rope?

A. The Table recommends under the heading of "Average Diameters Recommended" for a 6 × 19 rope 45 times the rope diameter.

Q. And since this was a half inch rope, then what would be the recommended diameter of a pulley for it?

A. In reference to this particular recommendation, which covers any form of operation of a wire rope, it would be twenty-two and a half inches in diameter.

[Mr. Stewart continued to read from the manual that the minimum recommended diameter would be *fifteen inches*.]

Q. So that the minimum recommended diameter for a half inch 6 × 19 rope, the minimum should be fifteen?

A. Yes, sir.

Q. As against the average recommended diameter of twenty-two and a half inches?

A. Yes, sir, that is what it says.

Q. And that is accepted in the industry and by you?

A. Yes, sir, absolutely.

Q. Because the smaller that pulley or sheave, the more that rope has to bend, or the sharper the bend, we will say?

A. Yes, that is right.

Q. And the sharper the bend, the more fatigue?

A. That is what I testified to, sir.

Q. And the shorter the life of the rope?

A. Yes, sir.

Q. And the ultimate separation of the rope and the breaking?

A. No sir, the shorter the life of the rope is what it says here (indicating).

Mr. Barron: That is all, thank you.

[Redirect examination, by Mr. McMath, plaintiff's counsel]

Q. Mr. Stewart, does the size of this sheave affect your findings as to the defective quality of this rope in question?

A. It does not, sir.

Q. Of course, all pulleys cause fatigue as the cable rolls over it, does it not?

A. Yes, I indicated that this morning in my testimony.

Q. And if a one-half inch rope is defective as it runs over a small pulley, it accelerates the fatigue of that rope?

A. Yes, it does. If it is defective — is that what you said?

Q. Yes, if it is defective?

A. Yes, that is correct.

Q. And, of course, the load that the cable was pulling would affect the degree of acceleration, would it not?

A. Definitely, sir.

[Recross-examination, by Mr. Barron, defendant's counsel]

Q. Did you intend to leave the impression that a small pulley below the minimum recommended only affects the fatigability of the rope if the rope is defective?

A. No, I didn't say that.

Q. Well, you left me with that impression. The fact is that a real small pulley will fatigue the rope?

A. Yes.

Q. And it will accelerate the fatigue?

A. It will, but the fact is that Mr. McMath's question went beyond just that one element, namely that of operation and load to which it is subjected. These diameter indicators here are designed up to the limit strength of the rope, as far as the load carrying ability is.[3]

Note on p. 188.

Keep in mind the foregoing is only a small fraction of the extended examination and cross-examination of engineer Stewart. And after the plaintiff had rested, defendant then called several expert witnesses of its own who were in turn examined and cross-examined extensively.

At the end of all the evidence the jury returned a verdict for the defendant wire company; the verdict was appealed but upheld by the appellate court, with extensive written briefs and oral arguments on appeal.[4]

NOTES

1. 383 F.2d 186 (8th Cir. 1967).
2. 1 L. Frumer and M. Friedman, *Products Liability* § 12.02(3), at 281.5–6 (1968).
3. *Ibid.*, 281.14–16.
4. *Supra,* note 1.

III

The Complexities of Compulsory No-Fault Medical Services Insurance

The cumbersomeness of any approach but elective no-fault insurance for injuries from medical treatment is illustrated by the proposal included in the report of the HEW Secretary's Commission on Medical Malpractice.[1] It will be recalled that the proposal was made to require health care producers to compensate for "any physical harm, bodily impairment, disfigurement, or delay in recovery which (i) is more probably associated in whole or in part with medical intervention rather than with the condition for which such intervention occurred, and (ii) is not consistent with or reasonably to be expected as a consequence of such intervention or (iii) is a result of medical intervention to which the patient has not given his informed consent."[2] Mention has already been made of the racking problems of separating under such a formula those injuries which should be compensated from those which should not.[3] Under the proposal under discussion it is suggested that ultimately there should follow "the establishment of schedules [of payment] of every conceivable medical injury, by type and severity."[4] But so formidable is drafting even more limited schedules that the authors in drafting proposed no-fault legislation for medical injuries do not attempt the task, announcing that "drafting of such schedules is beyond the scope of the [proposed] act and of commentary to the act."[5]

Trying thus by bureaucratic command at one stroke to formulate an appropriate amount of compensation for every medical injury from every medical treatment — or even for major injuries from major forms of treatments — would indeed be an incredibly difficult task. The HEW report refers to the analogy of sched-

Notes on p. 194.

uled benefits under workers' compensation,[6] but that precedent hardly portends a happy solution. In the words of an earlier work I coauthored: "In the first place, workmen's compensation involves payment by so-called 'scheduled benefits' — so much for loss of a finger, a different amount for a hernia, etc. . . . Such schedules by definition are arbitrary and unfair. To classify injuries with predetermined price tags really amounts to throwing up our hands in admitting that we can't award each according to his hurt. . . . Also, those schedules are usually too low. In these days of more or less continuous . . . price rises, the schedules get out of date after a few years, even if they are high enough for the average person at the start."[7] Scheduled benefits under workers' compensation have also meant prodigious infighting over just what category or slot in the schedules a given injury is to be assigned:

> [T]he extent of the disability resulting from, and attributable to, the accident is often the center of the dispute and presents in consequence the vexed question of *disability rating*. Not only . . . are the factual bases of the statutory benefit formulae frequently inconsistent or uncertain, but the methods of ascertaining them in the individual cases are costly and haphazard. One of the recognized leaders in the field of occupational medicine has voiced the following evaluation of the present state of practice: "The most common type of system of rating disability . . . is not disability rating but a tournament. It isn't a decision to the individual's working capacity or loss of working capacity, but a victory or defeat in a medical-legal tournament." This battle by teams of medical and legal experts is not only demoralizing, time consuming and expensive but produces of course unavoidable discrepancy and incongruity in the awards and in consequence thereof dissatisfaction among the injured.[8]

But the difficulties of scheduling adverse results from medical services are dwarfed, according to the HEW report, by the difficulties from alternative approaches:

> [Rick J.] Carlson proposes several middle-ground definitions based on the notion that compensation should be awarded for outcomes of medical intervention that deviate substantially from an expected outcome. Essentially the idea is that for a given medical condition of a patient a distribution of outcomes can be established

Notes on p. 194.

on the basis of aggregated experience and compensation can be based on some cut-off criterion. In Figure A-1 such a hypothetical distribution is shown. The abscissa [or horizontal coordinate] scale is the range of possible outcomes, and varies from death to complete recovery. The ordinate [or vertical coordinate] denotes the number of cases associated with each outcome. The dotted line represents a hypothetical dividing line which separates compensable outcomes (to the left of the line) and noncompensable outcomes (to the right of the line). The position of this line may be based on the outcome (degree of recovery) or on the relative number of cases contained under the curve to the left of the line. For instance, Carlson recommends that compensation be paid if no more than 33.3% of the interventions on record have resulted in such poor outcomes.

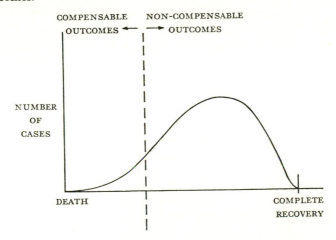

Figure A-1   OUTCOMES DISTRIBUTION

Given that a sufficiently large set of such distribution curves were available now, such a compensability definition would afford the advantage of determining compensability by using published tables and schedules, i.e. with a high degree of objectivity and predictability of application. However, although beginnings at collecting such data have been made and for instance a very detailed classification scheme for diseases exists,[9] the time when sufficient data for even partial application will be available, appears at least 5–10 years away. Some of the difficulties in establishing the necessary—

Note on p. 194.

sary data base are (1) the degree of recovery depends not only on the diagnosed disease but also on the state of the patient (age, sex, general state of health, economic conditions, climate, etc.) (2) in many cases patients suffer from more than one disease, a factor which tends to reduce the number of cases that can be plotted one distribution. Some of the difficulties are conceptual: no consistent scale is readily apparent for grading outcomes between complete recovery and death; severity of the disability must be rated separately if it is to be included in determining the amount of compensation. Other parameters, such as the time period between medical intervention and outcome measurement are not explicitly considered. The time parameter should include the notion of undue delay in recovery. (This difficulty may be overcome by applying the outcomes model in time steps, i.e. from first intervention till, say a first diagnosis of the disease, from a first diagnosis till a second diagnosis, etc.)

In sum, the introduction of statistical outcomes models as the basis for determining compensability, while attractive, is premature because the state-of-the-art of medical research does not provide the necessary data base and secondly, because certain conceptual problems have not yet been resolved. However, it appears possible to implement the concept on a subjective basis whereby a panel of medical experts adjudges the "normal" outcome of the particular case and the extent of deviation from the normal.[10]

Reference to the panel raises the recommendation of the HEW report that a Medical Injury Compensation Commission, analogous to a workers' compensation commission, administer the no-fault medical compensation system (note another expensive — and resented? — bureaucracy). The following summary conveys the complexity and cumbersomeness of the scheme:

> [The proposal is] . . . based on the establishment of a State Medical Injury Compensation Commission which directs a Medical Injury Compensation Board in accordance with a Medical Injury Compensation Law. Further, [the proposal is] . . . based on the assumption that the law is based on the principle of strict liability and contains explicit definitions of compensable medical injury. The costs of administering the Medical Injury Compensation Commission are borne by general taxes; all other costs are borne by insurance.

Note on p. 194.

... The following description follows the order of [procedure].
...

1) The system will be compulsory in the sense that it abolishes relief for compensable medical injury through tort-liability.

2) Claims may be filed by the injured party (or his representative). Assistance is provided through the Board in filing claims and (for hospital patients) in uncovering potential claims, although the decision to file still rests with the claimant.

3) A claim-screening mechanism functions to informally review all claims at an early stage. As a result, the abandonment of non-meritorious claims is encouraged, probably successful claims are supported; and settlement without further formal procedure is advised in non-disputed cases.

4) Claims not disposed of in the preceding screening stage advance to the referee (or hearing examiner) who, with the aid of expert medical staff, hears argument by claimant, health care providers and their advisors. The referee determines compensability based on the evidence presented to him and in accordance with the rules of the Commission.

5) Compensability is limited to special damages which include all costs incurred in treating the injury, loss of income, including present worth of future income, compensation for disabilities resulting from the injury, and rehabilitation.

6) The referee, usually at the hearing outlined under (4) above, also determines the amount of compensation awarded. To the extent possible, he makes the award following schedules which are established by the Commission. Where schedules do not apply he uses his own, or additionally, his medical advisor's judgment in making the award.

7) Claimant, health care providers and their insurance carriers may appeal the referee's decision to a Commission Review Board which examines questions of law and fact. The decision of the Review Board may be further appealed to court of law, but only on questions of procedure.

Incorporated in the recommended injury compensation system, which includes this mode, is provision for keeping a written record. This record will be used as a basis for a continuing process of improving the Commission's rules.[11]

Perhaps eventually we will move to such an ambitious, expensive, and revolutionary new scheme for medical compensation. But the

Note on p. 194.

sweep and scope and expense of such a proposal augurs, at the least, interminable delay in its adoption.[12]

NOTES

1. Roth and Rosenthal, "Non-Fault-Based Medical Injury Compensation Systems," U.S. Department of Health, Education, and Welfare, *Appendix, Report of the Secretary's Commission on Medical Malpractice* 450 (1973) [hereinafter cited as HEW Secretary's Commission Report]. Said the report itself about this study, "Our major study dealing with this subject was brought to our attention for discussion at our last meeting, and while it raised many of the important issues, it did not comprehensively explore all possible systems, nor did it suggest any definitive alternative for the Commission's consideration" (HEW Secretary's Commission Report 99).

2. *Appendix*, HEW Secretary's Commission Report, *supra* note 1, at 460.

3. *Supra*, ch. 7, notes 10–12 and accompanying text.

4. *Appendix*, HEW Secretary's Commission Report, *supra* note 1, at 466.

5. *Ibid.*, 484.

6. *Ibid.*, 466.

7. R. Keeton and J. O'Connell, *After Cars Crash: The Need for Legal and Insurance Reform* 79 (1967).

8. Reisenfeld, "Basic Problems in the Administration of Workmen's Compensation," 36 *Minn. L. Rev.* 119, 133–34 (1952).

9. 1 and 2 *International Classification of Diseases* (ICDA) (8th ed., Public Health Service Publication No. 1693, Dec., 1968).

10. *Appendix*, HEW Secretary's Commission Report, *supra* note 1, at 488–89.

11. *Ibid.*, 481, 483.

12. The former president of the Association of Trial Lawyers of America (ATL), Richard Markus, was a member of the HEW Secretary's Commission on Medical Malpractice. For his separate statement dismissing as impossible any attempt to define comprehensively medical injuries under which all such injuries could be compensated on a no-fault basis, see Markus, "Separate Statement," in HEW Secretary's Commission Report, *supra* note 1, at 131, 132–33.

IV

"Does Economics Help?"

It is interesting that turning to no-fault insurance or abolishing defenses based on the injured party's contributory fault offends not only traditional legal doctrine but some traditional economic doctrine as well.[1] Both doctrines seem equally vulnerable. It is fascinating that as the defense of the fault system by lawyers has seemed more and more beleaguered, some economists have leaped into the breach to attempt to provide an intellectually viable defense of the concept of fault as applied to accident compensation. Professor Richard Posner of the University of Chicago (both a lawyer and an economist) has, for example, argued against no-fault insurance, especially if it entails a concomitant abandonment of the defense of contributory negligence: "Economic theory provides no basis, in general, for preferring [no-fault] ... liability to negligence, or negligence to [no-fault] ... liability, provided that some version of a contributory negligence defense is recognized. ... [But] ... a [no-fault] ... liability standard without a contributory negligence defense is, in principle, less efficient than the negligence-contributory negligence standard."[2] (Note the almost perfect counterpoint: Posner is indifferent to whether no-fault liability is adopted but believes that, regardless of whether it is, the defense of contributory negligence must in any event be retained; I strongly urge that no-fault liability be adopted but believe that, regardless of whether it is, the defense of contributory negligence must in any event be abolished.)[3]

Traditional legal doctrine has long enshrined the mythical reasonable man as a model we must all follow at our peril. A. P. Herbert poked fun at the concept long ago:

Notes on p. 202.

The Common Law . . . has been laboriously built about a mythical figure — a figure of "The Reasonable Man." . . . He is an ideal, a standard, the embodiment of all those qualities which we demand of the good citizen . . . . He is one who invariably looks where he is going, and is careful to examine the immediate foreground before he executes a leap or bound; who neither star-gazes nor is lost in meditation when approaching trap-doors or the margin of a dock; . . . who never mounts a moving omnibus, and does not alight from any car while the train is in motion . . . and will inform himself of the history and habits of a dog before administering a caress; . . . who never drives his [golf] ball till those in front of him have definitely vacated the putting-green which is his own objective; who never from one year's end to another makes an excessive demand upon his wife, his neighbors, his servants, his ox, or his ass; . . . who uses nothing except in moderation, and even while he flogs his child is meditating only on the golden mean. Devoid, in short, of any human weakness, with not one single vice, sans . . . absence of mind, as careful for his own safety as he is for that of others, this excellent but odious character stands like a monument in our Courts of Justice, vainly appealing to his fellow-citizens to order their lives after his own example.[4]

Actually, the standard of the reasonable man may have had some basis in sound policy for the common law when it was advanced, drawing on the thinking of the rationalists of the eighteenth and early nineteenth centuries. But unfortunately, any sense in the concept as applied to accidents began to be undermined almost literally from the moment (in the early nineteenth century) that it began to be accepted. Before the industrial revolution it was generally true that one man did not ordinarily hurt another's person without some "unreasonable" — indeed, often intentional — wrongful act.[5] But with the coming of swift and lethal machinery, man's capacity to injure himself and others increased exponentially, and the individual person, injuring or injured, usually was guilty of no more than a slight, understandable, split-second error of judgment. Hence, the fallacy of the law's painstaking dissection of accidental incidents into seconds and minutes and feet and yards in a Kafkaesque endeavor to try to (1) re-create what happened in the agony of the moment of accident, and — even more fallaciously — (2) determine whether

Notes on p. 202.

compensation for accidents should be paid to accident victims on the basis of the desserts of how they supposedly reacted in that agonized moment. And, as I say, just as society begins to comprehend how fallacious is that sort of rationalization of the law of torts on the part of tort lawyers, some economists have come along with their justification of such analysis. Not only are we asked to imagine that individuals constantly, closely, and rationally calculate the risks of getting into accidents in a mechanized society, but we must also believe that they do so in finely tuned judgments calibrated in dollars and cents and based on an exquisite knowledge of the risks and an exhaustive knowledge of the law.[6]

A pedestrian starts across the street; if he is in a jurisdiction with a law of contributory negligence, wherein his own negligence will totally bar him from any payment regardless of his injurer's negligence, some economists would ask us to believe the pedestrian will be significantly more careful and less willing to dart across in the face of oncoming traffic than if he were in a jurisdiction adopting a rule of comparative negligence, where his damages would be decreased but not eliminated based on a mathematical comparison of his degree of negligence versus that of his injurer. Furthermore, some economists would have us to believe that if the pedestrian is in a comparative negligence state (like Wisconsin) that requires an injured party be less negligent than his injurer in order to have the comparison applied (and thus be eligible for payment), he would be significantly less inclined to carelessness than if he were in a so-called pure-comparative negligence state (like Mississippi), where the comparison is applied regardless of who is more careless. Lest it be thought I unfairly characterize the limits to which some economists go in hypothesizing a "reasonable man," listen to Posner:

> Suppose there is a class of automobile accidents in which the injurers are all very wealthy men. The opportunity costs of their time are so great that the expected accident costs are lower than the costs to them of preventing the accidents by driving more slowly, slower driving being the only method by which the accidents might be prevented. In these circumstances, which rule of liability would be more efficient: [No-fault]...liability with no contributory negligence defense; or no liability at all?[7]

Notes on p. 202.

> [Answer] No liability. Then the victims will take any precautions that cost less than the expected accident costs. Under [no-fault] ... liability with no contributory negligence, neither party in the circumstances hypothesized would take any precautions, the injurers because their precautions are not cost justified, the victims because they are fully compensated for their accident costs.[8]

There you have it: An economist telling us that if we compensate people regardless of their negligence, none of them "would take any precautions."

Actually, though, Posner has attempted to anticipate the objections I have raised: "[A] ... fundamental criticism of the behavioral effects of negligence law is that it is unrealistic to expect people who are not deterred from careless conduct by fear of bodily injury to be deterred by fear of a money judgment, or, in the case where the negligence of the victim is a bar to recovery, by inability to obtain compensation for the injury from the injurer. Several observations on this point are in order. First, the argument is inapplicable to injurers not themselves in any personal jeopardy, to employers of injurers (such as a truck or taxi company) and to accidents where the only significant danger is to property." Here, of course, Posner is confirming my points; namely, that deterrence is applicable to institutions "not themselves in any personal jeopardy" but in jeopardy to other than personal injury.[9] Posner continues, "Second, the argument [criticizing the behavioral effects of negligence law] ignores the accident prevention effect of liability insurance premium rates that are so high, reflecting the expected liability of the insured, that they discourage him from attempting to drive."[10] Here Posner ignores his own words in his immediately preceding paragraph, where he admits that liability rates for given individuals are so crudely set that they do not reflect "the expected liability" of any given insured. Concerning drivers, according to Posner (where the rates for individuals are infinitely more refined than for other categories of injurers), "partly because of administrative expense, partly because of regulatory hostility toward 'discriminatory' premium rate structure, partly because of assigned-risk pools that enable the most dangerous drivers to purchase liability insurance at rates only slightly higher than normal, liability insurance premiums seem not to be

Notes on p. 202.

tailored with any precision to the expected accident costs of particular drivers."

Third, continues Posner, in answer to criticisms of the behavioral effects of negligence law, "the proposition that the prospective victim of an accident will not be deterred from behaving carelessly by fear of not being compensated implies that tort compensation is never full compensation. . . . If damages fully compensated the victim, he would be indifferent as between being injured and not being injured and a rule of contributory negligence would be indispensable to the creation of incentives for careful behavior."[11]

And so Posner returns full cycle to his conclusion that if we compensate people regardless of their negligence, none of them "would take any precautions." If such thinking is rejected when it is offered by lawyers, why should our response be any different when it is offered by an economist? Of course, some economists defend themselves against the unreality of their hypothetical cases and the answers by telling us that "it pays . . . to understand the oversimplified situation before trying to make judgments about the more complex ones."[12] But, as Professor Grant Gilmore, then of the University of Chicago, commented: "This would be true, I should think, if we could move by easy stages from the simple to the complex and if the complex, when we arrived at it, was recognizably of the same family as the simple model. It would not be true if there was simply no relationship that could be perceived between the two. In such a case the only conclusions that could be drawn from a comparison of the simple model with the complex reality (so far as that could, in any case, be accurately described) would be false — or, if true, would be so by the purest [of all things!] accident."[13]

Perhaps it should not surprise us that the economists' Economic Man very often turns out to be — like the lawyers' Reasonable Man — so unrealistic. Each stems, as Paul Carrington has perceptively pointed out, from the same mold. Both Blackstone and Adam Smith were determined to pluck "reason" from that nettle "life." According to Carrington, an extensive economic analysis of a law by lawyer-economist Posner can be viewed as reuniting

two divergent strands of rational intellectual tradition, the classical

Notes on p. 202.

economic rationalism sired by Adam Smith and the common law rationalism which can be said to date from William Blackstone.

... Blackstone and Smith each wrote with an extraordinarily lucid, if somewhat oracular, style. ... While Smith analyzed markets and Blackstone analyzed court decision, both proceeded from the assumption that human behavior is essentially, if not completely, rational. ... Both Blackstone and Smith were prone to attribute to human rationality a commanding force over social institutions and relationships. ...

It is not hard to find a cause of the similarity between Blackstone and Smith. Smith was born in the early summer of 1723 in Scotland, Blackstone a month later in London. Blackstone studied at Oxford from 1738 to 1746, Smith was at Oxford from 1740 to 1748. Smith began lecturing in Glasgow in 1751, Blackstone at Oxford in 1753. Blackstone's great work was completed in 1769, Smith's in 1776. Smith was the more creative of the two and had much the greater impact, but the influence of both can be seen in the development of many ... thinkers who succeeded them. ...[14]

Of course, the law's Reasonable Man and the economists' Economic Man are by no means useless. Hypothesizing rationality makes sense, for example, in the law's determining whether someone has committed perjury or in the economist's determining the effect on supply of an increase in price for an item facing elastic demand. But economists wedded to Economic Man recognize the shortcomings as well as the strengths of the concept. Professor George Stigler of the University of Chicago has written: "When we assume that consumers, acting with mathematical consistency, maximize utility ... it is not proper to complain that men are much more complicated and diverse than that. So they are, but if this assumption yields a theory of behavior which agrees tolerably well with the facts, it must be used until a better theory comes along."[15] But *does* a theory of Economic Man yield "a theory of behavior which agrees tolerably well with the facts" in describing an individual's motivation and even instinct to avoid personal injury, especially if the theory is posited with a potential victim precisely — and predominantly — calculating the economic effects on himself of accidents? It was R. H. Tawney who described economics as "a body of occasionally useful truisms."[16] The key, of course, is trying to find the appropriate occasion for applying a given truism.

Notes on pp. 202-3.

Neither Posner nor I can offer definitive data proving or disproving, say, the effect of rules of contributory fault on the care taken by individuals in their daily lives to avoid personal injury. I would only suggest that what we can intuit seems strongly to indicate the lack of a significantly deterrent effect on unsafe conduct by potential accident victims of such rules of contributory fault. Recently Professor Peter Diamond, an M.I.T. economist, has undertaken "to begin the extension of equilibrium models to include tort liability for accidents. [His] . . . model building . . . represents an attempt to examine some of the elements of the way tort law affects resource allocation. . . ." Diamond says he "started this project as an attempt to set Calabresi to mathematics. . . ."[17] The development and refinement of economic models has come under vigorous attack recently, even from economists,[18] but one can scarcely dismiss all economic model building.[19] And thus anyone interested in the interaction of law and economics, particularly as it applies to the law of torts, is inclined to applaud Diamond for his pioneering efforts. But, at the conclusion of his paper, Diamond admits that "the model of individual behavior I have employed is highly simplified and excessively rational." The key problem, as Diamond sees it, is that in the area of accidents even normal rationality — not to speak of "excessive rationality" — and especially economic rationality, seems out of place. "Decisions about care," he says, "may be particularly subject to non-market forces. It is particularly in the realm of decisions involving low probability of events and involving one's own health and safety that the accuracy and rationality of individual choice are questionable."[20] Just so. Posner, in supporting the retention of contributory fault as a defense to personal injury claims seems, in Diamond's phrase, "excessively rational."

Recently, an anonymous reviewer of the (London) *Times Literary Supplement,* in reviewing an essay by E. F. Schumacher entitled "Does Economics Help?," stated, "if economics is to help, it must shake off its obsession with deriving the logical behavior-pattern of some mythical *homo economicus* from a set of conveniently simple assumptions, step outside its traditional boundaries and play a part in studying man in his wholeness."[21] Whether, with such a broader point of view, the resultant discipline would still be economics, or

Notes on p. 203.

so often helpful, strikes me as problematic. But while the economists are wrestling with that rather cosmic question, the rest of us — with a broader point of view than Posner would allow — should proceed apace to abolish contributory negligence (along with assumption of risk) as a defense to personal injury claims — either alone or, even better, in conjunction with a no-fault proposal.

NOTES

1. Concerning the abolishment of defenses based on the injured's fault, see *supra,* ch. 9, notes 44–47 and accompanying text.

2. Posner, "Strict Liability: A Comment," 2 *J. Legal Studies* 205, 221 (1973).

3. *Supra,* note 1.

4. A. P. Herbert, *Uncommon Law* 1–4 (7th ed. 1950).

5. "In short, in the mid-19th century, the common law of tort was well nigh inviolate, retaining an inordinate emphasis on damage to land and on intentional injuries" (Veitch, "Assault on the Law of Torts," 1974 *Modern L. Rev.* ——, ——; Malone, "Ruminations on the Role of Fault in the History of Torts," in *The Origin and Development of the Negligence Action* 1, 9 [U.S. Department of Transportation, Automobile Insurance & Compensation Study, 1970]; also printed in a slightly revised version in 31 *La. L. Rev.* 1, 11–12 [1970]).

6. But for an indication that in fact the public is woefully ignorant of the laws of negligence, including rules pertaining to contributory negligence, see *supra,* ch. 9, note 28 and accompanying text.

7. R. Posner, *Economic Analysis of Law* 97 (1973).

8. R. Posner, *Teacher's Manual for Economic Analysis of Law* 19 (1973). Posner goes on to say that "many readers will consider a rule under which the wealthier are excused from liability because they are unlikely to take precautions to be the height of unfairness."

9. *Supra,* ch. 9, note 31 and accompanying text. The Posner quote is found at Posner, *Economic Analysis of Law, supra* note 7, at 85.

10. *Ibid.*

11. *Ibid.,* 85–86.

12. McKean, "Products Liability: Trends and Implications," 38 *U. Chi. L. Rev.* 3, 31 (1970).

13. Gilmore, "Products Liability: A Commentary," 38 *U. Chi. L. Rev.* 103, 105–6 (1970).

14. Carrington, book review of Posner, *Economic Analysis of Law, supra* note 7, 1974 *U. Ill. L. Forum* 187.

15. G. Stigler, *The Theory of Price* 6 (3d ed. 1966). Professor Louis Schwartz of the University of Pennsylvania Law School has commented on the virtues of professional myopia: "The X-ray chooses not to see skin, fat, any tissue extraneous to the target of its probe. Intellectual specialists must similarly blind themselves to much that is ultimately relevant, in order to see

more deeply. The economist necessarily excludes from the range of his inquiry much that the lawyer cannot ignore. The mathematical economist excludes much that the institutional economist regards as vital." But, Schwartz goes on to say, "For me, the moral of all this is the necessity for professional modesty. The X-ray must not suffer the illusion that it sees all" (Schwartz, book review in 120 *U. Pa. L. Rev.* 584, 596 [1972]).

16. Johnson, book review of R. Terrill, *R. H. Tawney and His Times* (1973), in *N.Y. Times,* Dec. 30, 1973, § 7, p. 4, col. 4.

17. Diamond, "Single Activity Accidents," 3 *J. Legal Studies* 107 (1974).

18. B. Ward, *What's Wrong With Economics?* 50 (1972); see also O'Connell, book review of *ibid.,* in 1973 *U. Ill. L. Forum* 604.

19. See J. Simon, *Basic Research Methods in Social Science* 123–24 (1966). See also *supra* note 15.

20. Diamond, *supra* note 17, at 163.

21. Book review in *Times Literary Supplement,* Oct. 12, 1973, p. 1224. The problem, according to Professor Benjamin Ward of the Economics Department at the University of California, Berkeley, is that ignoring nonmonetary values has meant for economics "weakly developed and inherently implausible theories of man.... Straightening this out is a central problem [for economics, and]... the developing of a powerful theory of social influences on man is the primary desideratum" (B. Ward, *supra* note 18, at 233; see also O'Connell, book review of *ibid., supra* note 18).

V

Is It Constitutional?

*with James E. Souk**

There are at least several constitutional issues that will probably be raised to challenge elective no-fault liability under the United States and various state constitutions. As we are now seeing with state and federal auto no-fault bills and laws, these issues will be raised by well-financed and -organized opposition, whether the implementation of elective no-fault liability is attempted at the federal or state level. The elective feature of the plan can be expected to hold to a minimum much of the potential opposition of the medical and business communities, but constitutional issues will undoubtedly still have to be resolved.

As has been the case with some early no-fault auto laws,[1] it is possible that some elective no-fault liability plans will be enacted with poorly considered provisions which will render the laws unconstitutional. No attempt will be made to anticipate all possible variations of elective no-fault liability or to discuss additional constitutional problems that may be presented by such plans. Rather, the purpose of this discussion is merely to assert that the general plan of elective no-fault liability proposed here meets the requirements of the federal and state constitutions.[2] Generally speaking, the long constitutional history of workers' compensation and the limited decisions thus far available on auto no-fault laws strongly support an argument in favor of the constitutionality of elective no-fault liability at either the federal or state level.

* A.B., West Virginia University, 1966; J.D., University of Illinois, 1974.

Notes on pp. 231–32.

Due Process. A federal elective no-fault liability law would have to satisfy the requirements of the due process clause of the Fifth Amendment of the United States Constitution,[3] while a state law would be tested under the due process clause of the Fourteenth Amendment[4] and similar clauses found in the constitutions of most states.[5] The test to be employed is essentially the same for all these due process clauses[6] (though the manner in which the tests are applied varies from federal to state courts).[7] First, a presumption of constitutionality attaches to the statute; if a situation could exist which would justify the statute, then such a situation is presumed to have existed at the time of the statute's passage.[8] Then, "in the absence of other constitutional restriction,[9] a state[10] is free to adopt whatever economic policy may reasonably be deemed to promote public welfare, and to enforce that policy by legislation adapted to its purpose. The courts are without authority either to declare such policy, or, when it is declared by the legislature, to override it. If the laws passed are seen to have a reasonable relation to a proper legislative purpose, and are neither arbitrary nor discriminatory, the requirements of due process are satisfied. . . ."[11]

Since elective no-fault liability would alter preexisting common law rights, many courts will also require that the law provide a reasonable substitute for the common law rights that are lost.[12] An argument can be made that this additional test is not constitutionally required,[13] but such an argument is unnecessary since elective no-fault liability seems to satisfy this requirement.

It should prove helpful in discussing the constitutional issues to first review the common law rights which are altered by elective no-fault liability and to identify which parties affected by the law might validly claim a deprivation of "life, liberty or property without due process of law." The business or professional person who chooses to be covered by elective no-fault liability is subjected to liability without fault but of course has no real constitutional argument since he can retain full or partial common law rights — without sanction — merely by refraining from exercising his options under the law.[14] He can hardly complain when he is allowed to specify not only which injuries he will pay for on a no-fault basis but also the monetary limits of such no-fault coverage. Since he is under no illegitimate pressure to elect coverage, he clearly waives any constitutional rights, including due process, when he does make an election for no-fault coverage.

What about the consumer/patient who has suffered injury? If the business or professional has not elected no-fault coverage, then the consumer/patient likewise has no due process argument since he retains his full common law rights to sue in tort. If his injury is one for which the business or professional has elected no-fault coverage, then the consumer or patient loses his right to compensation for pain and suffering and can no longer benefit from the multiple recovery allowed by the "collateral source" rule. In exchange, he is assured compensation for medical expenses and wage loss without having to prove the product defective or, say, the doctor negligent.

Perhaps to some the most disturbing constitutional feature under elective no-fault insurance is that private persons — professionals or businesses — are allowed unilaterally to alter the common law rights of those they injure. At first blush this might seem to run counter to the rising tide of consumerism, until one realizes that the consumer movement has been in the vanguard of urging the substitution of no-fault insurance for traditional tort liability.[15] And the apparent novelty of such elective private power over others' common law rights to payment for personal injury is dissipated when the analogy of elective workers' compensation is recalled. Perhaps the most analogous situation is the West Virginia Workmen's Compensation Law, which is alone among the laws of the elective states in being compulsory for employees but elective for employers.[16] Here too, then, a private individual (or concern) is allowed unilaterally to alter the rights of those he injures by substituting guaranteed no-fault benefits for an uncertain tort remedy. Such unilateral power over one's victims' avenue to personal injury payment has been explicitly upheld as constitutional by the West Virginia Supreme Court.[17] And although in the other ten states with elective workers' compensation the employee retains the right to reject the employer's election, that right, as previously noted, is in reality a legal fiction, in that it is never as a practical matter asserted, nor would it be honored if it were.[18]

Even states with compulsory workers' compensation laws exempt certain occupations from compulsory coverage but allow exempt employment to be covered voluntarily. Indeed, in most compulsory-

Notes on p. 233.

law states where election is permitted for certain categories of employment, the employer's election, as in West Virginia, is binding on the employee.[19] In New York, for example, any exempt employer is also free to elect coverage under the workers' compensation statute.[20] However, the employee has no right of rejection[21] — the employer's unilateral decision terminates the employee's common law rights. The New York law originally required a joint election by employer and employee, but a 1941 amendment abrogated the employee's right of election.[22] Although never considered specifically on constitutional grounds, the amendment has been accepted by New York courts without question.[23]

As an additional point on this matter of the consumer/patient victim's loss of his common law rights by the unilateral action of another, the consumer/patient may also have no real constitutional claim since, it can be argued, he has the right to purchase his products and medical care from businesses and professionals who have not elected no-fault coverage, and he can thus elect to retain his full common law rights. On the other hand, it is entirely possible that enough businesses or professionals in certain fields will elect no-fault coverage so that the consumer/patient is effectively left with no choice.

In addition, an argument based on the consumer/patient's choice loses some of its force since it is unclear just how easily one will be able to discover who has elected what coverage. Granted, it is not entirely plain just what form of notice regarding no-fault elections will have to be given by the business or professional to the consumer/patient, but the following system is suggested as fair and feasible as well as sufficient to meet constitutional requirements:

(1) The business or professional must file a written copy of his elective no-fault policy with the state insurance commissioner. The fact and terms of the election of any business or professional would be available to the public on request, preferably through use of computer printouts for faster service. The terms of the notice would be in clear language, approved by the insurance commissioner, so as to be comprehensible by the typical consumer/patient.

(2) Each business or professional would be required to have on file at applicable places of business those same terms of the election,

Notes on p. 233.

plus a copy of the policy itself, available for inspection by any con-
sumer/patient on request.

(3) At least in some instances, where considered feasible, such
terms of election in summary form might be required to be promi-
nently displayed at the applicable place of business.

(4) Such terms of election would be included in the provisions
of any applicable warranty.

Recall the analogous West Virginia Workmen's Compensation
Law which is compulsory for employees but elective for employers.[24]
There, each electing employer must "post and keep posted in con-
spicuous places about his place or places of business typewritten or
printed notices stating the fact that he has made such election, and
the same when so posted shall constitute sufficient notice to all his
employees and to parents of any minor employees of the fact that he
has made such election."[25] Such notice has been held sufficient to
inform the employee of the situation so that he may elect whether
he will continue his present employment.[26]

New York has a similar notice provision for those employers who
are exempt from compulsory coverage but who nevertheless elect
workers' compensation.[27] In Illinois, however, with its provisions for
mutual election,[28] an exempt employer who elects coverage need
only file notice of his election with the industrial commission *or* just
insure himself in accordance with the Workmen's Compensation
Act. To reject workers' compensation, the employee simply files
notice with the industrial commission, which in turn notifies the
employer. But note that the statute does not require an employer
to post notices or personally notify employees concerning his election.
(Notice requirements are stricter when an electing employer wishes
to discontinue workers' compensation at the beginning of the next
year. He must first file notice of his intention with the industrial
commission at least sixty days prior to the end of the calendar year
and then must either post formal written notices in his place of
business or personally serve notice on each employee. An electing
employee who wishes to reject coverage for the next year still need
only file notice with the commission.)[29]

For marketing and professional reasons mentioned earlier,[30] it is
often even less feasible, as a practical matter, to require explicit

Notes on pp. 234–35.

notice in nonemployment situations. In light of that, the provisions suggested above for elective no-fault coverage would seem to suffice to adequately inform the consumer/patient of the situation so that he can elect whether to continue purchasing goods or services from a particular business or professional.

In point of fact the necessity of explicit notice of reasonable alteration in common law tort rights, for constitutional and practical purposes, would seem to be diminished when one realizes how little the average person — or accident victim — knows about or cares about his common law tort rights.[31]

Concerning notice, too, it also must be kept in mind what a "legal fiction" is the right of an employee to reject no-fault workers' compensation and to thereby retain common law rights.[32]

But finally, if no other course seems constitutionally possible, lacking a constitutional amendment, elective no-fault could be limited to those situations where actual notice seems readily feasible. (Not that actual notice will necessarily have to be proven in each case. Rather, the criterion would be general availability of notice, as under elective workers' compensation provisions.)

But apart from notice, if we assume that at least some consumers/patients can raise a possible due process objection to elective no-fault liability, can such a no-fault law satisfy the other requirements of due process? Using workers' compensation and no-fault auto cases as the most relevant authority on the question, it seems quite evident that elective no-fault liability bears a rational relation to a proper legislative purpose and provides a reasonable substitute for common law rights which are lost.

Most supporters of the constitutionality of no-fault auto insurance[33] have made extensive use of the workers' compensation cases, which long ago upheld the constitutionality of both elective and compulsory workers' compensation.[34] The supporters of elective no-fault liability have even greater reason to use these cases since elective no-fault liability bears greater resemblance to workers' compensation than does auto no-fault. Auto no-fault operates principally to cause each driver's insurer to pay that driver (and his passengers and any pedestrians he injures) for medical expenses and wage loss; existing liability insurance is thereby transformed into first-party insurance.[35]

Notes on p. 235.

The parties involved in an auto accident are essentially all in the same class and can constitute the injured, injurer, or both in any particular situation. If they are in different cars, for example, their relationship is neither planned nor voluntary, occurring only as a result of a totally fortuitous mishap. In workers' compensation and elective no-fault liability the relationship between the parties is usually voluntary, occurring before there is ever any injury and continuing even if no injury occurs. The product or activity of the employer, business, or professional always "causes" the injury, and the employee, consumer, or patient is always the party suffering the injury; there are two classes, and even when no-fault is introduced the injurer (or his insurer) continues in every instance to pay the injured.[36] Workers' compensation and elective no-fault liability thus do not transform existing liability insurance into first-party insurance. But such considerations are really peripheral, because the soundness of the analogy between all three concepts (auto no-fault, workers' compensation, and elective no-fault) depends really on one basic similarity: they all entail payment without fault and restrict or eliminate certain preexisting common law rights.[37]

Many early workers' compensation statutes were elective, largely due to concern that compulsory statutes were unconstitutional. The United States Supreme Court clearly upheld the constitutionality of workers' compensation statutes, including compulsory plans, in *Mountain Timber Co.* v. *Washington*,[38] *New York Central Railroad Company* v. *White*,[39] and *Arizona Employer's Liability Cases*,[40] all decided between 1917 and 1919. The language of Mr. Justice Pitney in *White* summarizes the position of the court:

> No person has a vested interest in any rule of law entitling him to insist that it shall remain unchanged for his benefit. . . .
>
>   . . . .
>
> . . . The statute under consideration sets aside one body of rules only to establish another system in its place. If the employee is no longer able to recover as much as before in case of being injured through the employer's negligence, he is entitled to moderate compensation in all cases of injury, and has a certain and speedy remedy without the difficulty and expense of establishing negligence or proving the amount of damages. . . . On the other hand, if the employer is left without defense respecting the question of fault,

Notes on pp. 235–36.

he at the same time is assured that the recovery is limited, and that it goes directly to the relief of the designated beneficiary. . . . We have said enough to demonstrate that . . . the particular rules of the common law . . . are not placed by the Fourteenth Amendment beyond the reach of the law making power of the State; and thus we are brought to the question whether the method of compensation that is established as a substitute transcends the limits of permissible state action.

. . . .

. . . It is plain that, on grounds of natural justice, it is not unreasonable for the State, while relieving the employer from responsibility for damages measured by common-law standards and payable in cases where he [is] at fault, to require him to contribute a reasonable amount . . . by way of compensation for the loss of earning power incurred in the common enterprise, irrespective of the question of negligence. . . . Nor can it be deemed arbitrary and unreasonable, from the standpoint of the employee's interest, to supplant a system under which he assumed the entire risk of injury in ordinary cases, and in others had a right to recover an amount more or less speculative upon proving facts of negligence that often were difficult to prove, and substitute a system under which in all ordinary cases of accidental injury he is sure of a definite and easily ascertained compensation, not being obliged to assume the entire loss in any case. . . .

Much emphasis is laid upon the criticism that the act creates liability without fault. . . . [L]iability without fault is not a novelty in the law. The common-law liability of the carrier, of the innkeeper, of him who employed fire or other dangerous agency or harbored a mischievous animal, was not dependent altogether upon questions of fault or negligence. Statutes imposing liability without fault have been sustained.[41]

Such reasoning seems fully applicable to auto no-fault and elective no-fault liability. In holding the Massachusetts auto no-fault law constitutional in *Pinnick* v. *Cleary*,[42] the Supreme Judicial Court of Massachusetts relied heavily on *White*. The court first found that the law clearly was a rational solution to a legitimate legislative objective, recognizing the existence of three major problems whose solution could have been the goal of the legislation: (1) court congestion caused by auto cases, (2) the high cost of auto insurance, and (3) inequities to claimants under the tort system. Additionally the court observed:

> The Legislature was also presumably aware of the long delays in getting financial aid to the injured person, confronted with medical and subsistence bills during a period of no employment for him and want for his family. The time spent in investigation, the time required for proof of negligence, the exaggerated claims, the all too common suspicion of perjured testimony, the horse and buggy approach to a twentieth century dilemma — all of this might well have influenced the Legislature, recognizing the right and need of all accident victims to simple and speedy justice, toward reform.
>
> It cannot be seriously argued that it was beyond legislative competence to assess this situation and to effect the necessary statutory repair. What we have discussed are evils which it was within the province of the Legislature to consider and which it endeavored to correct or eliminate. We do not intimate that the legislative determination . . . was the only answer or solution to the problem, but it cannot be successfully maintained that its salient provisions . . . are not a rational approach to the solution of these patent inefficiencies and inequities.[43]

The court then held that the Massachusetts law also provided a reasonable substitution for the common law rights which were affected: "[T]he exchange of rights involved with respect to the driver in an accident in which he was not negligent bears considerable resemblance to that effected by the statute in the *White* case with respect to employees. . . . The effect . . . on Massachusetts motorists thus is to provide benefits in return for affected rights at least as adequate as those provided to New York employers and employees in return for rights taken by the act in the *White* case."[44]

It is significant that the other no-fault auto cases do not question this basic holding of *Pinnick* and *White* that the no-fault concept does not violate the standards of due process. Those auto no-fault laws which have been found unconstitutional had particular provisions which were defective; the general no-fault idea was not found unconstitutional.[45]

As previously noted, then, there is a strong analogy between elective no-fault liability, workers' compensation, and auto no-fault. All three alter common law rights, allowing recovery on a no-fault basis to at least some extent. There seems no doubt that under

Notes on p. 236.

White, Pinnick, and related cases elective no-fault liability can avoid due process problems by merely meeting the standards required by those cases.

First, does elective no-fault liability attempt a solution to a legitimate legislative objective? Although the problems created by the products liability and medical malpractice compensation systems, for example, are not identical to those created by common law systems of compensation for auto and industrial injuries, they are clearly quite similar in nature and have become serious enough to merit legislative attention.[46] To some the problems stemming from nonindustrial and non-auto accidents may not appear to be as serious as those caused by industrial and auto accidents. To us, they seem worse, but perhaps have simply not received as much publicity; it matters little which. The welfare of thousands of citizens is already being threatened, and the state, exercising its police power,[47] or the federal government, exercising its power over interstate commerce,[48] can clearly attempt to remedy the situation. Elective no-fault liability, then, is a solution to a "legitimate legislative objective."

But is the solution proposed by elective no-fault liability a rational solution? And does that solution, even if rational, also provide a reasonable substitute for those preexisting common law rights which are lost? Elective no-fault liability is designed to compensate more people in less time at a lower cost. Rather than paying so much insurance money to lawyers and experts to fight in the courts over who gets paid, the insurance dollar is used to pay victims of product, medical, and other injuries for their actual pecuniary loss. A legislature has great leeway in determining just what is a rational solution to a problem. The solution chosen does not have to be the best one available; it need only be rational, and *White* and *Pinnick* clearly indicate that either an elective or a compulsory no-fault approach to such problems is indeed a rational solution.

In those instances under elective no-fault liability where common law rights are lost, the substitute is also clearly reasonable in light of *White* and *Pinnick.* Manufacturers, doctors, or others who elect to forego their common law defenses and compensate those injured on a no-fault basis will pay less to each claimant since no recovery is allowed for pain and suffering and since the "collateral source"

Notes on p. 236.

rule is eliminated. They will save substantial amounts now spent for lawyers and other experts and will avoid the stigma now associated with defective products and medical malpractice or other forms of negligence. And of course they could hardly complain about the substitution since they have complete freedom to retain all common law rights merely by choosing to do so. The consumer/patient also has a reasonable substitution when the business or professional elects no-fault coverage. In return for the uncertain right to recover for pain and suffering and for amounts already received from collateral sources, the consumer/patient is guaranteed payment for his actual losses which are not covered by other sources — without the long delay, expense, and difficulty of legal proceedings.

Indeed, not only is elective no-fault liability a rational solution to a legitimate legislative objective which provides a reasonable substitute for preexisting common law rights, but it seems to be the only solution which is legally feasible (from the point of view of proximate cause)[49] as well as economically and politically feasible at the present time.[50] Solving problems one step at a time is both constitutionally permissible and often practically wiser.[51] Elective no-fault is an experimental first step, and if its implementation is a success then perhaps compulsory no-fault liability for at least many injuries can follow as a more complete solution to the problems created by product and medical injuries. If the experiment is a failure, the damage done will be minimal compared to more sweeping, compulsory solutions,[52] and alternative solutions to the existing "horse and buggy approach to a twentieth century dilemma"[53] can then be assayed.

Equal Protection. A state elective no-fault liability law must meet the requirements of the equal protection clause of the Fourteenth Amendment[54] and similar clauses contained in most state constitutions.[55] Although the Fifth Amendment of the United States Constitution contains no equal protection clause, the concept of equal protection is embodied in the due process clause of that amendment, so a federal law still has to meet equal protection standards.[56] As was the case with the various due process clauses, equal protection standards are supposedly substantially identical no matter which particular clause may be applicable.[57] But here, again, state implementation is often far different from federal implementation.[58]

Notes on p. 236.

Equal protection becomes an issue only when the classification of persons affected by the law results in different treatment for persons who are similarly situated. Elective no-fault liability treats all businesses and professionals alike since each has complete freedom to choose the type and amount of no-fault coverage he desires, if any. True, after businesses and professionals make their election they will be treated differently, but only as a result of their own election, not as a result of a compulsory classification by the law. They clearly have no equal protection argument. It can also be contended that consumers/patients all receive similar treatment since each has the total freedom to elect which products he will consume and which doctors he will patronize. But as previously indicated, the reality of the system could mute the practicality of choice.[59] Therefore, in order to fully discuss the constitutional issues, let us assume that elective no-fault liability forces different treatment for injured consumers/patients who are similarly situated.

It should be noted at the outset that the consumer/patient has no equal protection argument because he is not given the free election that the business or professional is allowed. In *Hawkins* v. *Bleakly*,[60] the U.S. Supreme Court held that the elective Iowa Workmen's Compensation Act did not deprive the employer of equal protection of the laws. Workers' compensation was applicable only if both employer and employee elected coverage. However, the act withdrew the employer's common law defenses of assumption of risk, contributory negligence, and negligence of fellow servants if both employer and employee or the employer alone rejected the act. Only if the employer accepted and the employee rejected workers' compensation were the common law defenses available. In rejecting the employer's equal protection argument, the Court stated that "[a]ll employers are treated alike, and so are all employees. . . ."[61] Under elective no-fault, all businesses and professionals are treated alike, and the only complaint of consumers/patients can be that they are treated differently from each other in an arbitrary or discriminatory fashion.

A simple example should illustrate the different treatment possible for consumers/patients under elective no-fault liability. A, B, C, and D each suffers identical eye injury when struck by rocks thrown by their power mowers while mowing their lawns. Each has $10,000 in

Notes on p. 236.

out-of-pocket losses (medical expenses and lost wages) and an additional $10,000 in pain and suffering but recovers only $7,000 from collateral sources. The four different mowers are similar models manufactured by Companies W, X, Y, and Z, respectively. Company W has elected against any no-fault coverage, so A can recover only by suing under his traditional tort remedy and if successful could receive $10,000 for out-of-pocket losses and $10,000 for pain and suffering. Adding that $20,000 to the $7,000 from collateral sources, A has a possible total recovery of $27,000. Company X has chosen no-fault coverage for some injuries caused by their power mowers, but not for those caused by thrown rocks, so B is also restricted to the traditional tort system, and his total possible recovery is also $27,000. Note that A and B will both have to pay a lawyer approximately one-third of the $20,000 recovered in the tort suit, so their actual net possible recovery will be reduced by $6,667 to $20,333.

Company Y has elected no-fault coverage for thrown-rock injuries, but only to the extent of $5,000. Since C has already received $7,000 from collateral sources, Company Y would pay on a no-fault basis only the remaining $3,000 of C's out-of-pocket losses. C could then sue in tort and recover an additional $12,500 as follows: (1) $5,000 for the out-of-pocket losses exceeding the $5,000 tort exemption created by the no-fault election and (2) $7,500 for pain and suffering, assuming a tort exemption of one-half the no-fault election, or $2,500. Thus, C's possible recovery is $7,000 from collateral sources plus $3,000 for no-fault recovery plus $12,500 tort recovery for a total of $22,500 — reduced by $4,167 (one-third of $12,500 for his lawyer's contingent fee) to a net total of $18,333. Company Z has elected no-fault coverage for thrown-rock injuries to the extent of $10,000, but it still has to pay D only $3,000 of no-fault to cover the out-of-pocket losses remaining after payment from collateral sources. However, Company Z gets a $10,000 tort exemption since it elected $10,000 of no-fault coverage, and D cannot recover anything additional in tort for out-of-pocket losses. Company Z, however, has only a $5,000 exemption in tort for pain and suffering (one-half of the other tort exemption created by the no-fault election) and thus D can possibly recover an additional $5,000 in tort for pain and suffering. His recovery then is $7,000 from collateral sources plus $3,000 in no-fault benefits plus $5,000 in tort for a total of $15,000 — reduced by $1,667 (one-third of $5,000 for the lawyer's contingent fee) to $13,333. Thus, under elective no-fault liability, even though A, B, C, and D have received identical injuries and damages, their *potential* recoveries vary greatly.

To carry the example just one step further, assume that B's wife is injured by the same lawnmower that caused B's loss, but that she loses several of her toes when the mower runs over her foot. She, too, suffers $10,000 in out-of-pocket losses and $10,000 in pain and suffering and recovers $7,000 from collateral sources. However, Company X has elected no-fault coverage for this type of injury to the extent of $10,000, so her potential recovery is $13,333 (identical to that of D). Even though she and her husband were injured by the very same mower, suffering identical money damages, their *potential* recoveries also vary greatly under elective no-fault liability.

It is easy to see from this example that the number of different treatments becomes enormous with each business and professional making multiple elections involving thousands of different products and possible injuries.[62] Thus, there can be no question that elective no-fault liability does, indeed, classify consumers/patients so that similarly situated persons — all suffering injuries from products or medical procedures — are compensated for their injuries in a variety of different ways. This conclusion means only, however, that an equal protection issue can be expected to be raised, not that elective no-fault liability violates the equal protection clause. In order to determine whether elective no-fault does in fact violate equal protection, it is necessary to examine the equal protection tests used by the courts and then apply the proper test.

The courts utilize two major tests to determine when a violation of equal protection has occurred; both are very similar to the due process tests already discussed. The traditional equal protection test allows differentiation between similarly situated persons if the classification bears a rational relationship to a legitimate purpose. If, however, a "fundamental interest" or a "suspect classification" is involved, the "strict scrutiny" test is applied, requiring that the classification created by the law serve a "compelling state interest."[63] A review of the history of the two standards leaves little doubt that the traditional approach should be applied to elective no-fault liability which involves no rights or classifications that are even remotely

Notes on p. 236.

similar to those considered "fundamental" or "suspect" by the U.S. Supreme Court.[64] Thus, the different treatment accorded to consumers/patients is permissible if the classification bears a rational relationship to a legitimate legislative purpose.

We have already seen that a legitimate legislative purpose exists. A major problem has been created by product, medical, and other injuries, and the state or federal government has a right and duty, using the police power and interstate commerce power, respectively, to seek solutions to that problem.[65] The classification created by the law does, indeed, bear a rational relationship to the legislative purpose. Presently existing data are insufficient to determine the economic feasibility of mandatory universal no-fault coverage in the products liability, medical malpractice, and other areas. We can be almost certain that compulsory no-fault is unfeasible politically. Even if it were feasible, an initial stage of experimentation seems the wiser course — and surely a rational one — when the economic consequences are so uncertain.[66] The elective feature allows the necessary experimentation and renders the use of no-fault politically feasible — but is also responsible for the different treatment afforded injured consumers/patients since they are classified on the basis of elections made by businesses and professionals. Since the elective feature of the plan represents a reasonable and wise approach in achieving a legitimate legislative purpose, the resulting classification bears a rational relationship to that purpose.

Viewing the situation after recovery, it is obvious that there are unequal and perhaps even arbitrary results. However, the crucial focus should be at the time preceding the accident, when the fairness of insurance options can best be measured. True, potential recoveries vary and indeed decrease as no-fault coverage increases, but the important point is that greater *potential* recoveries may result in smaller *actual* recoveries. Trading higher possible recoveries (or payments from businesses and professionals) for guaranteed lower recoveries and payments under no-fault is surely a fair exchange. "A classification having some reasonable basis does not offend [the Constitution] merely because . . . in practice it results in some inequality."[67]

Compulsory auto no-fault laws do not have the same equal protection problems as elective no-fault liability, but most of them do

Notes on pp. 237–38.

have provisions which create an equal protection problem even more serious than that of elective no-fault liability. For example, the Massachusetts auto no-fault law contains a provision permitting recovery for pain and suffering only if medical expenses exceeded $500.[68] If, however, the injury results in a fracture, death, loss of a body member, permanent and serious disfigurement, or loss of sight or hearing, the plaintiff can recover for pain and suffering in any case without regard to the amount of medical expenses. Such a classification is arguably even more arbitrary than the classification of elective no-fault liability in which the consumer/patient can at least purchase the products and medical care of his choice. And even though the basis for the classification is different, both have a similar result in denying to certain persons a possible recovery for pain and suffering allowed under common law.

Confronted with this equal protection issue, the *Pinnick* court first recognized a legitimate legislative purpose: "It was clearly proper for the Legislature to conclude that the benefits of compensating an injured person for relatively minor pain and suffering, which as such entails no monetary loss, did not warrant continuation of the practice when balanced against the evils it had spawned."[69]

The court next decided that the exemption for the five types of serious injury — although perhaps allowing recovery for minor claims for pain and suffering while denying recovery for many substantial claims for pain and suffering — was not a violation of equal protection: "Some inequality in result is not enough to vitiate a legislative classification grounded in reason. . . . It seems to us that the Legislature has employed criteria rationally related to seriousness of injury in general, and thereby to seriousness of pain and suffering. Whether fracture should be included as a category, at the risk of allowing some minor claims for pain and suffering, is within the permissible range of judgment."[70] The court also found that the five-hundred-dollar threshold did not violate equal protection, relying on famous language of Mr. Justice Holmes: "When a legal distinction is determined, as no one doubts that it may be, between night and day, childhood and maturity, or any other extremes, a point has to be fixed or a line has to be drawn, or gradually picked out by successive decisions, to mark where the change takes place. Looked at by itself without regard to the necessity behind it the

Notes on p. 238.

line or point seems arbitrary. It might as well or nearly as well be a little more to one side or the other. But when it is seen that a line or point there must be, and that there is no mathematical or logical way of fixing it precisely, the decision of the Legislature must be accepted unless we can say that it is very wide of any reasonable mark."[71] Similarly, the lines drawn by elective no-fault liability do not appear "very wide of any reasonable mark."

Several recent cases have held long-established legislative classifications in violation of the equal protection clause and should be examined to determine their effect on the equal protection arguments just advanced favoring the constitutionality of elective no-fault liability. In *Brown* v. *Merlo*,[72] the California Supreme Court held the state's automobile "guest statute" unconstitutional as a violation of the equal protection clauses of the U.S. and California constitutions. The statute contained three levels of classification: (1) automobile guests were treated differently from paying passengers, (2) automobile guests were treated differently from other social guests, and (3) some automobile guests were treated differently from other automobile guests.[73] The court recognized two possible legislative justifications for the classifications: (1) to promote hospitality by barring suits for ordinary negligence against a generous driver by an ungrateful passenger, and (2) to prevent collusive lawsuits in which a host fraudulently admits negligence so that his passenger — a friend or relative — can recover from the driver's insurance company. The court held that "the classifications which the guest statute creates between those denied and those permitted recovery for negligently inflicted injuries do not bear a substantial and rational relation to the statute's purposes. . . ."[74]

Does *Merlo* cast doubt on the constitutionality of elective no-fault liability? We think not. First, "guest statutes" have long been under constitutional attack since they single out injured automobile guests for very "special" treatment.[75] Instead of receiving an alternative form of recovery, as is the case for workers' compensation, auto no-fault, and elective no-fault liability, the automobile guest is denied any recovery unless he can prove willful and wanton negligence or intoxication, which he is usually unable to do. In addition, that guest statutes remain constitutional in many states indicates that

Notes on p. 238.

elective no-fault liability — with far more rational classifications relating to more serious legislative purposes — would withstand constitutional attack in those states. Also, the California court's concluding remarks in *Merlo* reveal no antipathy toward no-fault laws: "Nothing we have said is intended to imply that only the common law rules of negligence can govern automobile liability. We hold only that in undertaking any alteration or reform of such rules the Legislature may not irrationally single out one class of individuals for discriminatory treatment."[76] Not only does elective no-fault liability not "irrationally single out one class of individuals for discriminatory treatment," but it also very rationally provides potentially fairer treatment for every class involved in product, medical, and other injury cases.

In *Gallegos* v. *Glaser Crandell Co.*,[77] the Michigan Supreme Court held that the agricultural exclusion section of the Michigan Workmen's Compensation Act of 1969[78] violated the equal protection clauses of the Michigan and U.S. constitutions. That statute provided full workers' compensation coverage only for those agricultural workers who were paid an hourly wage or salary (and not on a piecework basis) and who worked thirty-five or more hours per week for thirteen or more consecutive weeks for the same employers as long as the employer hired at least three such regular employees. The statute also provided medical and hospital coverage for only those agricultural employees working at least thirty-five hours a week for five or more consecutive weeks for the same employer who had at least one such employee within his hire. The court held:

> There is no basis for distinguishing the work of a laborer who drives a truck at a factory from a laborer who drives one on the farm or for any one of numerous other labor activities "on the farm" as distinguished from the same activity in industry, wholesaling, retailing, or building. There is no basis for singling out for an exclusion piece work "on the farm" but not elsewhere. There is no basis for a special definition of "weekly wage" for farm labor as distinguished from any other type of labor. "All private employers" come under the act if they regularly employ 3 or more employees at one time. On the other hand, only "agricultural em-

Notes on p. 239.

ployers" who employ 3 or more employees, not on piece work, 35 or more hours per week by the same employer for 13 or more weeks during the preceding 52 weeks come under the act.

. . . .

. . . Agricultural employers, regardless of the skills of their employees or the activities engaged in, are accorded a special treatment and classification of their employees not accorded any other private or public employer. Such treatment is impermissible, clearly discriminatory and has no rational basis.[79]

Although this situation is far more analogous to elective no-fault liability than was the California guest statute, in that no-fault liability is extended to some but excluded from others, it, too, can be distinguished. The Michigan statute singles out one occupation for "special" treatment. Although there were arguably rational reasons for doing so when most workers' compensation statutes were passed,[80] those reasons — at least in Michigan — in the court's view have ceased to exist. Workers' compensation laws are now well established, and once-proper classifications or exclusions may no longer be proper in light of changed circumstances. This is not to concede, however, that elective no-fault liability contains improper classifications. At least for the present the classifications resulting from the elective feature of an unproven plan requiring experimentation are far less arbitrary and discriminatory than the exclusion of a particular class of workers from the proven benefits of workers' compensation. And, of course, there are forty states in which such agricultural exclusions in workers' compensation statutes remain constitutional — Gallegos stands alone.[81] Elective no-fault liability would not seem, then, to be necessarily threatened by Gallegos, Merlo, or similar cases.

But it must be admitted that the tendency of some state courts to strike down legislation in this and other areas — as illustrated not only by the Illinois[82] and Florida[83] no-fault cases but also by Gallegos, Merlo, and other cases[84] — may incline one to urge federal enactment of elective or extrahazardous no-fault liability insurance since federal courts would probably give more sympathetic constitutional consideration to such legislation. On the other hand, the tide of state decisions on the constitutionality of no-fault auto laws seems now rather clearly to be running heavily in favor of upholding

Notes on p. 239.

them.[85] Here again, though, the adverse decisions on the rather more novel and complex car damage no-fault provisions, even by state courts willing to uphold no-fault laws applicable to personal injury,[86] can cause fear concerning the arguably novel and complex provisions under elective no-fault liability for personal injury. Not that the features of the car damage laws are directly analogous to elective no-fault liability for personal injury. On the contrary, elective no-fault, unlike the car damage option, takes care not to leave the victim without any remedy.[87] But in each instance variations even more novel than auto no-fault applicable to personal injury are employed, and the hostility of some courts to such novelty, when coupled with the other decisions mentioned above, can give one pause — not about what state courts *should* do, but about what they *might* do.

Other State Constitutional Provisions. Although some might argue that federal elective no-fault liability would exceed the congressional power over interstate commerce,[88] there is simply no doubt about state power to enact an elective no-fault liability law (assuming it to be otherwise constitutional) utilizing the police power which allows broad authority to legislate for the health and welfare of the people of the state.[89] There are, however, special provisions in the constitutions of some states which do present thornier constitutional problems for elective no-fault liability.

Section 54 of the Kentucky Constitution, for example, states: "The General Assembly shall have no power to limit the amount to be recovered for injuries resulting in death, or for injuries to persons or property."[90] Arizona, Arkansas, Pennsylvania, and Wyoming have similar provisions prohibiting limitations on the amount to be recovered in both injury and death cases.[91] Four other states — New York, Ohio, Oklahoma, and Utah — have constitutional provisions which prohibit such a limitation on recovery only for cases resulting in death.[92] For example, Article I, § 16 of the New York Constitution reads: "The right of action now existing to recover damages for injuries resulting in death, shall never be abrogated; and the amount recoverable shall not be subject to any statutory limitation."[93] Such provisions have formerly, at least, been viewed as posing a serious constitutional obstacle for various types of no-fault legislation. In Kentucky, for example, the workers' compensation law remains

Notes on pp. 239–40.

elective because it has been held that a compulsory law would violate the prohibition of Section 54.[94]

Several of the other states — before enacting compulsory workers' compensation — amended such provisions to allow an exception for workers' compensation.[95] It was thought, on first impression, that (1) such provisions "would seem to stand clearly in the way of enacting [a no-fault auto] ... system [and t]hus further amendments would be needed to enact [such a] ... system,"[96] and (2) "without modification of the [Keeton-O'Connell] basic protection [no-fault auto] plan,[97] a constitutional prohibition against altering the death action might very well interfere with the application of the basic protection system to death actions."[98] Elective no-fault liability is, of course, faced with the same problem, since — once an election for no-fault coverage is made by the business or professional — the right of the consumer/patient to recover for pain and suffering and collateral sources is substantially affected. One might therefore conclude that an elective no-fault liability law in these nine states must be preceded by an amendment of the applicable constitutional provisions.

However, it has recently been suggested by Joel Martel, a member of the Pennsylvania bar, that this cursory examination is inadequate and that a more searching analysis of the problem produces substantial support for the position that a constitutional amendment will not be necessary after all.[99] After a specific exception for workers' compensation cases, Article 3, Section 18, of the Pennsylvania Constitution goes on to provide: "[I]n no other cases shall the General Assembly limit the amount to be recovered for injuries resulting in death, or for injuries to persons or property, and in case of death from such injuries, the right of action shall survive, and the General Assembly shall prescribe for whose benefit such actions shall be prosecuted. No act shall prescribe any limitations of time within which suits may be brought against corporations for injuries to persons or property, or for other causes different from those fixed by general laws regulating actions against natural persons, and such acts now existing are avoided."[100] The original purpose of this constitutional terminology was apparently to reverse the effect of the act of April 4, 1868,[101] which had limited the amount an injured person could recover in a negligence action against railroad com-

Notes on pp. 240–41.

panies and common carriers to $3,000 for injury and $5,000 for death.[102] Martel argues that Article 3, Section 18, should be restricted to similar laws placing an arbitrary upper limit on recovery and not applied to no-fault laws:[103]

> Clearly the term "limit" would be applicable to a law such as the Act of 1868, which set an upper ceiling or boundary on the amount a victim could recover when suing a negligent railroad. On the other hand, the term "limit" does not seem applicable to a law which sets no upper boundary on the amount recoverable in an action, but rather merely attempts to exclude minor or small claims.... The language ... does not say "the General Assembly shall not *abolish* causes of action for injuries to person or property"; rather, it speaks only of placing no *limit* on the amount to be recovered. Therefore, one may fairly conclude that the framers intended that, so long as the legislature considered a tort cause of action a useful social mechanism for the achievement of justice, no legislation be passed that would place a limit on the amount to be recovered in such an action. The language of the provision does not compel the conclusion that an antiquated and anachronistic cause of action cannot be wiped out by the legislature. Such an interpretation would freeze the law of torts in a rigid, inflexible mold and prevent its adaptation to changing social conditions. The total abolition of all tort actions in cases of automobile accidents, to be replaced with a no-fault system of compensation, would not be the type of legislation which article 3, section 18, expressly or impliedly forbids.[104]

In addition to historical support, Martel contends that his thesis is further strengthened by the fact that Pennsylvania has abolished a number of common law tort actions — including alienation of affections and breach of promise to marry[105] — without encountering constitutional problems.[106] But no-fault laws such as the no-fault auto laws or elective no-fault liability are less restrictive than laws abolishing a common law cause of action since they only affect the amounts recoverable for pain and suffering and collateral sources in some cases without completely abolishing recovery for these items in all cases. Martel admits that his case is weakened by the fact that a constitutional amendment was considered necessary before a compulsory workers' compensation law was passed in Pennsylvania.[107]

Notes on p. 241.

Consequently, the compulsory law was never tested under Article 3, Section 18, but several cases do contain strong dicta[108] indicating that such a law would have violated Article 3, Section 18, without the exception for workers' compensation. Martel candidly concludes, "This is truly a case where the legal arguments on both sides carry considerable weight, and it cannot be predicted with confidence which side would prevail in the Pennsylvania Supreme Court."[109] Additionally, he finds that his theory has even less chance for acceptance in some other states with similar constitutional provisions.[110] It should be noted, though, that Dean Griswold not only finds merit in the Martel theory as applied to the Pennsylvania Constitution, but also contends that the constitutional obstacles facing similar provisions in other states are not insurmountable either.[111] Even so, it should be obvious that elective no-fault liability faces more serious constitutional tests in the nine states with such limitation provisions.[112]

A less serious, but nonetheless arguable, constitutional obstacle to elective no-fault liability is found in the "redress of injury" clauses of about twenty-five state constitutions.[113] Article I, Section 21, of the Florida Constitution is a typical example: "The courts shall be open to every person for redress of any injury, and justice shall be administered without sale, denial or delay."[114] But in *Lasky* v. *State Farm*,[115] the Florida Supreme Court held that a no-fault auto law and its tort exemption did not violate this provision. Similarly, the "redress of injury" clause in the Massachusetts Declaration of Rights guarantees "a certain remedy, by having recourse to the laws, for all injuries or wrongs which [one] may receive...."[116] In *Pinnick* v. *Cleary*,[117] the Massachusetts Supreme Judicial Court quickly rejected the contention that the Massachusetts auto no-fault law violated the clause: "The article is clearly directed toward the preservation of procedural rights and has been so construed.... [C]hanges in prior law are necessary in any ordered society, and to argue that [the "redress of injury" clause] prohibits alterations of common law rights as such, especially in the face of the specific provision to the contrary in art. 6 [contemplating revision of the common law by the legislature], flies in the face of all reason and precedent."[118]

Decisions in other states interpreting "redress of injury" provisions lend additional and powerful support to the proposition that elective no-fault liability would not violate such provisions.[119] For example, the Texas "redress of injury" provision was interpreted in *Lebohm* v. *City of Galveston*[120] to validate a city charter granted by the state legislature conferring tort immunity on the city. The court held that a legislature is allowed to abolish a common law cause of action if a reasonable substitute is provided or if the abolition is a reasonable exercise of the police power. Martel noted that cases such as *Lebohm* really amount "to a restraint upon legislative power no greater than the restraint to which legislatures are subject under the general requirements of due process and equal protection"[121] and "that the consensus of the state courts have construed ["redress of injury"] provisions . . . as not posing a bar to legislation designed to implement a no-fault automobile accident compensation system."[122] And so just as elective no-fault liability readily satisfies due process and equal protection standards, it just as readily satisfies the standards of "redress of injury" provisions found in the constitutions of one-half the states.

Congressional Power to Enact Elective No-Fault Liability. With a federal auto no-fault law now being considered by the United States Congress, a federal elective no-fault liability law is a possibility the constitutional implications of which should be discussed. Since the U.S. Constitution does not grant to the federal government the police power possessed by the states, the Congress can pass an elective no-fault liability law only if justified by the Commerce Clause of the Constitution.[123] That clause has been broadly interpreted to allow Congress far-reaching control over any matters even remotely affecting interstate commerce,[124] and it should present no significant constitutional obstacle for elective no-fault liability.

On first glance, however, it might appear that many product, medical, and other injuries which are the focus of elective no-fault liability are strictly intrastate occurrences. But, of course, the actual problem is the inadequacy of the system of compensation for those injuries. And in reality — even though the underlying liabilities are controlled by state law — the vast majority of businesses and professionals are covered by liability insurance which pays the overwhelming amount of tort compensation presently available to those injured.[125] Thus, elective no-fault liability in effect is nothing more

Notes on pp. 243–44.

than the regulation of a presently existing system of liability insurance, and the United States Supreme Court has clearly held that insurance is an interstate business subject to congressional regulation. Said the Court in 1944 in the famous *South-Eastern Underwriters* decision: "Our basic responsibility in interpreting the Commerce Clause is to make certain that the power to govern intercourse among the states remains where the Constitution placed it. That power, as held by this Court from the beginning, is vested in the Congress, available to be exercised for the national welfare as Congress shall deem necessary. No commercial enterprise of any kind which conducts its activities across state lines has been held to be wholly beyond the regulatory power of Congress under the Commerce Clause. We cannot make an exception of the business of insurance."[126] The power to regulate the insurance business would, however, be meaningless if the underlying reason for the inadequacy of the liability insurance system — the state laws controlling liability in products liability, medical malpractice, and other tort cases — were beyond the reach of congressional power. Those laws presently constitute a burden on interstate commerce because they contribute significantly to the deficiencies of the insurance business. Congress can thus legislate in the areas affected by such laws in light of their effect on interstate commerce, and once a federal law is passed, any conflicting state laws would be rendered inoperative under the Supremacy Clause of the U.S. Constitution.[127]

Additionally, it is clear that at least the products liability aspects of elective no-fault liability would be constitutional even if insurance were not pervasively involved. Indeed, the products causing injuries are the very "stuff" of interstate commerce. When those products cause injury and death — with the victims largely uncompensated — the effects on interstate commerce are considerable. Not only can Congress act to relieve those effects, but the Supreme Court has specifically held that Congress can do so by regulating the liabilities of parties involved in injuries arising out of interstate commerce.[128] And that power can clearly reach even those products which are produced, sold, and consumed without ever crossing a state line. Indeed, the long constitutional history of the Commerce Clause is replete with examples of activities which appeared to be totally intrastate in nature but were nonetheless subject to Congressional

Notes on p. 244.

control.[129] In that regard, the practice of medicine can also be seen as an interstate business — or at least as having a significant effect on interstate commerce — such that it, too, is subject to congressional control regardless of the involvement of insurance.

A final comment to put these constitutional issues in perspective. It is quite easy to become discouraged about the prospects of personal injury law reform in light of even the few decisions holding no-fault auto reform unconstitutional. Many opponents of no-fault reform are inclined to emphasize the threat of unconstitutionality to forestall reform. Thus, James Kemper, Jr., president of the Kemper Insurance Companies, writing in 1967, stated, ". . . our attorneys are of the opinion that the . . . analogy to workmen's compensation insurance will not stand up, and that [a no-fault auto] . . . plan will be struck down as a violation of the due process and equal protection clauses of the federal and state constitutions. . . . One consequence of the doubt in this area could be disastrous: If a state legislature passed [a no-fault] . . . statute, the system might be instituted and operating before a ruling of the . . . Supreme Court on its constitutionality; and [a no-fault] . . . plan represents an irrevocable step. Trying to return to the tort liability system to meet constitutional requirements would be like trying to unscramble an egg."[130] And thus Paul Blume, Vice President and general counsel of the National Association of Independent Insurers, an organization opposing federal no-fault insurance, according to a press report, "in testimony before a Senate Judiciary Committee . . . said court rulings that voided the Illinois no-fault law and a section of the Florida law cost auto insurers and ultimately their policyholders well over $75 million. Should all or part of a federal law be invalidated, the costs in 50 states would be astronomical, Blume said. These expenses could bankrupt hundreds of small companies, lessening competition in the auto-insurance business and encouraging a monopoly of large companies. And even the companies that survive would be forced to pass on their higher costs of business to the consumer in the form of higher rates, he said."[131]

The forbidding nature of constitutional arguments — especially to the nonlawyer legislator — was highlighted a few years ago by then Representative Michael Dukakis of the Massachusetts House of Representatives, a leading sponsor of no-fault auto insurance in

Notes on p. 244.

Massachusetts. In discussing the process by which the Massachusetts bill he sponsored was opposed, Dukakis said "[Lawyers in the
legislature] . . . can often baffle a nonlawyer legislator with plausible
arguments about constitutionality and due process. We have one
prominent lawyer-legislator in Massachusetts who has repeatedly
questioned the constitutionality of the [no-fault auto insurance] . . .
bill on the grounds that it compels people to insure themselves. Apparently he has never heard of Social Security or Medicare.[132] But
such arguments, particularly if delivered with an aura of legal
authority, can raise doubts in the minds of the legislator who is not
an attorney."[133]

But those who are fainthearted or those discouraged by possible
constitutional pitfalls must keep such issues in context. No one seriously questions today that workers' compensation should have been
considered constitutional when it was proposed in the early part of
this century. And yet it took many years — with many defeats in
many states and occasional resort to constitutional amendments —
before the courts began to acknowledge that workers' compensation
was indeed a legitimate exercise of legislative discretion and therefore constitutional. We have seen some of those same frustrations
recently — in Illinois and Florida — with reference to some aspects
of no-fault auto insurance laws. And the same frustrations *may*
accompany some attempts at elective or extrahazardous no-fault
laws. But in fact, an objective examination of the arguments against
the constitutionality of replacing the common law tort liability system with no-fault laws — in light of the way the common law
actually works — would seem to justify the almost impatient (while
thorough and painstaking) dismissal of those objections by Erwin
Griswold, surely one of the ablest and most versatile legal scholars
of his age, in his recent Senate testimony on federal no-fault auto
insurance.[134] Said Griswold at the outset of his testimony:

> Before going further, . . . I would like to say that, though consti-
> tutional questions are always important, they should not be over-
> emphasized. The fact that there are possible constitutional ques-
> tions does not mean that they will necessarily arise if [the federal
> no-fault bill under consideration, Senate Bill 354] is enacted. . . .
> I have endeavored to examine the constitutional questions care-
> fully and thoroughly. The mere length of what I have done may

Notes on pp. 244–45.

make it seem that the constitutional problems are more serious than I think they really are. . . . [T]hus . . . I do not think that the constitutional questions should be allowed to dominate the consideration of this bill. Of course, [a legislature] . . . must operate within the Constitution. Nevertheless, many of the constitutional questions which have been raised . . . seem to me to be more theoretical than practically real.[135]

Indeed, at bottom, to insist that a constitution prevents the change that no-fault entails in the common law fault system — with all the fault system's cruelty, waste, and delay — is to tarnish that constitution.

NOTES

1. See Grace v. Howlett, 51 Ill.2d 478, 283 N.E.2d 474 (1972). The Illinois auto no-fault law required that only private passenger automobiles be covered by no-fault policies but restricted recovery of general damages (mostly pain and suffering) for all cases of injury by any kind of motor vehicle, whether covered by a no-fault policy or not. This provision was held unconstitutional as a violation of the Illinois Constitution's restriction on passage of special legislation when a general law could be made applicable. Additionally, the law's provision establishing mandatory arbitration of claims not exceeding $3,000 was held to violate several other constitutional requirements, including the right to trial by jury. But see the convincing dissent by Underwood, C.J., 51 Ill.2d at 491, 283 N.E.2d at 481 (1972).

In Manzanares v. Bell, No. 122, 937 (Dist. Ct. First Div., Shawnee County, Kan., Jan. 4, 1974), a Kansas trial court held the Kansas auto no-fault law unconstitutional as a denial of due process and equal protection. The Kansas legislature then passed a new no-fault bill remedying the supposed "flaws" even though the case was on appeal to the Kansas Supreme Court (National Underwriter [Property and Casualty ed.], Feb. 15, 1974, p. 41). See also Kluger v. White, 281 So. 2d 1 (Fla. 1973) holding the property damage section of the Florida auto no-fault law unconstitutional.

But as this book goes to press, three decisions (including Supreme Court cases in Kansas and Florida) upholding no-fault laws have been handed down. On May 7, 1974, the Kansas Supreme Court upheld the constitutionality of both the old and new laws (Manzanares v. Bell, —— Kan. —— [1974]).

In April the Florida Supreme Court had upheld the Florida no-fault law as it applies to personal injury (Lasky v. State Farm, 296 So. 2d 9 [Fla. 1974]). On May 20, 1974, a Michigan state trial court in Detroit declared the property damage section of the Michigan no-fault law unconstitutional, but most of the bodily injury portion of the law was found constitutional except for the provision excluding two-wheeled vehicles from no-fault coverage and several other minor provisions (Shavers v. Kelley [Cir. Ct. Wayne County, Mich., May 20, 1974]).

Furthermore, the concepts of elective no-fault liability need not be affected by the above-mentioned adverse decisions since the general plan of elective no-fault is arguably unburdened by the kind of "technical" flaws which rendered those laws questionable.

2. Certain provisions in some state constitutions present special problems whose resolution *may* require a constitutional amendment in those particular states. See *infra* notes 88–112 and accompanying text for a full discussion of these special limitation provisions found in the constitutions of only nine states.

3. "[N]or shall any person . . . be deprived of life, liberty, or property, without due process of law . . ." (*U.S. Const.* amend. V).

4. "[N]or shall any state deprive any person of life, liberty, or property, without due process of law . . ." (*U.S. Const.* amend. XIV, § 1).

5. See, e.g., *Utah Const.* art. I, § 7; *Wyo. Const.* art. I, § 6; *Ill. Const.* art. I, § 2; and *Conn. Const.* art. I, § 8.

6. United States v. Carolene Products Co., 304 U.S. 144 (1938); Howes Bros. Co. v. Unemployment Compensation Comm., 296 Mass. 275, 283–84, 5 N.E.2d 720, 726 (1936); Opinion of the Justices, 304 A.2d 881, 886 (1973); State v. Doe, 149 Conn. 216, 226, 178 A.2d 271, 276 (1962); People v. Brown, 407 Ill. 565, 95 N.E.2d 888 (1950); Untermyer v. State Tax Commission, 102 Utah 214, 222–23, 129 P.2d 881, 885 (1942). See also *Hearings on S. 354 before the Senate Committee on the Judiciary*, 93d Cong., 1st and 2d Sess. 770–71 (1974) [hereinafter cited as *Hearings on S. 354*].

7. State presumption of constitutionality is often, in modern times, considerably less rigorous than is federal. Paulsen, "The Persistence of Substantive Due Process in the States," 34 *Minn. L. Rev.* 92 (1950); Heatherington, "State Economic Regulation and Substantive Due Process of Law," 53 *Nw. L. Rev.* 13, 226 (2 pts., 1958). See *infra* notes 72–86 and accompanying text. There seems to be, in fact, little problem of elective no-fault meeting the requirements of federal due process.

8. Nebbia v. New York, 291 U.S. 502, 537–38 (1934); O'Gorman & Young, Inc., v. Hartford Fire Ins. Co., 282 U.S. 251, 257–58 (1931).

9. Note added: If the legislation affects a right which the courts deem "fundamental," then the federal or state government must show that it has a "compelling interest" before the legislation can satisfy due process standards. In challenging the Massachusetts auto no-fault law, plaintiffs attempted to find some impairment of a fundamental right of personal security and bodily integrity, using as support the concurring opinion of Mr. Justice Goldberg in Griswold v. Connecticut, 381 U.S. 479, 486 (1965). The Supreme Judicial Court of Massachusetts quickly disposed of the argument: "Whatever may be the fundamental 'right of personal security and bodily integrity' to which the plaintiff refers, it is not affected [here]. . . . [Our no-fault law] . . . merely limits the common law right in the automobile accident situation to obtain money damages on account of unintentionally inflicted pain and suffering and modifies the procedure for obtaining damages according to the common law measure for all other elements of recovery" (Pinnick v. Cleary, 271 N.E.2d 592, 600 [Mass. 1971]).

Similar reasoning precludes the application of the "compelling interest" test to elective no-fault liability, especially considering the types of laws which have been subjected to this stricter constitutional standard. See, e.g., Griswold,

381 U.S. 479, holding that a Connecticut statute forbidding use of contraceptives denied due process because it violated the fundamental right of marital privacy; Shelton v. Tucker, 364 U.S. 479 (1960), holding that an Arkansas statute requiring teachers to file an annual affidavit listing organizational affiliations violated due process because it deprived the teachers of the fundamental right of associational freedom; Sherbert v. Verner, 374 U.S. 398 (1963), holding that state denial of unemployment compensation to a Seventh Day Adventist, who could not keep a job because of his refusal to work on Saturday, was a denial of due process as a violation of the fundamental right of freedom of religion; and Roe v. Wade, 410 U.S. 113 (1973) and Doe v. Bolton, 410 U.S. 179 (1973), holding that state abortion laws violated due process because they infringed upon the fundamental right of privacy. These cases in which the U.S. Supreme Court has applied the "compelling interest" test are arguably not analogous to situations such as workers' compensation, auto no-fault, and elective no-fault liability, which affect no such fundamental constitutional right.

10. NOTE ADDED: The same due process standard applies to the federal government except that, unlike the states, the federal government has no constitutionally based police power to legislate for the general welfare. Thus, federal legislation must be justified under some provision of the U.S. Constitution such as the Commerce Clause. See *infra* notes 123–24 and accompanying text.

11. Nebbia, 291 U.S. at 537. See also West Coast Hotel Co. v. Parrish, 300 U.S. 379, 391 (1937).

12. Pinnick, 271 N.E.2d at 602.

13. *Ibid.* The argument relies on cases upholding automobile "guest statutes" and laws abolishing actions for breach of promise, seduction, alienation of affections, and criminal conversation which do not provide any substitute for the common law rights they abolish.

14. See *supra,* ch. 8, notes 23–25 and accompanying text.

15. E.g., "No-Fault Automobile Insurance: A Progress Report," *Consumer Reports,* Oct., 1973, p. 642.

16. W.Va. Code Ann. ch. 23 (1970). But see *infra* notes 19–23 and accompanying text for similar provisions in compulsory states.

17. Rhodes v. J. B. B. Coal Co., 79 W.Va. 71, 90 S.E. 796 (1916). See also DeFrancesco v. Piney Mining Co., 76 W.Va. 756, 86 S.E. 777 (1915).

18. See *supra,* ch. 9, note 17 and accompanying text.

19. U.S. Chamber of Commerce, Analysis of Workmen's Compensation Laws 12 n. 1 (1973).

20. N.Y. Workmen's Compensation Law § 3 (McKinney 1965).

21. *Ibid.*

22. L. 1941, c. 639, § 1 (1941).

23. See Murphy v. Elmwood Country Club, 183 Misc. 332, 51 N.Y.S.2d 260 (1944). In addition to the many states, like New York, which simply allow the exempt employer's unilateral election to bind the employee, Illinois, for example, has further variations in allowing such personal injury rights to be unilaterally altered by another private party. In Illinois any employer exempt from compulsory coverage can elect workers' compensation coverage for his employees, who then have thirty days to reject such coverage (Ill. Rev.

Stat. ch. 48, § 138.2 [1973]). However, even if the employee rejects coverage, the liability of the employer is determined by the Workmen's Compensation Act until he receives notice from the industrial commission of the employee's rejection (*ibid.*). Thus, even a rejecting employee has his common law rights unilaterally affected for at least the time needed to comply with the rejection provisions of the act. If he is injured during those few days, his only means of recovery is workers' compensation. If both employer and employee initially elect workers' compensation coverage, either can later reject coverage for the next calendar year (*ibid.*). In that situation, personal injury compensation rights are altered by the unilateral action of another individual or concern. (But rather than common law rights being altered — indeed, they are restored — the existing statutory rights of an employer or employee under workers' compensation are altered by the unilateral action of another individual or concern.) Note, too, that if the employer never elects workers' compensation, his unilateral decision forecloses the employee from ever enjoying the benefits of workers' compensation. (A separate question is whether employees not covered by compulsory workers' compensation are denied equal protection of the law. For a discussion of this question, see *infra* notes 80–84 and accompanying text.

It might also be noted there already exist many other instances in which one individual has the right to modify unilaterally the common law rights of another vis-à-vis himself. One example is the privilege against testifying against one's spouse about acts which occurred prior to marriage even when the marriage was entered into to gain this privilege (8 J. Wigmore, *Evidence in Trials at Common Law* §§ 2230, 2235 [rev. by J. McNaughton, 1961]; McCormick, *Handbook of the Law of Evidence* § 66 [2d ed. rev. by E. Cleary, 1972]). A second example occurs when a person voluntarily enters the armed forces. The Soldiers and Sailors Civil Relief Act (50 U.S.C. Appendix 501 et seq. [1964]), among other things, prevents eviction of a service member's family, stays execution of judgments, and sets a maximum rate of interest on obligations. This has been held a valid exercise of the congressional power to wage war (Erickson v. Macy, 231 N.Y. 86, 131 N.E. 744 [1921]; Hoffman v. Five Cents Savings Bank, 231 Mass. 324, 121 N.E. 15 [1818]; Pierrard v. Hoch, 997 Ore. 71, 191 P. 328 [1920]; Bell v. Parker, 260 S.W. 158 [Tex. 1924]). A third example is the delegation of eminent domain power to private corporations, which has been held valid (e.g., Chicago Burlington & Quincy Railroad v. Cavanagh, 278 Ill. 609, 116 N.E. 128 [1917]).

24. W.Va. Code Ann. ch. 23 (1970).

25. *Ibid.*, § 23-2-7.

26. Daniels v. Charles Boldt Co., 78 W.Va. 124, 88 S.E. 613 (1916).

27. N.Y. Workmen's Compensation Law § 51 (McKinney 1965).

28. See *supra* note 23.

29. Ill. Rev. Stat. ch. 48, § 138.2 (1973). For decisions holding, on constitutional grounds, that regardless of whether an employer under elective workers' compensation provides notice in accordance with the statutory requirements and regardless of whether the employee actually receives notice, the employee is bound by the employer's election of workers' compensation, see Young v. Duncan, 218 Mass. 346, 106 N.E. 1 (1914); Mackin v. Detroit-Timken Axle Co., 187 Mich. 8, 153 N.W. 49 (1915). (Both decisions con-

cerned laws under which the employee was empowered to reject the employer's election of workers' compensation provided he got notice, acted in a timely fashion, etc.)

30. See *supra,* ch. 8, note 8; ch. 9, note 16; and ch. 11, notes 17–20 and accompanying text. But see ch. 8, note 32.

31. See *supra,* ch. 9, notes 2–11 and accompanying text.

32. See *supra,* ch. 9, note 17 and accompanying text.

33. See, e.g., R. Keeton and J. O'Connell, *Basic Protection for the Traffic Victim: A Blueprint for Reforming Automobile Insurance* 485 (1965); *Hearings on S. 354, supra* note 6, at 772–75; Cowen, "Due Process, Equal Protection and 'No-Fault' Allocation of the Costs of Automobile Accidents," and Bishop, "The Validity Under the Constitution of the United States of Basic Protection Insurance and Similar Proposals for the Reform of the System of Compensating Victims of Automobile Accidents," in U.S. Department of Transportation, *Constitutional Problems in Automobile Accident Compensation Reform* 28–33 and 44–53, respectively (Automobile Insurance and Compensation Study, 1970).

34. New York Central Railroad Company v. White, 243 U.S. 188 (1917); Mountain Timber Co. v. Washington, 243 U.S. 219 (1917); Arizona Employers Liability Cases, 250 U.S. 400 (1919).

35. For an attempt to refine the meaning(s) of "first party insurance" (a refinement that apparently has not caught on), see R. Keeton and J. O'Connell, *supra* note 20, at 343–51.

36. But see *supra,* ch. 8, notes 31–32 and accompanying text.

37. Dean Griswold finds merit in such an analogy: "The power of a legislature to replace the common law action for damages with specified benefits payable without regard to fault is amply supported by the Supreme Court decisions sustaining the constitutional validity of Workmen's Compensation Acts against challenge under the due process clause" (*Hearings on S. 354, supra* note 6, at 772).

In answer to those who attack the analogy between auto no-fault and workmen's compensation, the authors of the basic no-fault protection plan (Keeton and O'Connell, *supra* note 20, at 486) had this reply: "Nor does the constitutionality of workmen's compensation acts turn on their involving employer-employee relationships. 'Such a suggestion magnifies the importance of the relationship out of which the injury may arise and minimizes the social consequences of the injury itself' [Dowling, "Constitutional Questions," 32 *Colum. L. Rev.* 785, 816–17 (1932)]. Moreover, 'it is now well settled that the constitutionality of compensation legislation rests not upon the private employment contract but upon public welfare and police powers' [1 Larson, *Law of Workmen's Compensation* § 49.22, at 734 (1964)]."

Griswold continues: "It is also said ... that workmen's compensation is different because the equities require the employer to bear the loss. Again, this is not a valid distinction. No-fault seeks to allocate the costs of automobile accidents among all persons who operate automobiles. Although the first party must bear (through insurance) the costs of injuries to himself (in the situation in which no-fault applies) he is relieved of liability to others, in the same situations; and there is a benefit to all through the elimination of the issue of fault with its attendant costs. Thus there is a benefit to the first party, and

Congress could reasonably conclude that the no-fault plan provides, over-all, a more equitable basis for allocating the accident costs inherent in the operation of motor vehicles" (*Hearings on S. 354, supra* note 6, at 775–76 n. 6).

38. 243 U.S. 219.
39. 243 U.S. 188.
40. 250 U.S. 400.
41. 243 U.S. at 198–204.
42. 271 N.E.2d 592.
43. *Ibid.*, 605.
44. *Ibid.*, 606–7.
45. See *supra* note 1.
46. See *supra* chs. 2–4.
47. See *infra* note 89 and accompanying text.
48. See *supra* note 10 and accompanying text.
49. See *supra*, ch. 6, note 2; ch. 8, note 23; and accompanying text.
50. See *supra* chs. 6–9.
51. Williamson v. Lee Optical of Oklahoma, Inc., 348 U.S. 483 (1955); Railway Express Agency v. New York, 336 U.S. 106 (1949).
52. See *supra*, ch. 8, notes 24–30 and accompanying text.
53. Pinnick, 271 N.E.2d at 605.
54. "No state shall . . . deny to any person within its jurisdiction the equal protection of the laws" (*U.S. Const.* amend. XIV, § 1).
55. E.g., *Mass. Const.* pt. 1, art. 10 ("Each individual of the society has a right to be protected by it in the enjoyment of his life, liberty and property, according to standing laws"); *Fla. Const.* art. I, § 2; *Mich. Const.* art. I, § 2; *Ill. Const.* art. I, § 2.
56. Bolling v. Sharpe, 347 U.S. 497 (1954).
57. Opinion of the Justices, 257 N.E.2d 94, 95 (Mass. 1970); State v. Mason, 94 Utah 501, 507, 78 P.2d 920, 923 (1938); Bargain City U.S.A. v. Dilworth, 407 Pa. 129, 179 A.2d 439 (1962).
58. See *supra* note 7 and accompanying text. See also *infra* notes 72–86 and accompanying text.
59. See *supra*, text following note 23.
60. 243 U.S. 210 (1917).
61. *Ibid.* at 218.
62. Note that the number of different treatments is immaterial as long as the classification still meets equal protection standards by bearing a rational relationship to a legitimate legislative purpose. Of course, a wide variation in the number of treatments can bear heavily in determining whether the relationship is rational. But in elective no-fault liability, the many variations result from the elective feature of the plan, which is a most reasonable approach to the existing problem. See San Antonio Independent School Dist. v. Rodriguez, 93 S.Ct. 1278, 1299 (1973), in which the U.S. Supreme Court — using the traditional "rational basis" test — held that the Texas system of financing public schools did not violate the equal protection clause even though the effect of the system was to allow different levels of financing in each school district and hence numerous different treatments for school children depending on the school district in which they lived.
63. *Ibid.* at 1288. But see case note, 21 *U.C.L.A. L. Rev.* 1566 (1974).

64. "Suspect" classifications include: (1) race (McLaughlin v. Florida, 379 U.S. 184 [1964]); (2) national ancestry (Korematsu v. United States, 323 U.S. 214 [1944]); (3) alienage (Sei Fujii v. State, 38 Cal. 2d 718, 242 P.2d 617 [1952]); and (4) illegitimacy (Gomez v. Perez, 93 S.Ct. 872 [1973]). "Fundamental interests" include: (1) interstate travel (Shapiro v. Thompson, 394 U.S. 618 [1969]); (2) right to vote (Reynolds v. Sims, 377 U.S. 533 [1964]); (3) right to procreate (Skinner v. Oklahoma, 316 U.S. 535 [1942]); and (4) procedural rights of criminals (Griffin v. Illinois, 351 U.S. 12 [1956]). Several recent decisions indicate that the Supreme Court will be very reluctant to extend the "compelling interest" test to additional rights and classifications. A Maryland statute denied additional welfare payments on a per child basis once the family reached a maximum size. Using the "rational basis" test to hold the law constitutional, the Court held that the "compelling interest" test was inapplicable, "[f]or here we deal with state regulation in the social and economic field, not affecting freedoms guaranteed by the Bill of Rights . . ." (Dandridge v. Williams, 397 U.S. 471, 484 [1970]). If the payment of welfare benefits involves no fundamental rights or suspect classifications, it seems certain that neither does the payment of compensation for product, medical, and other injuries. The Court has also held that education is not a fundamental right, despite the implication of Brown v. Board of Education, 347 U.S. 483 (1954), in San Antonio Independent School Dist., 93 S.Ct. at 1299. Nor is wealth a suspect classification (93 S.Ct. at 1294). Cases such as Harper v. Virginia Bd. of Elections, 383 U.S. 663 (1966) and Douglas v. California, 372 U.S. 353 (1963), which applied the "compelling interest" test in which wealth was the basis of classification, had also involved a valid "fundamental interest" such as voting rights and criminal defense rights.

Particularly persuasive are four recent decisions by state supreme courts refusing to apply the "compelling interest" test: (1) Brown v. Merlo, 106 Cal. Rptr. 388, 392 (1973), holding the California automobile "guest statute" unconstitutional; (2) Gallegos v. Glaser Crandell Co., 388 Mich. 654, 202 N.W.2d 786 (1972), holding the Michigan workers' compensation law unconstitutional; (3) Pinnick, 271 N.E.2d at 609, upholding the constitutionality of the Massachusetts auto no-fault law; and (4) Opinion of the Justices, 304 A.2d at 886, advising the New Hampshire House of Representatives that the proposed auto no-fault law was constitutional. The language of the California Supreme Court in *Merlo* illustrates very well the type of reasoning likely to be applied to elective no-fault liability: "[The plaintiff] cites neither authority nor persuasive reasoning either for the proposition that "automobile guests" constitute a "suspect classification" comparable to racial or sexual classifications, or for his claim that his right to sue for negligently inflicted injuries is a "fundamental interest" analogous to voting rights. . . . Under these circumstances, we conclude that the strict scrutiny analysis is not applicable" (106 Cal. Rptr. at 392, n. 2). See *infra* notes 72–81 and accompanying text.

In Grace v. Howlett, 51 Ill. 2d 478, 283 N.E.2d 474 (1972), holding the Illinois auto no-fault law unconstitutional, the plaintiffs alleged that the law violated equal protection because it discriminated against the poor. Their argument was twofold: (1) medical services for the poor cost less; thus, the poor would be less able to accrue the $500 in medical expenses necessary before being eligible to recover general damages; and (2) since Illinois was not a compulsory insurance state, many people, especially the poor, would receive no benefits under the law but would be subject to severe limitations if attempting recovery through a tort action. The trial court, using the "rational basis" test, found the classification arbitrary and invidious and ruled the law unconstitutional as a violation of the equal protection clause. Several observations are relevant to elective no-fault liability: (1) after *Rodriguez* it is clear that the "rational basis" test must be applied when wealth is the classification; (2) it is not at all clear that the Illinois trial court was correct, since the Illinois Supreme Court ruled the law unconstitutional on other grounds and the *Pinnick* court refused to honor a similar argument (271 N.E.2d at 611; (3) the whole argument does not affect elective no-fault liability since medical expenses do not determine eligibility to recover for pain and suffering and the insurance coverage is maintained by businesses and professionals, not consumers/patients (but see *supra,* ch. 8, note 30).

It is also interesting to note that Jesse Jackson's civil rights organization, People United to Save Humanity (PUSH), and an organization of black insurance brokers of Chicago filed an *amicus* brief with the Illinois Supreme Court in support of the Illinois no-fault law, despite its tort limitation tied to amount of medical bills, arguing that, while the law was far from perfect, it vastly improved benefits for the poor when compared to their situation under the tort liability system. In a recent no-fault debate, Robert Begam, a prominent Phoenix personal injury lawyer, upon learning of the brief, stated, "This is the first time I ever realized that Jesse Jackson was an authority on Constitutional Law," whereupon his opponent replied, "I think it fair to say that Jesse Jackson knows at least as much about Constitutional Law as the American Trial Lawyers know about poverty."

65. See *infra,* notes 68, 102–8 and accompanying text.

66. See *supra,* ch. 8, notes 22–29 and accompanying text.

67. Lindsley v. Natural Carbonic Gas Co., 220 U.S. 61, 78 (1911).

68. Mass. Stat. ch. 670, § 5 (1970). The New Hampshire Supreme Court considered the constitutionality of a very similar section (proposed Section 407-C:9 of House Bill No. 79) in Opinion of the Justices, 304 A.2d 881, finding it to be in compliance with equal protection standards.

69. 271 N.E.2d at 610.

70. *Ibid.*

71. Louisville Gas & Elec. Co. v. Coleman, 277 U.S. 32, 41 (1928).

72. 106 Cal. Rptr. 388.

73. The California "automobile guest statute" (West's Ann. Vehicle Code § 17158) deprived an injured automobile guest of any recovery for the negligent driving of his host unless the host was guilty of willful misconduct or intoxication. Paying passengers as well as social guests in other circumstances were allowed to recover for the ordinary negligence of their driver or host. Thus, the ordinary automobile guest received different treatment not only from paying passengers and other social guests, but also from those few automobile guests "fortunate" enough to be injured by a host guilty of willful misconduct or intoxication.

74. 106 Cal. Rptr. at 407. See case note, 21 *U.C.L.A. L. Rev.* 1566 (1964).

75. *Ibid.* at 407–8. See, e.g., W. Prosser, *The Law of Torts* § 34, at 186–87 (4th ed. 1971); Pedrick, "Taken for a Ride: The Automobile Guest and

Assumption of Risk," 22 *La. L. Rev.* 90 (1961); White, "The Liability of an Automobile Driver to a Non-Paying Passenger," 20 *Va. L. Rev.* 326 (1934); Stevens v. Stevens, 355 Mich. 363, 94 N.W.2d 858 (1959).

76. 106 Cal. Rptr. at 407.

77. 388 Mich. 654, 202 N.W.2d 786.

78. 1969 P.A. 317, § 115(d)(M.C.L.A. § 418.115[d]; M.S.A. § 17.237 [115][d]).

79. 202 N.W.2d at 791.

80. See Note, "Workmen's Compensation Laws and Equal Protection: Does *Gallegos* Portend the Demise of the Agricultural Exclusion?" 1973 *Duke L.J.* 705, 708–10 (1973), suggesting several justifications for the agricultural exclusions found in most states: (1) the exclusions were politically necessary to gain the rural support required to pass the first workers' compensation laws (similar to one of the justifications for elective no-fault liability; see *supra,* ch. 8, note 14 and accompanying text); (2) it was administratively impractical to include agricultural workers; (3) the farmer could not add the compensation paid to the price and pass it on to the consumer; (4) farming was not considered a hazardous occupation; and (5) it was feared that compensation coverage would have to be provided for family members on family farms.

81. See *ibid.,* 710–11 for a comprehensive summary of the agricultural exclusion sections in the various state workers' compensation laws.

82. Grace v. Howlett, 51 Ill. 2d 478, 283 N.E.2d 474 (1972). For discussion, see *supra* note 1.

83. Kluger v. White, 281 So. 2d 1 (Fla. 1973). For discussion, see *infra* note 115.

84. See *infra* note 132 and accompanying text. See also *supra* notes 7 and 58 and accompanying text.

85. See *supra* notes 1 and 42 and accompanying text.

86. See *supra* note 1.

87. *Supra* notes 40–44 and accompanying text.

88. "The Congress shall have power . . . (3) To regulate Commerce with foreign Nations and among the several States, and with the Indian tribes; . . . (8) To make all Laws which shall be necessary and proper for carrying into Execution the foregoing Powers, and all other Powers visited by this Constitution in the Government of the United States, or in any Department or Officer thereof" (*U.S. Const.* art. I, § 8). As to federal authority to enact elective no-fault insurance, see *infra* notes 124–29 and accompanying text.

89. Many states have specific constitutional provisions relating to the police power: "As the health and morality of the people are essential to their well-being, and to the peace and permanence of the state, it shall be the duty of the legislature to protect and promote these vital interests by such measures for the encouragement of temperance and virtue, and such restrictions upon vice and immorality of every sort, as are deemed necessary to the public welfare" (*Wyo. Const.* art. 7, § 21). The Wyoming Supreme Court has held that the constitutional provision is not a necessity because the police power "is an attribute of sovereignty, is essential for every civilized government, is inherent in the legislature except as expressly limited, and no express grant thereof is necessary" (State v. Langley, 53 Wyo. 332, 343, 84 P.2d 767, 770 [1938]).

In fact, some states have no such constitutional provision, relying solely on case law to establish the police power: "The police power of a state is recognized by the courts to be one of wide sweep. It is exercised by the state in order to promote the health, safety, comfort, morals, and welfare of the public. The right to exercise this power is said to be inherent in the people of every free government. It is not a grant derived from or under any written constitution. It is not, however, without limitation, and it cannot be invoked so as to invade the fundamental rights of a citizen" (State ex rel. Cox v. Board of Educ., 21 Utah 401, 414, 60 P. 1013, 1016 [1900]). The key question for elective no-fault liability is thus not whether the state has the basic power to enact such a measure but whether that power must be limited because the plan invades the fundamental rights of the citizens of the state.

90. *Ky. Const.* § 54.

91. *Ariz. Const.* art. II, § 31; *Ark. Const.* art. V, § 32; *Pa. Const.* art. III, § 21; *Wyo. Const.* art. X, § 4.

92. *N.Y. Const.* art. I, § 16; *Ohio Const.* art. I, § 19a; *Okla. Const.* art. XXIII, § 7; *Utah Const.* art. XVI, § 5. But see *infra* note 97.

93. *N.Y. Const.* art. I, § 16.

94. Kentucky State Journal Co. v. Workmen's Compensation Bd., 161 Ky. 562, 170 S.W. 1166 (1914). As this book goes to press, Kentucky has passed a noncompulsory no-fault auto law "to get around potential challenges to the constitutionality of the law" (*National Underwriter* [Property and Casualty ed.], April 15, 1974, p. 39, cols. 2–3). But see *infra* note 99.

95. *Ariz. Const.* art. 18, § 8; *Ark. Const.* art. V, § 32; *Okla. Const.* art. XXIII, § 7; *N.Y. Const.* art. I, § 18; *Pa. Const.* art. 3, § 18; *Wyo. Const.* art. 10, § 4. Utah's amendment has a broader exception for "cases where compensation for injuries resulting in death is provided for by law" (*Utah Const.* art. XVI, § 5). The language seems applicable to workers' compensation, auto no-fault, and elective no-fault liability, but for a decision indicating that the amendment is limited to workers' compensation, see Henrie v. Rocky Mountain Packing Corp., 113 Utah 415, 196 P.2d 487 (1948).

96. R. Keeton and J. O'Connell, *Basic Protection for the Traffic Victim: A Blueprint for Reforming Automobile Insurance* 505 (1965).

97. Note added: For those jurisdictions with prohibitions against limiting recovery in death cases, the Keeton-O'Connell basic protection no-fault auto plan included alternate paragraph 4.2(a) preserving the tort action in every case in which the injury caused death (*ibid.*, 508–11). The same could conceivably be done for elective no-fault liability, although a serious problem still exists in those states which also forbid limitation on recovery in injury cases. Also note that it is the "prevailing view that constitutional protection afforded to death actions does not extend to survival actions" (*ibid.*, 513).

98. *Ibid.*, 508.

99. Martel, "No-Fault Automobile Insurance in Pennsylvania: A Constitutional Analysis," 17 *Vill. L. Rev.* 783 (1972). A similar theory was advanced by attorney and insurance executive Harold Baile, testifying before the Pennsylvania Legislature on Feb. 10, 1972, on the constitutionality of the proposed Pennsylvania auto no-fault bill. This impression is reinforced by the recent passage of a no-fault auto law in Pennsylvania. *Supra*, ch. 2, note 6.

100. *Pa. Const.* art. 3, § 18.

101. Act of April 4, 1868, Pub. L. No. 58.

102. Martel, *supra* note 78, at 801–9.

103. "Thus, several very important distinctions should be drawn between proposals for no-fault accident compensation and legislation similar to the Act of 1868. No-fault proposals are designed to promote fairer and more adequate compensation for the victims of car accidents. A proposal such as the Keeton and O'Connell basic protection plan would not ordinarily reduce the net amount that a seriously injured person could recover (R. Keeton and J. O'Connell, *supra* note 96, at 446–49). The Act of 1868, on the other hand, restricted even the most seriously maimed or disfigured victim to a maximum recovery of $3000. Furthermore, the Act of 1868 was not part of a legislative reform designed to improve compensation for victims of railroad accidents; the limit on recovery could only be justified as an economy measure, sacrificing full and adequate compensation for the severely injured victim. No-fault proposals, in marked contrast, are designed to *improve* compensation for those seriously set back by auto accidents, at the cost only of abolishing claims for small amounts of pain and suffering, which are often exaggerated and without merit and which, statistics show, are foreseeable for almost all vehicle occupants at some time during their lifetime" (*ibid.,* 806).

104. *Ibid.,* 805–7.

105. Pa. Stat. tit. 48, §§ 170, 171 (1935). This abolition of common law tort actions was ruled constitutional in McMullen v. Nannah, 49 Pa. D. & C. 516 (C. P. Beaver Co. 1943).

106. *Ibid.,* 812–15. In addition to abolishing the cause of action for alienation of affections and breach of promise to marry, Pennsylvania has passed the following statutes: (1) Medical Good Samaritan Act, Pa. Stat. tit. 12, § 1641 (Supp. 1972), abolishing a negligence action against a physician who injures a person while rendering aid in an emergency; (2) Nonmedical Good Samaritan Act, Pa. Stat. tit. 12, § 1643 (Supp. 1972), abolishing a negligence action against firemen, policemen, or members of a rescue squad for injuries caused while rendering emergency care; (3) Disease Prevention and Control Law of 1955, Pa. Stat. tit. 35, §§ 521.1–21 (1964), abolishing a cause of action against a physician who treats a minor for veneral disease without parental consent; and (4) Pa. Stat. tit. 37, § 61 (1954), which changed the liability of innkeepers and hotel proprietors for loss of the personal property of their guests and was declared constitutional in Sherwood v. Elgart, 383 Pa. 110, 117 A.2d 899 (1955).

107. Martel, *supra* note 99, at 809. But see *supra,* ch. 2, note 6.

108. See Burgan v. Pittsburgh, 373 Pa. 608, 96 A.2d 889 (1953), holding that pain and suffering are substantive losses, and DeJesus v. Liberty Mutual Insurance Co., 439 Pa. 180, 183–85, 268 A.2d 924, 926–27 (1970), in which the court specifically indicated that the amendment was necessary for the enactment of workers' compensation and "precludes the enactment of legislation limiting the amount of compensation payable to employees for injuries other than those 'arising in the course of their employment.' "

109. Martel, *supra* note 99, at 808.

110. New York has the following provision: "The right of action now existing to recover damages for injuries resulting in death, shall never be

abrogated; and the amount recoverable shall not be subject to any statutory limitation" (*N.Y. Const.* art. I, § 16).

Martel says that the New York language is more explicit and compelling than the language of the Pennsylvania Constitution ("in no other cases shall the General Assembly limit the amount to be recovered for injuries resulting in death, or for injuries to persons or property, and in case of death from such injuries, the right of action shall survive..." [*Pa. Const.* art. 3, § 18]) and that "the difference in language... is a substantial indicator that a different result was intended in Pennsylvania, at least as to non-fatal injuries" (Martel, *supra* note 99, at 816).

He also notes differing language in the Arizona Constitution and that the Arizona legislature has not passed legislation abolishing causes of action for alienation of affections, seduction, or breach of promise to marry. Arizona does have a "Good Samaritan" act which Martel believes would be unconstitutional if the Arizona Supreme Court adhered to its dictum about compulsory workers' compensation: "A statute which would attempt to forcibly limit the amount recoverable for personal injuries suffered would be in direct conflict with these plain, simple provisions of the state Constitution. Statutes which provide a limited amount in satisfaction of damages and leave to the parties interested the right to elect to abide by its provisions are controlled by other principles of law and should not be confused with statutes imperative in their terms" (Inspiration Consol. Copper Co. v. Mendez, 19 Ariz. 151, 167, 166 P. 278, 284–85 [1917], *aff'd sub nom.*, Arizona Employer's Liability Cases, 250 U.S. 400 [1919], *overruled on other grounds,* Consolidated Ariz. Smelting Co. v. Egich, 22 Ariz. 543, 199 P. 132 [1921]). But concerning the reality of the employee's choice under elective workers' compensation, see *supra,* ch. 9, note 17 and accompanying text.

In Ludwig v. Johnson, 243 Ky. 533, 49 S.W.2d 347 (1932), the Kentucky Supreme Court held that the Kentucky automobile "guest statute" violated § 54 of the Kentucky Constitution. Since other constitutional provisions were involved in the decision, it can be strongly argued that the court was not as concerned with the abolition of a common law cause of action as it was with the failure to provide a substitute remedy.

The situation is more favorable in Arkansas and Wyoming. Arkansas's automobile "guest statute" was held to be constitutional in Roberson v. Roberson, 193 Ark. 669, 101 S.W.2d 961 (1937). Wyoming, in addition to a "guest statute," has statutes abolishing actions for alienation of affections and breach of promise to marry, none of which have been challenged on constitutional grounds (Martel, *supra* note 99, at 817–19). Finally, although Martel cites only the specific Pennsylvania constitutional history regarding the purpose of such limitation sections, is it not probable that a similar impetus was behind other limitation provisions?

111. *Hearings on S. 354, supra* note 6, at 805–10. At the same time, one must consider that Griswold was discussing the constitutionality of the proposed *federal* auto no-fault legislation (S. 354) and felt that "to the extent that any provision of a state constitution is in conflict with S. 354, it would be rendered invalid by the Supremacy Clause..." (*ibid.,* 814).

112. Ultimately, resort to constitutional amendment may be necessary. This is not to suggest that the passage of a constitutional amendment is a short

and simple process. For example, in Arizona an amendment is introduced in either house of the legislature or proposed by an initiative petition signed by 15 percent of the voters in the last gubernatorial election. After approval by a majority of both houses, the amendment must then be submitted to a vote of the people at either a general or a special election and must be approved by a majority of those voting upon it. Amendment by constitutional convention is also allowed, but this requires action in at least two sessions of the legislature and referral to a popular vote both as to the calling of the convention and approval of the convention's action, thereby rendering the process even longer than that for amendments proposed through the legislature (*Ariz. Const.* art. XXI). The other states with limitation provisions have similar procedures for amendment of their constitutions. See Auto Insurance Reform, *Statement of the American Mutual Insurance Alliance before the Senate Commerce Committee,* Exhibit VI (1973), for a brief summary of the amendment procedures in these states. However, as was demonstrated in those states passing special exceptions for workers' compensation laws, an amendment is more than just a remote possibility when the issue is sufficiently important. For example, a recent newsletter of the Florida Association of Insurance Agents, after commenting on the possibility that Florida's no-fault law applicable to personal injury might be held unconstitutional (a possibility later foreclosed by Lasky v. State Farm, 296 So. 2d 9 [Fla. 1974]), said such a result "would make legislative attention, probably in special session, imperative" to rectify the bill, and hinted indeed at constitutional amendment, if necessary. "Whatever happens," the publication concluded, "it's a safe bet Florida is not going back to the old tort system. Not for long anyway" (Florida Association of Insurance Agents, Vol. 23, bull. 10, Nov. 28, 1973).

113. See, e.g., *Ala. Const.* art. I, § 13; *Minn. Const.* art. I, § 8; *Neb. Const.* art. I, § 13; *Tenn. Const.* art. I, § 17. For a complete list of states having such a provision see *Hearings on S. 354, supra* note 6, at 810, n. 13.

114. *Fla. Const.* art. I, § 21.

115. 296 So. 2d 9 (Fla. 1974). The court had no difficulty distinguishing *Kluger* v. *White* (287 So. 2d 1 [1973]), which had held the Florida no-fault law applicable to car damage unconstitutional. But under Florida's triple option car damage provisions, a motorist through his own option could be left without any remedy — either one in tort or under a no-fault claim — for out-of-pocket loss stemming from damage to his car. Even so, as the dissent in *Kluger* pointed out, the provision could well have been viewed as constitutional (281 So. 2d 1, 5 [1973]). See also Keeton and O'Connell, "Alternative Paths toward Nonfault Automobile Insurance," 71 *Colum. L. Rev.* 243, 260–62 (1971), also printed in J. O'Connell, *The Injury Industry and the Remedy of No-Fault Insurance* 157–60 (1972).

116. *Mass. Const.* pt. I, art. XI.

117. 271 N.E.2d 592.

118. *Ibid.* at 600.

119. Smith v. Hill, 12 Ill. 2d 588, 147 N.E.2d 321 (1958); Goldberg v. Musim, 162 Colo. 461, 427 P.2d 698 (1967); Vogts v. Guerrette, 142 Colo. 527, 351 P.2d 851 (1960). See *Hearings on S. 354, supra* note 6, at 810–12, and Martel, *supra* note 99, at 792–800, for a complete discussion of these cases.

120. 275 S.W.3d 951 (Tex. 1955).

121. Martel, *supra* note 99, at 795.

122. *Ibid.*, 797.

123. *U.S. Const.* art. I, § 8.

124. Gibbons v. Ogden, 22 U.S. 1 (1824). (In holding that the commerce power included power to regulate navigation, Chief Justice Marshall held that it also included the power to control an intrastate activity which affected interstate commerce.) Houston, East and West Texas Railway Company v. United States, 234 U.S. 342 (1914). (Power granted to ICC by Congress extends to regulation of intrastate railroad rates.) Champion v. Ames, 188 U.S. 321 (1903). (Interstate commerce includes the interstate transportation of lottery tickets.) NLRB v. Jones & Laughlin Steel Corp., 301 U.S. 1 (1937). (Congress can control the collective bargaining process.) United States v. Darby, 312 U.S. 100 (1941). (Congress can control the working conditions of those who produce goods for interstate commerce.) Perez v. United States, 402 U.S. 146 (1971). (Congress can control loan-sharking in order to control the interstate crime which is partially financed by loan-sharking.) Heart of Atlanta Motel, Inc., v. United States, 379 U.S. 241 (1964). (Congress can regulate hotel and motel accommodations because discriminatory treatment impedes blacks from traveling interstate.)

125. James and Law, "Compensation for Auto Accident Victims: A Story of Too Little and Too Late," 26 *Conn. B. J.* 70, 78–79 (1952).

126. United States v. South-Eastern Underwriters Ass'n, 322 U.S. 533, 552–53 (1944).

127. "This Constitution, and the Laws of the United States which shall be made in Pursuance thereof; . . . shall be the supreme Law of the Land; and the Judges in every State shall be bound thereby, . . . any Thing in the Constitution or Laws of any State to the Contrary notwithstanding" (*U.S. Const.* art. VI, § 2).

128. Mondou v. New York, N.H. & H.R. Co., 223 U.S. 1 (1912), which held that the Employers Liability Act regulating the liability of common carriers by railroad to their employees was constitutional.

129. Wickard v. Filburn, 317 U.S. 111 (1942) is perhaps the best example. The Supreme Court held that Congress could restrict (through the Agricultural Adjustment Act) the amount of wheat a farmer could grow even though he was growing the wheat solely to feed his own animals on his own farm with none of the wheat ever entering the stream of commerce. After such cases it is exceedingly difficult to imagine what local activity is not regulable. We have come close to the point where there are no constitutional limitations on the power of Congress to regulate local activities under the Commerce Clause.

130. Kemper, "The Basic Protection Plan: Reform or Regression?" in *Crisis in Car Insurance* 99, 105–6 (ed. R. Keeton, J. O'Connell, and J. McCord, 1968); also printed at 1967 *U. Ill. L. Forum* 459, 465–66 (1967). Kemper — and his companies — subsequently changed their minds and became advocates of at least limited no-fault insurance.

131. *Chicago Sun-Times,* Feb. 4, 1974, p. 54, col. 1.

132. NOTE ADDED: But see American Motorcycle Association v. Davids, 11 Mich. App. 351, 158 N.W.2d 72 (1968) and People v. Fries, 42 Ill. 2d 446,

250 N.E.2d 151 (1969), ruling unconstitutional legislative enactments requiring motorcyclists to wear protective helmets on similar grounds. The decisions, though, seem clearly unsound. See Comment, "Police Power in Illinois: The Regulation of Private Conduct," 1972 *U. Ill. L. Forum* 158 (1972).

133. Dukakis, "Legislators Look at Proposed Changes," in *Crisis in Car Insurance, supra* note 130, at 222, 228; also printed in 1967 *U. Ill. L. Forum* 582, 588 (1967).

134. See *Hearings on S. 354, supra* note 6, at 743–894. But see the elegant argument of Professor Norman Dorsen of New York University Law School on the possible unconstitutionality not of no-fault insurance but of a law whereby federal law is to be imposed on and then implemented and administered by state officials (*ibid.,* 1216–23).

135. *Ibid.,* 725, 740.

Index

Abnormally dangerous activities, 58
"Acts of God," 140
Actuaries, 147
Advance payment, 50
Adverse selection, 116-17, 162
Advisory committees on elective no-fault coverage, 155
Agricultural workers, 221-22
Airplane crashes, 60
Alexander, Ruth, 30-31
Alienation of affection, 225
Ambulance chasing, 53
Amendment, constitutional, 209, 224, 225, 230
American Hospital Association, 156
American Medical Association, 44
American Trial Lawyers' Association. *See* Association of Trial Lawyers of America
Amputation, 99, 118, 119
Analgesics, 114
Anesthesia, 93, 100
Arbitration, 39
Architectural glass, 18, 91, 127-28
Arizona Constitution, 223
Arizona Employer's Liability Cases, 210
Arkansas Constitution, 223
Assault and battery. *See* Battery
Association of Trial Lawyers of America, 118
Assumption of risk, 121, 125, 127, 173, 202, 215. *See also* Contributory fault.
Atchison, Topeka and Sante Fe Railroad, 177
Atiyah, Patrick, 142-43
Atomic Energy Act, 140
Attorneys. *See* Lawyers
Australia, 73
Auto insurance. *See* Auto liability insurance; No-fault auto laws
Auto liability insurance, 21, 50, 79, 80, 100, 115
Auto safety, xii, xiv-xv, xviii, 130

Basic protection no-fault auto plan. *See* Keeton-O'Connell no-fault plan
Battery, 156
Bell, Daniel, xxii, 38, 75
Belli, Melvin, 39, 178-82
Bengis, Ingrid, 95
Bernzweig, Eli, 41
Bicycles, 18, 91
Blackstone, William, 200
Blasting. *See* Dynamite
Bliven, Naomi, xxii
Blue Cross, 21, 116. *See also* Health and accident insurance
Blume, Paul, 229
Boehm, Herbert, 52-53
Boston University Law-Medicine Institute, 31
Bottle, exploding, 129
Brandeis, Louis, 161

Breach of promise to marry, 225
Brown v. *Merle*, 220-22
Bureaucracies, 78-79, 104, 189-94
Burnett, Warren, 40
Bystander, liability to, 60-62

Calabresi, Guido, 76, 89, 121, 122, 123, 125
California, 177; Supreme Court, 220
Cardiac arrest, 93, 99
Cardozo, Benjamin, 64
Carlson, Rick, 190-91
Car rental companies, 100
Carrington, Paul, 199-200
Cavers, David, 140
Center for the Study of Democratic Institutions, 41, 42
Charge-back schemes, 78, 80
Churchill, Winston, 120-21
Cigarettes, 72
Claims, medical malpractice: adversary nature of, xx, 29, 38, 44; delay in, 29; resistance to, 29, 30-34, 38-39, 40-41, 46, 158; complexity of, 29-30, 39-40, 57, 158
Collateral sources, 50-52, 80, 90, 92, 98, 102, 106, 112, 115-16, 119, 120, 126, 139-40, 141-47, 168, 169, 173, 206, 213-14, 216, 217, 224, 225
Collision insurance, 140
Coming of Post-Industrial Society, The, 75
Commerce Clause, U.S. Constitution. *See* Interstate Commerce
Commissioner of insurance. *See* Insurance commissioner
Commissioners on Uniform State Laws. *See* National Conference of Commissioners on Uniform State Laws
Comparative negligence, 48-49, 125, 126, 168, 197. *See also* Pure comparative negligence
"Compelling state interest" test, 217. *See also* Equal protection clauses
Conard, Alfred, 11, 49, 115
Conflict of laws, 162-63
Congress, 74, 100, 227, 228

Consent forms, 157. *See also* Informed consent
Consortium, loss of, 58
Conspiracy of silence, 30-34, 38, 57
Constitutional amendment. *See* Amendment, constitutional
Constitutionality, 101, 103-4, 139, 204-31. *See also* Amendment, constitutional; Constitutional prohibitions on limitation of tort recovery; Due process clauses; Equal protection clauses; Interstate commerce; Police power; "Redress of injury" clauses
Constitutional prohibitions on limitation of tort recovery, 223-26
Consumer movement, xiv-xix, 60-61, 128-29, 206
Consumer Product Safety Act, 127
Consumer Product Safety Commission, xv, xvii, 91, 127-30
Consumer Protection Agency, xv, xvi, xvii
Contributory fault, 15, 48-49, 112, 119, 120, 121, 123, 124, 125-27, 147, 155, 173, 195, 197, 201, 202, 215
Contributory negligence. *See* Contributory fault
Corboy, Philip, 1-4, 9, 21, 53

Daggett, John, 177
Daggett, Paula, 177
Daggett v. *The Atchison, Topeka and Santa Fe Railroad,* 177-82
Damages, law of, 49, 98
Dangerous products, 18-20, 58-60, 71, 89, 91
Davis, Glynn, 159-61
Davis v. *Wyeth Laboratories,* 159-61
Death actions. *See* Wrongful death claims
Defect. *See* Defective product
Defective product, 1-2, 13, 21, 57, 62, 63, 64, 65, 77, 89, 90, 98, 99, 117, 118, 119, 123, 129, 130, 147, 171, 173, 206, 214
Defensive medicine, 43-44
Delaware no-fault auto law, 106

Delay in claims and litigation, 1, 14, 15-16, 22, 29, 30, 49-50, 89, 103, 115, 117, 119, 124, 130, 147, 171, 212, 214, 231
Denenberg, Herbert, 23
Dentists, 42
Department of Health, Education and Welfare (HEW). *See* Health, Education and Welfare
Department of Transportation, 130, 146; auto insurance study, 11-12, 20, 146
Depression, 114
Derbyshire, Robert, 44
Deterrence, 21-24, 42-44, 76-80, 89, 120-26, 130, 141-44, 158, 197-99, 200-202. *See also* Market deterrence
Diamond, Peter, 201
Disability insurance, 124. *See also* Sick leave
Disability rating, 190
Drugs, 72, 100, 101, 130, 153, 159-61
Due process clauses, 205-14, 217, 227
Dukakis, Michael, 229-30
Duplication of payment. *See* Collateral sources
Dynamite, 58-60, 63, 65

Economic man, 199, 200
Economics, xix, 129, 142, 144, 195, 197-202
Economists, 128-29, 195, 197-202
Education, 75
Elective no-fault liability, 97-106, 113-27, 131, 139-47, 152-63, 168, 169, 170, 173-75, 204, 205-31; costs of, 98, 99, 117, 119, 139, 173-74, 213; fairness of bargain of, 154-56; notice of coverage, 158-59, 161, 207-9. *See also* Constitutionality; Elective workers' compensation
Elective workers' compensation, 101, 102, 116, 117, 173, 206-7, 208, 209, 210. *See also* Workers' compensation
Elias, Antonio, 53
Emergency aid, 42-43
Emergency rooms. *See* Hospital emergency rooms
Empirical studies. *See* Polls

Employers' liability acts, 124-26
Energy crises, 75
Enterprise liability, 62, 89-95, 174. *See also* No-fault liability
Epidemiology, xii
Equal protection clauses, 214-23, 227. *See also* "Compelling state interest" test; "Fundamental interest" test; Police power; "Rational relationship to a legitimate purpose" test; "Strict scrutiny" test
Europe: social insurance in, 76, 169-70; tort liability in, 168, 169-70
Excess insurance, 145-47
Experimental reform, 95, 101, 103, 104, 214, 218
Expert witnesses, 2, 5-6, 12-13, 17, 21, 29-30, 49, 58, 98, 117, 183-88, 213, 214
Externalization, 123, 129, 141-44
Extrahazardous no-fault liability, 127-32, 139-47, 153, 155, 161-63, 168, 169, 170, 174-75; costs of, 131, 174

Falls, 48, 70, 71, 100
Federal Employer's Liability Act (FELA), 125
Federal government, 95, 128, 161-63, 204, 213, 214, 218, 222, 223, 227-29
Federal no-fault auto bill, 11, 162, 227, 230
Fifth Amendment, 205, 214
Fire insurance, 50, 116, 121, 155
Fireworks, 18, 91
First party insurance, 209-10
Floor furnaces, 18, 91
Florida: no-fault auto law, 115, 222, 226, 229, 230; constitution, 226; Supreme Court, 226
Food and Drug Administration, 130; survey by, 18
Food, deleterious, 100
"Forum shopping," 162
Fourteenth Amendment, 205, 211, 214
Frankfurter, Felix, xix-xx
Franklin, Marc, 141, 142
Freud, Sigmund, 52, 65
Fuld, Stanley, 59

"Fundamental interest" test, 217, 218.
  See also Equal protection clauses

Galbraith, J. K., 78
Gallegos v. *Glaser Crandell Co.*, 221
General deterrence. *See* Market deterrence
Gilmore, Grant, 199
Glass. *See* Architectural glass
Great Britain, 73
Gregory, Charles, 65
Griswold, Erwin, 226, 230-31
Gross negligence, 154, 155, 220
Group insurance, 124
Guest statute, 154, 220, 222

Halberstam, David, 157
Halberstam, Michael, 156-57
Harney, David, 29
Harper, Fowler, 65-66
Harvard Law Review, 57
Hawkins v. *Bleakly*, 215
Health, Education and Welfare, 74;
  Secretary's Commission on Medical
  Malpractice, 30, 39, 41, 42, 43, 101,
  104, 156, 157, 189-94
Health and accident insurance, 21, 50,
  51, 71, 77, 79, 80, 89, 90, 121, 124,
  145-46, 155, 167, 175
Hellner, Jan, 167
Henningsen v. *Bloomfield Motors, Inc.*,
  56, 57
Herbert, A. P., 195-96
Holmes, Oliver Wendell, 219
Hospital emergency rooms, 127
Hospitals, 42, 43, 157

Illinois, 113; no-fault auto law, 222,
  229, 230
Illinois Workmen's Compensation Act,
  208
Illness, 123
Impeachment of witness, 177-82
Industrial accidents. *See* Workers'
  compensation
Inflation, 125
Informed consent, 92, 94, 156-59
Insurance. *See* Auto liability insurance; Blue Cross; Elective no-fault
  liability; Fire insurance; Health and
  accident insurance; Insurance commissioner; Medical malpractice; No-fault auto laws; No-fault liability;
  Product liability
Insurance commissioner, 155, 207
Intentional injuries, 99, 154-55, 173,
  196
Internalization, 129, 142-44
International College of Surgeons, 39
Interstate commerce, 162, 213, 218,
  223, 227-29
Intrafamily immunity, 106
Iowa Workmen's Compensation Act,
  215
Ives v. *South Buffalo Ry.*, 101

James, Fleming, 65-66
Jensen, Malcom, 128
Jiminez, Lydia, 52
Judiciary Committee, U.S. Senate, 229
Jury trials, 2-5, 49, 53-54, 66

Kafka, Franz, 196
Kalven, Harry, 58-60, 63
Keeton-O'Connell no-fault plan, 224
Keeton, Robert, xi-xii, xx, 73, 224
Keiser, Lester, 115
Kemper, James, Jr., 229
Kemper Insurance Companies, 229
Kennedy, Edward, 74
Kentucky, 118; Constitution, 223-24
Kidney ailments, 74
King, Larry, 40

"Laboratories" of the states, 161
Ladders, 19, 71, 90
Laing, Jonathan, 3, 6
Larson, Arthur, 102
Lasky v. *State Farm*, 226
Law enforcement, 75
Lawnmowers, xiii-xiv, 19, 77, 78, 90,
  128, 215-17
Lawyer, Verne, 53
Lawyers, xiv, 17, 39, 51, 53, 56, 63-
  67, 70, 102, 106, 114, 115, 117, 119,
  123, 127, 161, 169, 197, 213, 229,

230; fees, 3, 4, 13, 21, 29, 41, 51, 98, 119, 214, 216, 217. *See also* Association of Trial Lawyers of America
Lebohm v. *City of Galveston,* 227
Liberal party, 120
Life insurance, 90, 98, 121, 124, 146
Lloyd George, David, 120
Locality rule, 57
Louisville, Kentucky, 118
Lump sum damages. *See* Damages, law of

Malingering, 49, 51-52
Malraux, Andre, xix
Market decisions, 75-76, 143, 201, 208. *See also* Market deterrence
Market deterrence, 76-80, 89, 120, 141-44, 167, 168
Martel, Joel, 224-26, 227
Massachusetts, 117; no-fault auto law, 10, 11, 106, 211-12, 218, 226, 229-30; Supreme Judicial Court, 211, 226; Constitution, 226
Mass transit, 75
Medicaid, 11, 74
Medical Injury Compensation Commission, 104, 192-93
Medical malpractice. *See* Claims, medical malpractice; Conspiracy of silence; Defensive medicine; Dentists; Emergency aid; Expert witness; Health, Education and Welfare, Secretary's Report on Medical Malpractice; Hospitals; Informed consent; Locality rule; Medical malpractice insurance; Screening panels
Medical Malpractice: The Patient Versus the Physician, xx, 39
Medical malpractice insurance, 38, 73, 79; costs of, 29, 42
Medical profession, 38, 44, 100, 155
Medicare, 11, 74, 118, 119, 230
Merit rating, 124, 198-99
Metzgar, W. R., 18
Michigan, 115; no-fault auto law, 10; Supreme Court, 221
Michigan Workmen's Compensation Act, 221

Minnesota no-fault auto law, 10
Mississippi, 197
Models, economic, 201
Moore, Beverly, Jr., 129
Mountain Timber Co. v. *Washington,* 210
Moynihan, Daniel Patrick, xxi-xxii, 75, 95, 127
Multiple causes, 152-53
Multiple payment. *See* Collateral sources

Nader, Ralph, 129
National Association of Independent Insurers, 229
National Commission on Product Safety, xiii, 9, 18, 21, 22, 23, 91, 127, 128, 162
National Commission on Workmen's Compensation, 103, 142
National Conference of Commissioners on Uniform State Laws, 11
National Electronic Injury Surveillance System (NEISS), xvii, 91, 127, 130, 162
National health insurance, 73, 74, 75, 146
National Highway Traffic Safety Administration, 130
Netherlands, 170
Neurosurgery, 100
New York, 74; no-fault auto law, 9-10; Court of Appeals, 59-60, 64, 65, 101; workmen's compensation law, 207, 208, 212; Constitution, 223
New York Central Railroad Company v. *White,* 210-11, 212
New Zealand, 73-74, 76, 80
Nixon, Richard, 74
No-fault auto laws, xi-xiii, xxi-xxii, 9-11, 66, 90, 92, 95, 97, 99, 100, 101, 105, 106, 115, 120, 127, 147, 152, 153, 154, 161, 171, 173, 204, 209-10, 211-12, 218, 220, 224, 225, 226, 227, 229-30; costs of, 11, 70, 71, 172
No-fault liability, 60, 63, 66, 70-73, 89-95, 101, 104, 125, 174, 189-94, 195, 202, 211, 214, 218; costs of,

71, 72-73, 92, 94-95, 173, 193-94, 218. *See also* Elective no-fault liability; Enterprise liability; Extrahazardous no-fault liability; Auto liability insurance
Nuclear accidents, 60, 140
Nuisance claims, 17, 51-53, 100, 171
Nurses, 43, 119

O'Connell, Jeffrey, xi-xiii, xviii, xix-xx, xxi, 224
Odessa Country Club, 40
Ohio Constitution, 223
Oklahoma Constitution, 223
One-car accidents, 106
Oregon no-fault auto law, 106
Orthopedics, 100
Oxford University, 200

Pain and suffering, 10, 51-53, 90, 92, 98, 102, 105, 112-15, 118, 119, 120, 121-22, 125, 139, 147, 169, 171, 173, 206, 213, 214, 216, 217, 219, 224, 225
Palsgraf v. *Long Island R. Co.*, 64
Passell, Peter, 78
Patient's Bill of Rights, 156
Pennsylvania: Constitution, 223, 224-26; Supreme Court, 226
Pensions, 146
Periodic payment. *See* Damages, law of
Pharmaceutical houses. *See* Drugs
Pinnick v. *Cleary*, 211-13, 219, 226
Pitney, Mahon, 210
Police power, 213, 218, 227
Polio vaccine, 159-61
Polls, 112-16, 118
Pollution, 75, 78
Posner, Richard, 195, 197-202
Power lawnmowers. *See* Lawnmowers
Power tools, 19, 90, 99, 118, 121, 152
Pre-existing condition, 73
Presenting complaint, 72, 93
Primary payers, 145-47
Procaccini, Italo, 1-3, 9, 10

Product liability, xii, 12-24, 53, 56-65, 77, 171, 213, 218. *See also* Defective product; Delay in claims and litigation; Expert witnesses; National Commission on Product Safety; Product liability insurance
Product liability insurance, 20-24, 57, 71, 79, 228; complexity of claims, 12-18, 21, 119, 130, 183-88; costs of, 13, 18, 21; resistance to claims, 17-18
Product Safety Commission. *See* Consumer Product Safety Commission
Professional Standards Review Organizations (PSROs), 130-31
Property damage, 116, 121, 139-41, 223
Prosser, William, 56, 61, 64, 66, 125
Prosthetic devices, 118, 155
Proximate cause, 64, 73, 152
Psychiatry, 114, 118
Public opinion polls. *See* Polls
Punishment, 155
Pure comparative negligence, 197

Rabb, William, 52
Rabb and Zeitler (law firm), 52
Railroad accident cases, 124-25, 177-82, 224-25
Railroad employees, 125, 224-25
"Rational relationship to a legitimate purpose" test, 217-20, 222. *See also* Equal protection clauses
Reasonable Man theory, 195-96, 200
"Redress of injury" clauses, 226-27
Rehabilitation, 49-50, 114, 118, 123, 155, 193
Renal dialysis. *See* Kidney ailments
Resource allocation, 125, 143, 201
Retailers, 152-53
Retired persons, 118-19
Ring, Leonard, 118, 119
Ritter, Lawrence, 75
Robling Wire Rope Manual, 185
Roddis, Richard, 143-44
Ross, Leonard, 77, 78, 153
Rostow, Eugene, 75-76

Rubsaman, David, 41

Safety, 77, 89, 127-28, 129, 141, 201.
  See also Auto safety; Deterrence
San Diego County, 93
Schauer, J., 181-82
Scheduled benefits, 103
Schumacher, E. F., 201
Screening panels, 39, 193
Seletz, Emil, 39
Sick leave, 50, 79, 90, 98, 112, 121,
  126, 145, 146
Smith, Adam, 200
Smith v. Wire Rope Corporation of
  America, Inc., 183-88
Social insurance, 65, 73-80, 89, 145,
  146, 167-70, 172; costs of expansion,
  73-80, 168, 172. See also Social
  security
Social security, 21, 73, 74-75, 76, 77-
  78, 79, 80, 90, 94, 132, 175, 230.
  See also Social insurance
Soft drinks, 129
South-Eastern Underwriters case. See
  United States v. South-Eastern Un-
  derwriters Ass'n
Spain, 170
Spinal anesthesia, 93
Spinal fusion, 93
Sponges, left in patient, 154, 155
State government, 95, 128, 161-63,
  204, 213, 214, 218, 222-23, 227,
  229
Stewart, Isaac, 183-88
Stigler, George, 200
Stigma of liability, 98-99, 101, 173,
  214
Stoves, 64, 65, 71, 79
Strict liability, 56-66
"Strict scrutiny" test, 217. See also
  Equal protection clauses
Subrogation, 77, 144, 167-68, 169.
  See also Indemnity
Supreme Court, United States. See
  United States Supreme Court
Surgeon general, 160
Surgeons, 42, 154, 155, 157

Surgical needles, left in patient, 154,
  155
Survey Research Laboratory. See Uni-
  versity of Illinois Survey Research
  Laboratory
"Suspect classification" test, 217-18.
  See also Equal protection clauses
Sweden, 167, 168, 169

Tawney, R. H., 200
Technology, xiii-xv
Texas Constitution, 227
Theft insurance, 116
Times Literary Supplement, 201
Tort exemption, 10, 90, 97, 101, 102,
  103, 105, 106, 119, 129, 216, 218,
  226
Tort liability insurance, costs of, xii,
  10, 116, 171. See also Medical mal-
  practice insurance; Product liability
  insurance
Trade associations, 78, 153
Traumatic neurosis, 115
Trial lawyers. See Association of Trial
  Lawyers of America; Lawyers
Trial tactics, 1-7, 12-13, 177-82

Unconscionable contracts, 155
Unconstitutionality. See Constitution-
  ality
Underwriters, 147
"Unholy trinity" of defenses, 102
Uniform Commercial Code, 140
Uniform state laws. See National Con-
  ference of Commissioners on Uni-
  form State Laws
United States, 76, 167, 168, 170. See
  also Federal government
United States Congress. See Congress
United States Constitution. See Con-
  stitutionality
United States Supreme Court, 210-11,
  215, 228
United States v. South-Eastern Under-
  writers Ass'n, 228
University of Illinois Survey Research
  Laboratory, 115

University of Rochester, 128-29
Utah Constitution, 223

Vaccination, 159-61
Vaporizers, 19, 91
Veblen, Thorstein, xviii

Wage loss, 75, 76, 77, 99, 113, 118, 153, 155, 175, 193, 206, 216
Warranty, 208
West Virginia Workmen's Compensation Law, 206, 207, 208
Whitford, William, 22
Wholesalers, 153

Wildman, Max, 4-6, 7, 9, 53
Wisconsin, 197
Workers' compensation, 48, 49, 58, 72, 79, 80, 92, 97, 102, 103, 120, 124, 125, 127, 128, 131, 142, 143, 147, 152, 155, 170, 189-90, 204, 206-7, 209, 210-11, 215, 220-22, 224, 225, 229, 230. *See also* Elective workers' compensation
Wrongful death claims, 224
Wyeth Laboratories, 159-61
Wyoming Constitution, 223

X-rays, 43